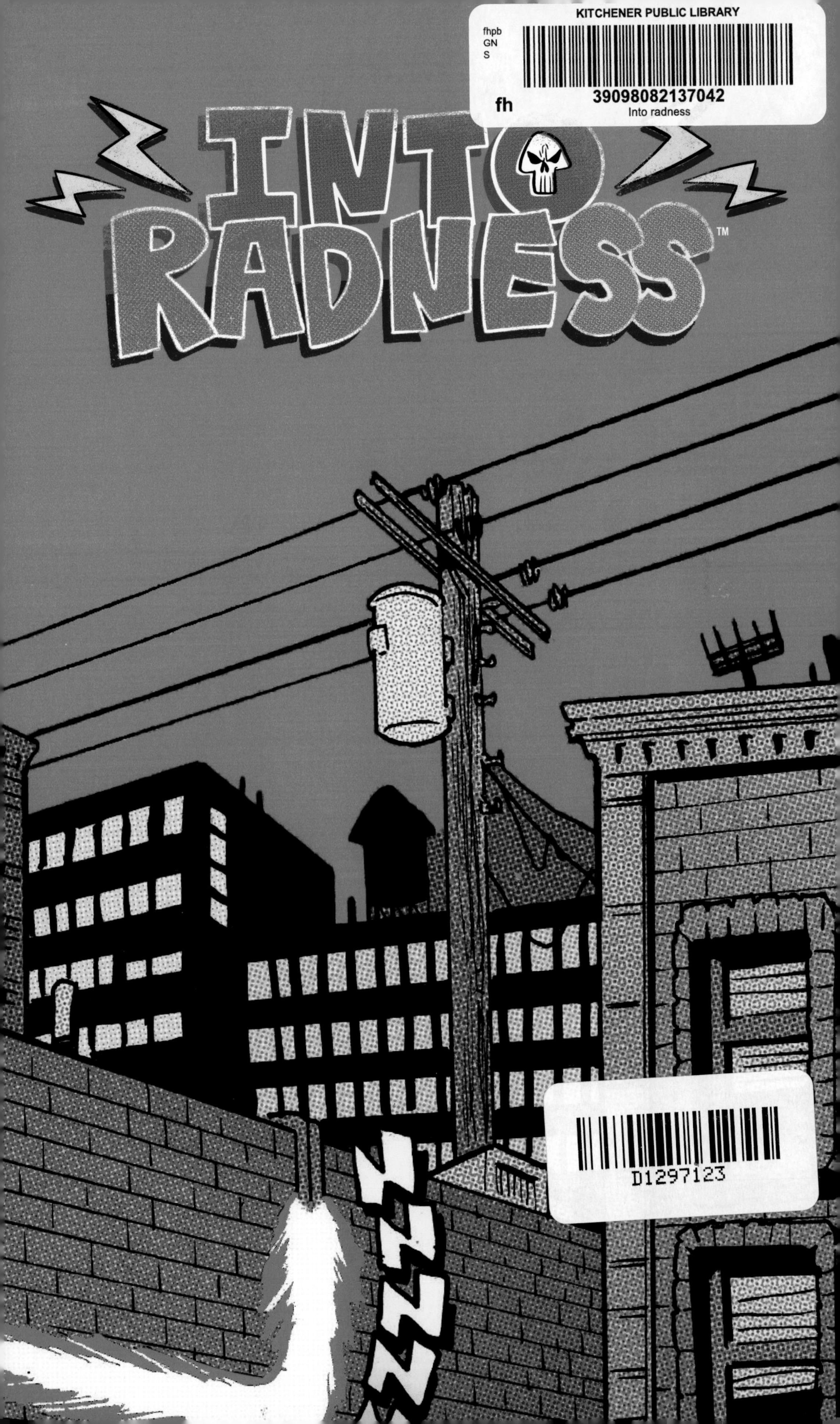
INTO RADNESS™

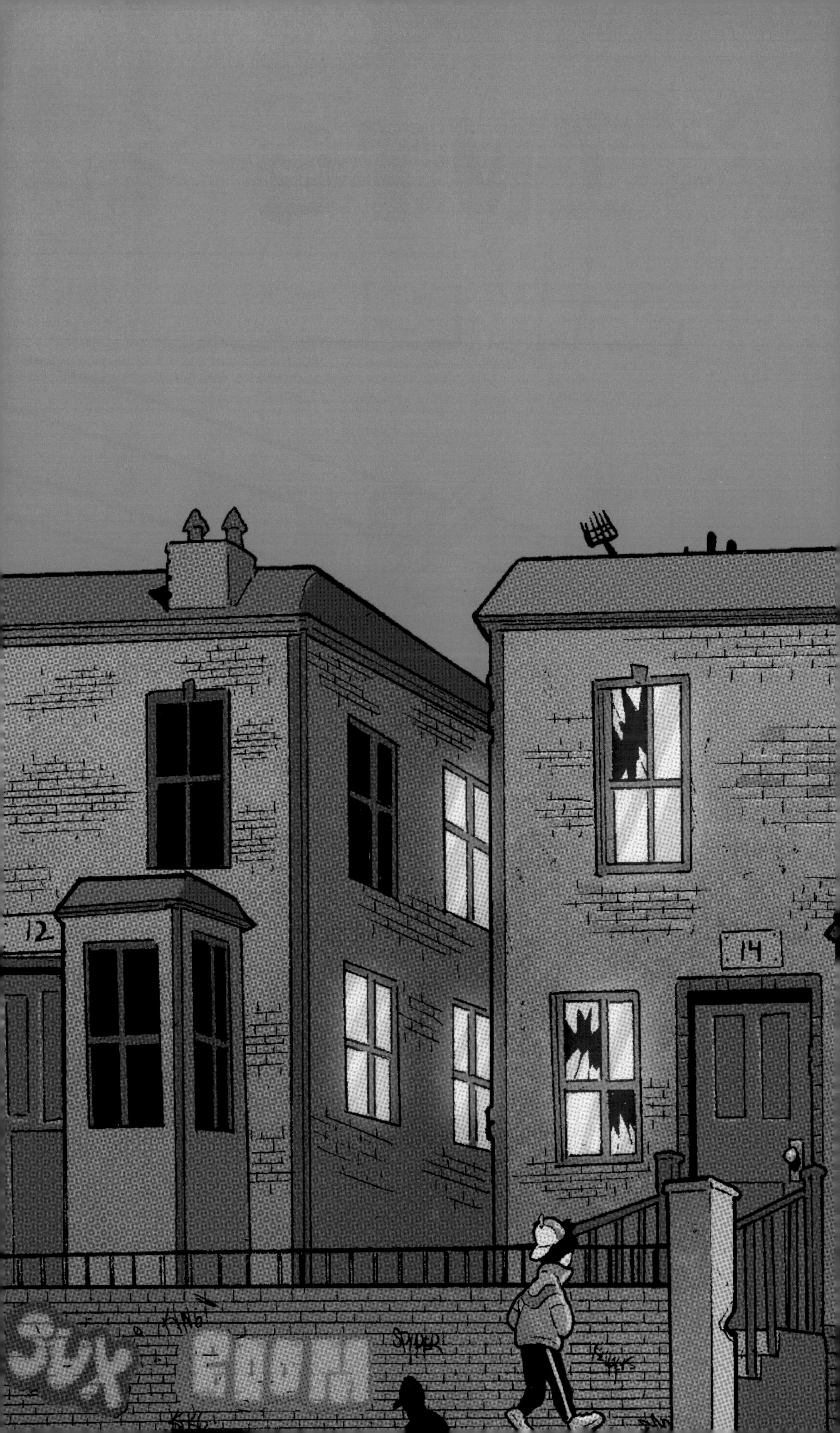
12
14
SPIDER

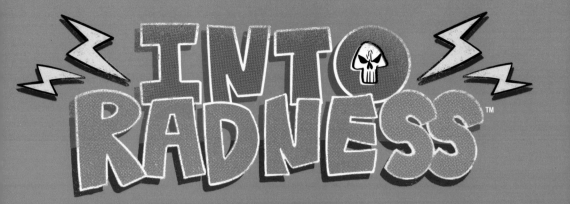

INTO RADNESS™

WRITTEN BY
KYLE STRAHM

ART BY
JAKE SMITH

LETTERS BY
CRANK!

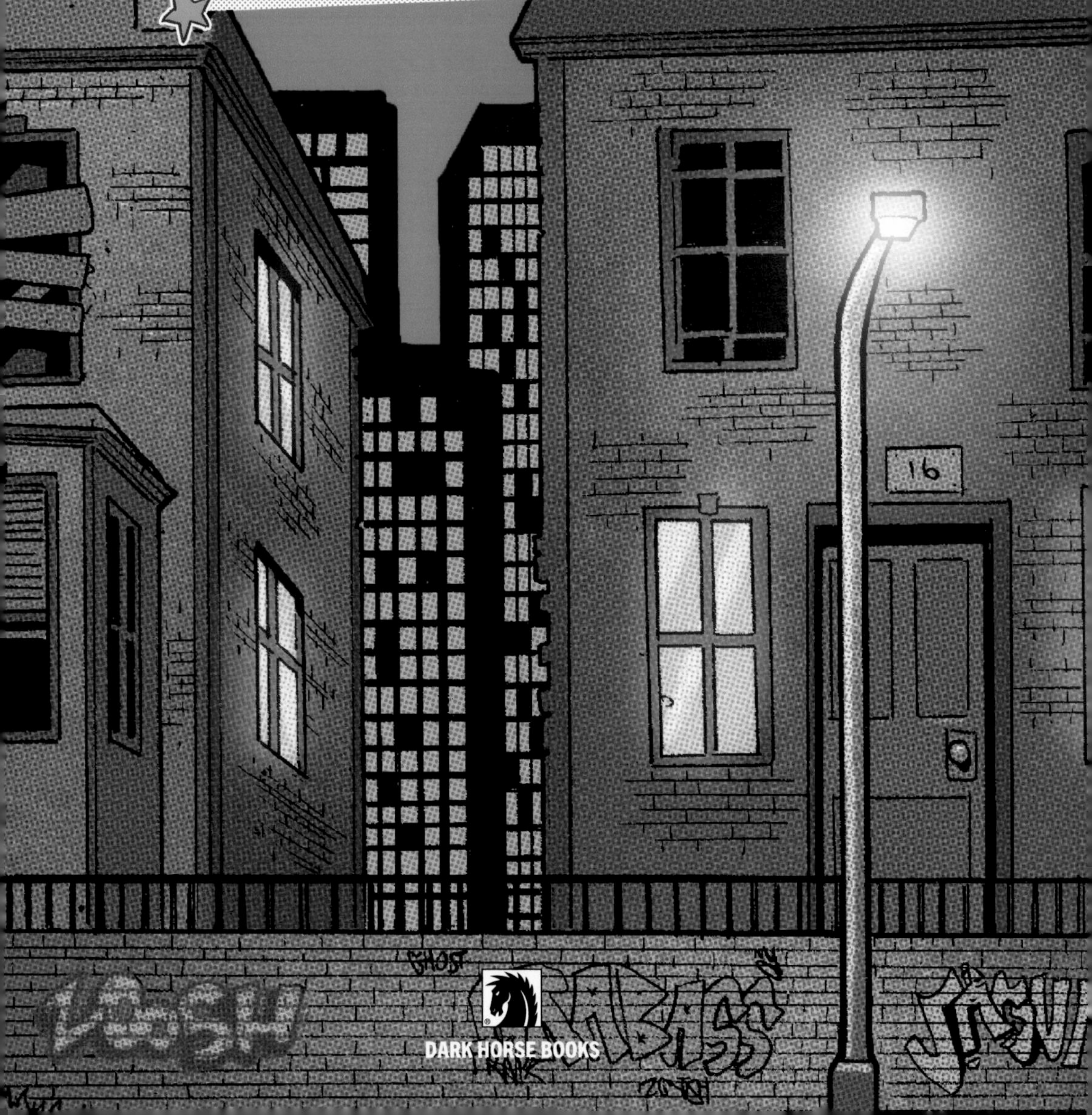

DARK HORSE BOOKS

PRESIDENT AND PUBLISHER
MIKE RICHARDSON

EDITOR
BRETT ISRAEL

ASSISTANT EDITOR
SANJAY DHARAWAT

DIGITAL ART TECHNICIAN
BETSY HOWITT

COLLECTION DESIGNER
MAY HIJIKURO

NEIL HANKERSON EXECUTIVE VICE PRESIDENT **TOM WEDDLE** CHIEF FINANCIAL OFFICER **DALE LaFOUNTAIN** CHIEF INFORMATION OFFICER **TIM WIESCH** VICE PRESIDENT OF LICENSING **MATT PARKINSON** VICE PRESIDENT OF MARKETING **VANESSA TODD-HOLMES** VICE PRESIDENT OF PRODUCTION AND SCHEDULING **MARK BERNARDI** VICE PRESIDENT OF BOOK TRADE AND DIGITAL SALES **RANDY LAHRMAN** VICE PRESIDENT OF PRODUCT DEVELOPMENT **KEN LIZZI** GENERAL COUNSEL **DAVE MARSHALL** EDITOR IN CHIEF **DAVEY ESTRADA** EDITORIAL DIRECTOR **CHRIS WARNER** SENIOR BOOKS EDITOR **CARY GRAZZINI** DIRECTOR OF SPECIALTY PROJECTS **LIA RIBACCHI** ART DIRECTOR **MATT DRYER** DIRECTOR OF DIGITAL ART AND PREPRESS **MICHAEL GOMBOS** SENIOR DIRECTOR OF LICENSED PUBLICATIONS **KARI YADRO** DIRECTOR OF CUSTOM PROGRAMS **KARI TORSON** DIRECTOR OF INTERNATIONAL LICENSING

Published by Dark Horse Books
A division of Dark Horse Comics LLC
10956 SE Main Street, Milwaukie, OR 97222

First edition: June 2022
Ebook ISBN 978-1-50671-962-7 || Trade Paperback ISBN 978-1-50671-961-0

1 3 5 7 9 10 8 6 4 2
Printed in China

Comic Shop Locator Service: comicshoplocator.com

INTO RADNESS

Library of Congress Cataloging-in-Publication Data

Names: Strahm, Kyle, writer. | Smith, Jake, 1995- artist. | Crank!
(Letterer), letterer.
Title: Into radness / written by Kyle Strahm ; art by Jake Smith ; letters
by Crank!.
Description: First edition. | Milwaukie, OR : Dark Horse Books, 2022. |
Summary: "Dylan, Trixie, and their friends want to be Internet famous,
but their show, INTO RADNESS, has 12 subscribers and it's terrible.
Blowing up old VHS tapes and setting slime on fire just doesn't bring in
the views. But freaky things are starting to happen in the city of Back
Alley. When the teens are filmed defending themselves from an oozing
ZONKED creature, they become overnight celebrities. Oh, and that
creature? There are a lot more of those roaming the streets! Friendships
are strained and battle plans drawn as six teens descend INTO
RADNESS!!"-- Provided by publisher.
Identifiers: LCCN 2021050352 | ISBN 9781506719610 (trade paperback) | ISBN
9781506719627 (ebook)
Subjects: LCGFT: Graphic novels.
Classification: LCC PN6727.S7636 I58 2022 | DDC
741.5/973--dc23/eng/20211108
LC record available at https://lccn.loc.gov/2021050352

CHAPTER ONE

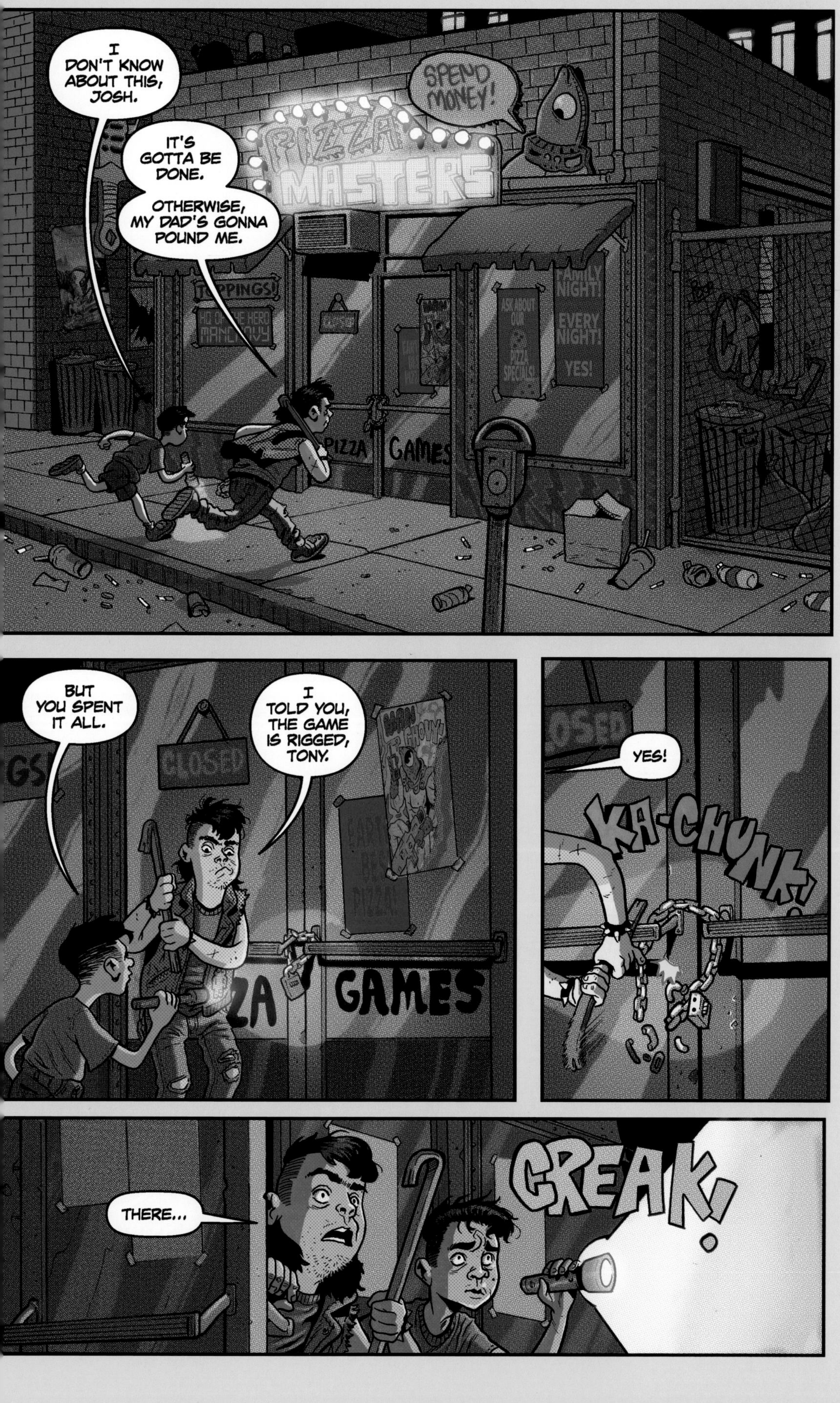

I DON'T KNOW ABOUT THIS, JOSH.
SPEND MONEY!
PIZZA MASTERS
IT'S GOTTA BE DONE.
OTHERWISE, MY DAD'S GONNA POUND ME.
TOPPINGS!
ASK ABOUT OUR PIZZA SPECIALS!
FAMILY NIGHT! EVERY NIGHT! YES!
PIZZA
GAMES
BUT YOU SPENT IT ALL.
CLOSED
I TOLD YOU, THE GAME IS RIGGED, TONY.
ZA
GAMES
YES!
KA-CHUNK!
THERE...
CREAK!

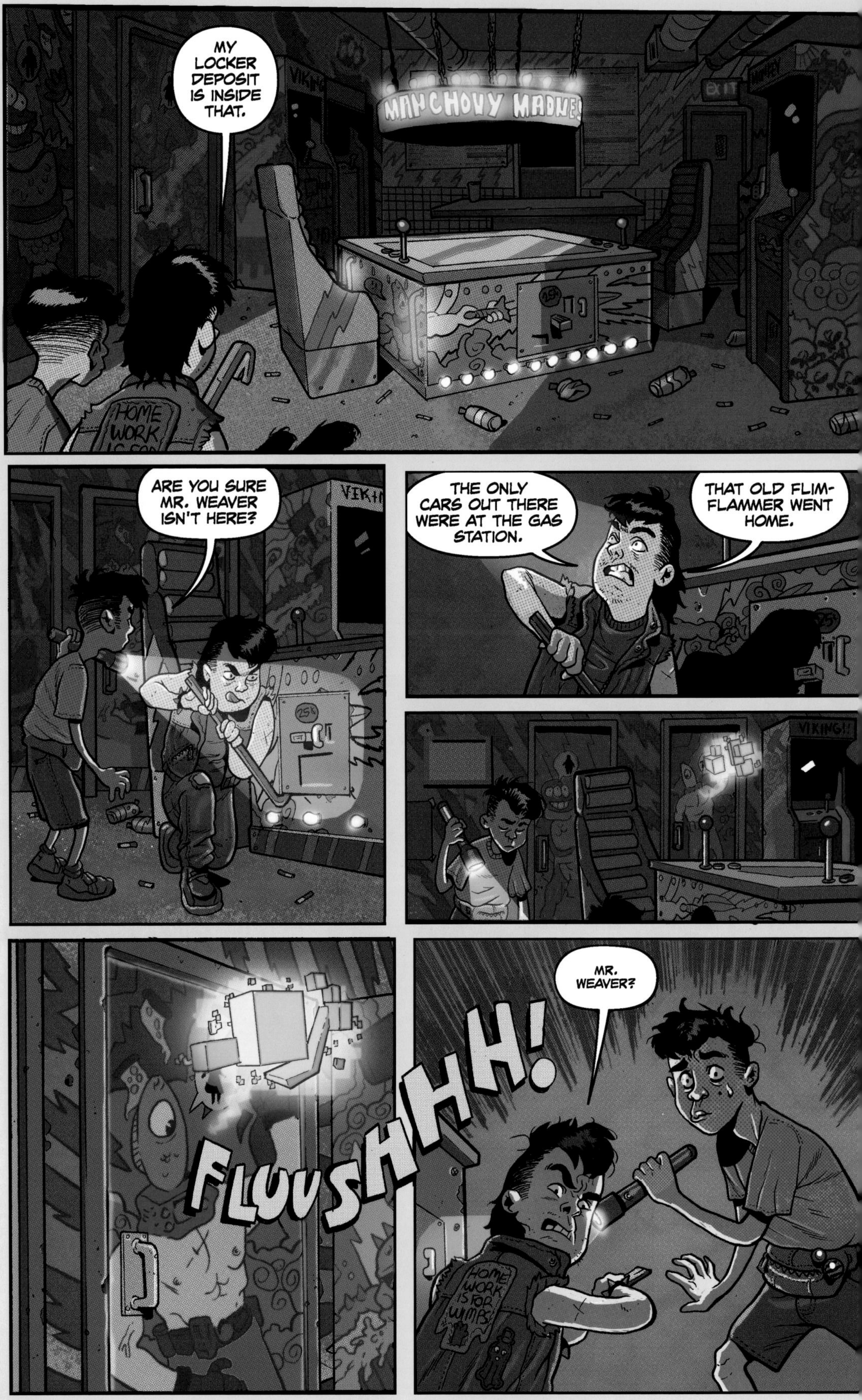
MY LOCKER DEPOSIT IS INSIDE THAT.
MANCHOVY MADNES
HOME WORK
VIKING
ARE YOU SURE MR. WEAVER ISN'T HERE?
THE ONLY CARS OUT THERE WERE AT THE GAS STATION.
THAT OLD FLIM-FLAMMER WENT HOME.
VIKING!!
FLUUSHHH!
MR. WEAVER?
HOME WORK IS FOR WIMPS!

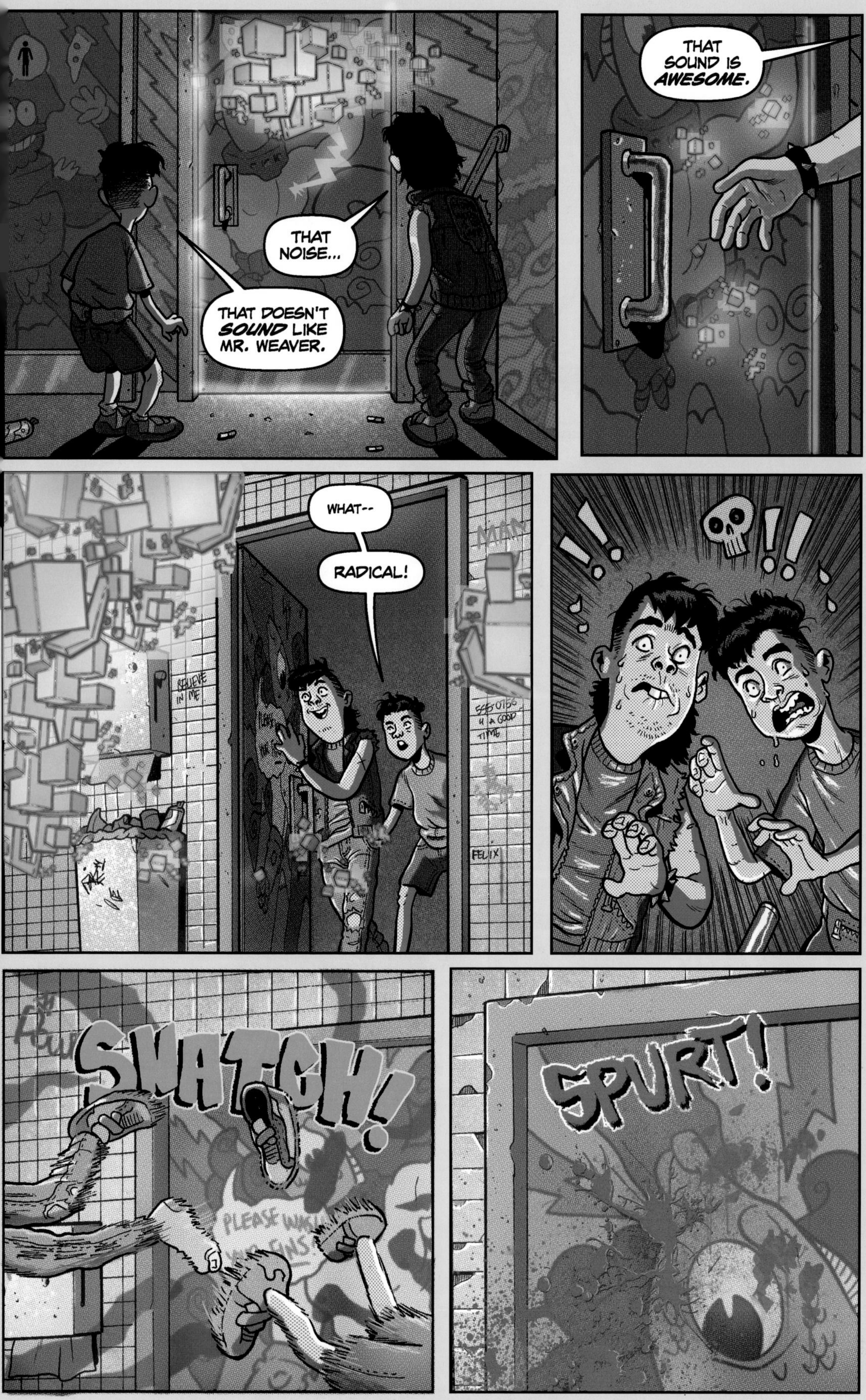
THAT NOISE...
THAT DOESN'T *SOUND* LIKE MR. WEAVER.
THAT SOUND IS *AWESOME*.
WHAT--
RADICAL!
BELIEVE IN ME
FELIX
SNATCH!
SPURT!

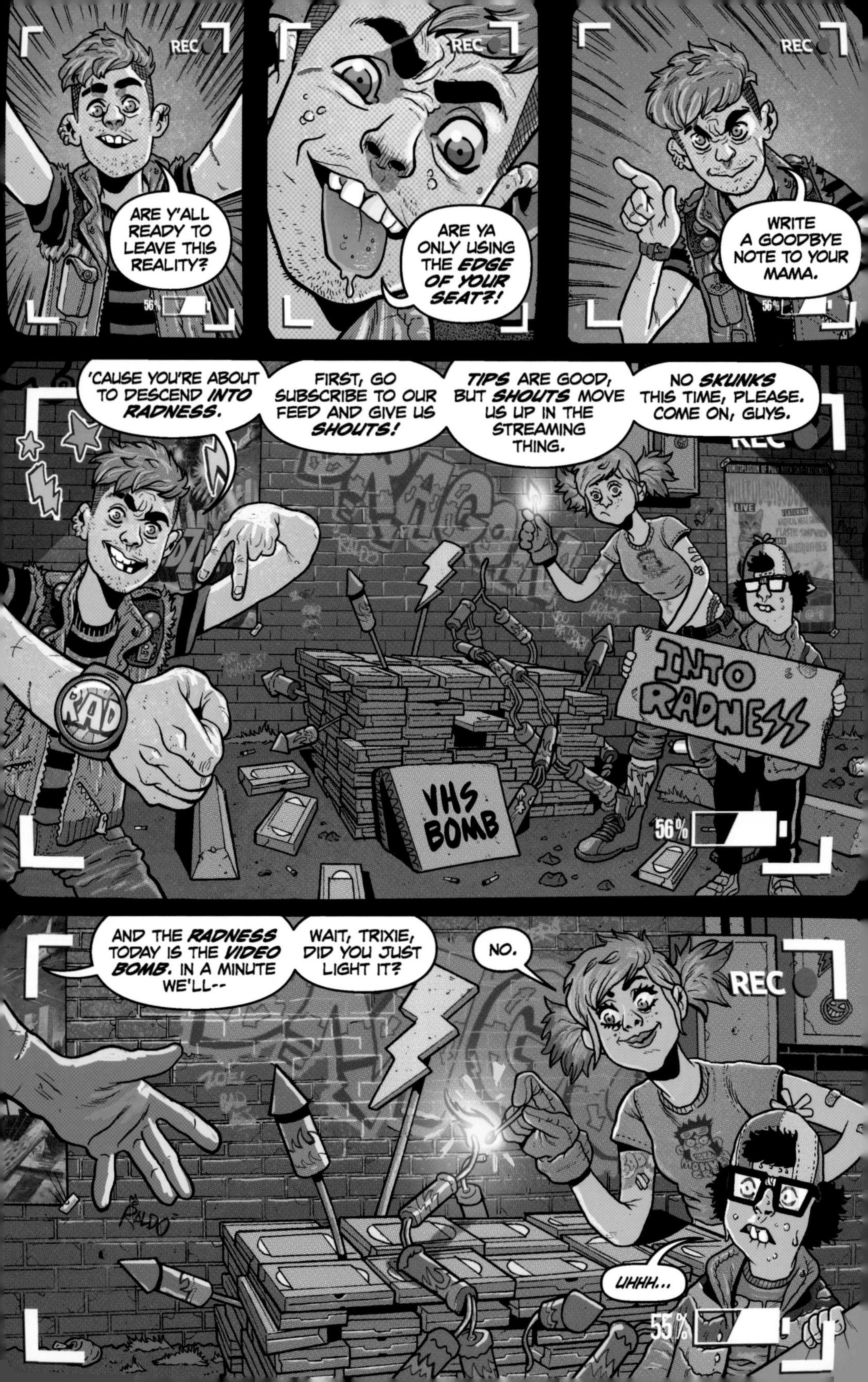

REC
ARE Y'ALL READY TO LEAVE THIS REALITY?
56%
REC
ARE YA ONLY USING THE *EDGE OF YOUR SEAT?!*
REC
WRITE A GOODBYE NOTE TO YOUR MAMA.
56%
'CAUSE YOU'RE ABOUT TO DESCEND *INTO RADNESS.*
FIRST, GO SUBSCRIBE TO OUR FEED AND GIVE US *SHOUTS!*
TIPS ARE GOOD, BUT *SHOUTS* MOVE US UP IN THE STREAMING THING.
NO *SKUNKS* THIS TIME, PLEASE. COME ON, GUYS.
REC
RAD
INTO RADNESS
VHS BOMB
56%
AND THE *RADNESS* TODAY IS THE *VIDEO BOMB.* IN A MINUTE WE'LL--
WAIT, TRIXIE, DID YOU JUST LIGHT IT?
NO.
REC
UHHH...
55%

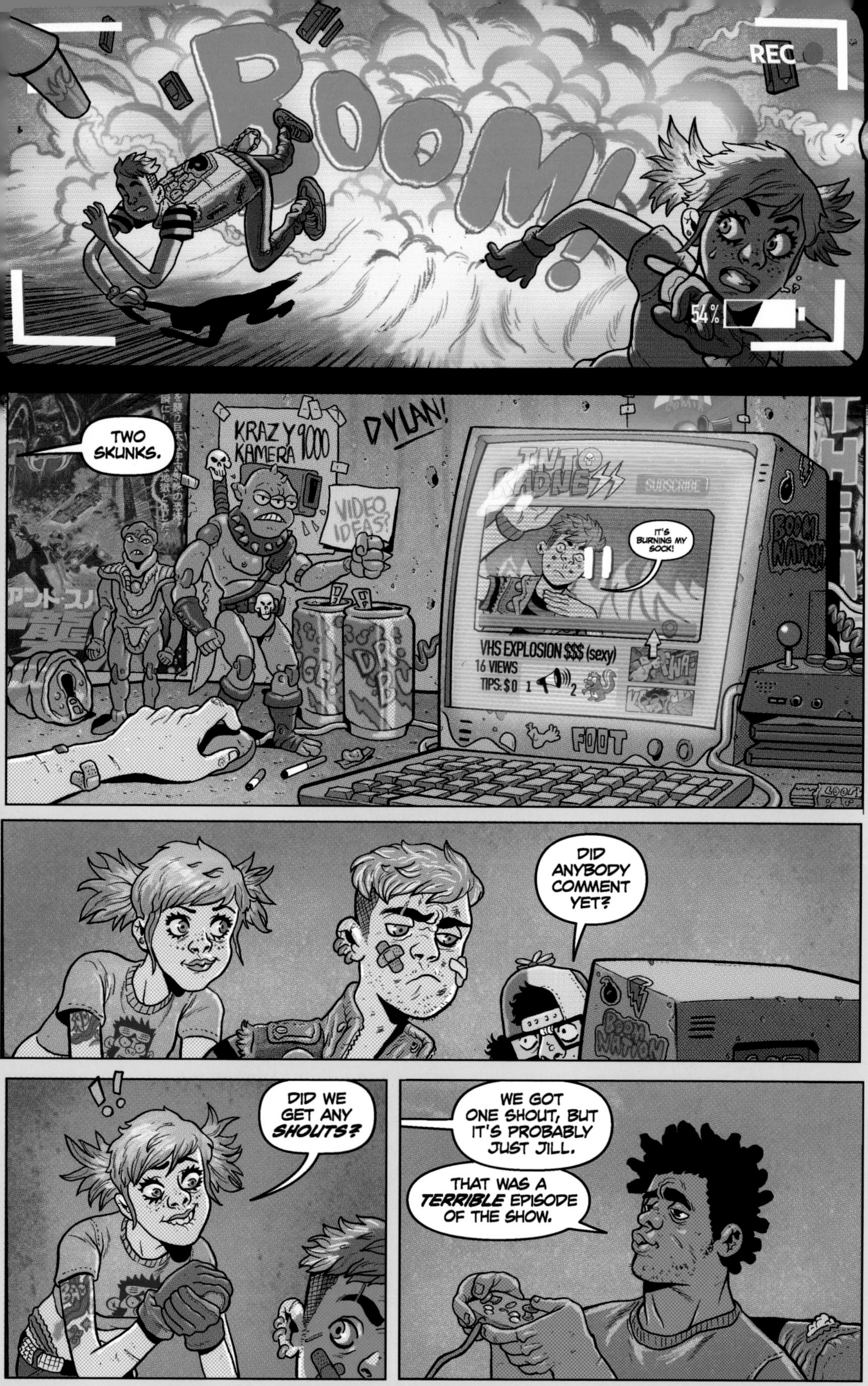
REC
BOOM!
54%
TWO SKUNKS.
KRAZY 9000 KAMERA
DYLAN!
VIDEO IDEAS?
SUBSCRIBE
IT'S BURNING MY SOCK!
VHS EXPLOSION $$$ (sexy)
16 VIEWS
TIPS: $0
FOOT
DID ANYBODY COMMENT YET?
DID WE GET ANY *SHOUTS?*
WE GOT ONE SHOUT, BUT IT'S PROBABLY JUST JILL.
THAT WAS A *TERRIBLE* EPISODE OF THE SHOW.

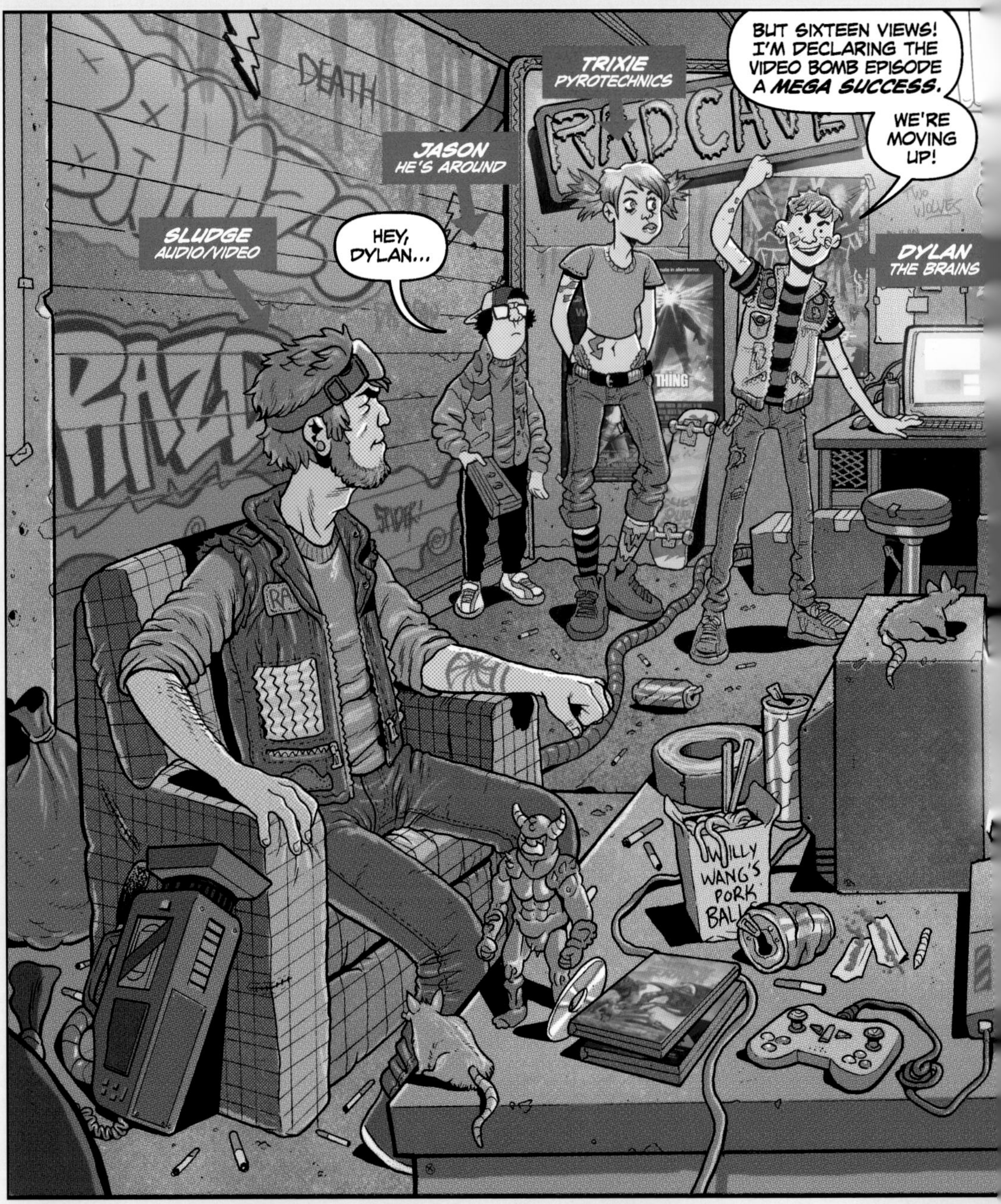
BUT SIXTEEN VIEWS! I'M DECLARING THE VIDEO BOMB EPISODE A ***MEGA SUCCESS.***
WE'RE MOVING UP!
TRIXIE PYROTECHNICS
RADCAVE
JASON HE'S AROUND
SLUDGE AUDIO/VIDEO
HEY, DYLAN...
DYLAN THE BRAINS
DEATH

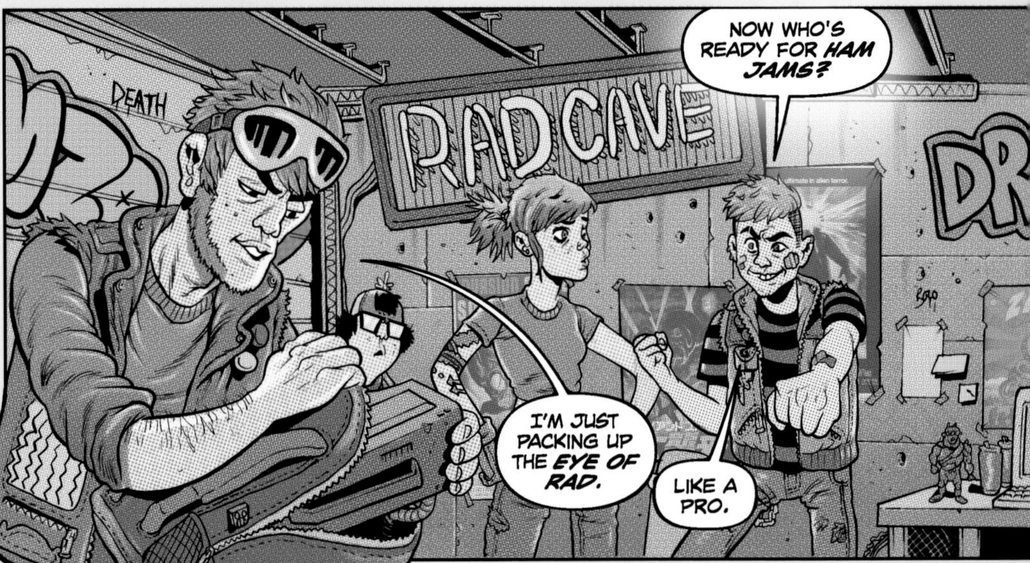
DEATH
RADCAVE
NOW WHO'S READY FOR ***HAM JAMS?***
I'M JUST PACKING UP THE ***EYE OF RAD.***
LIKE A PRO.

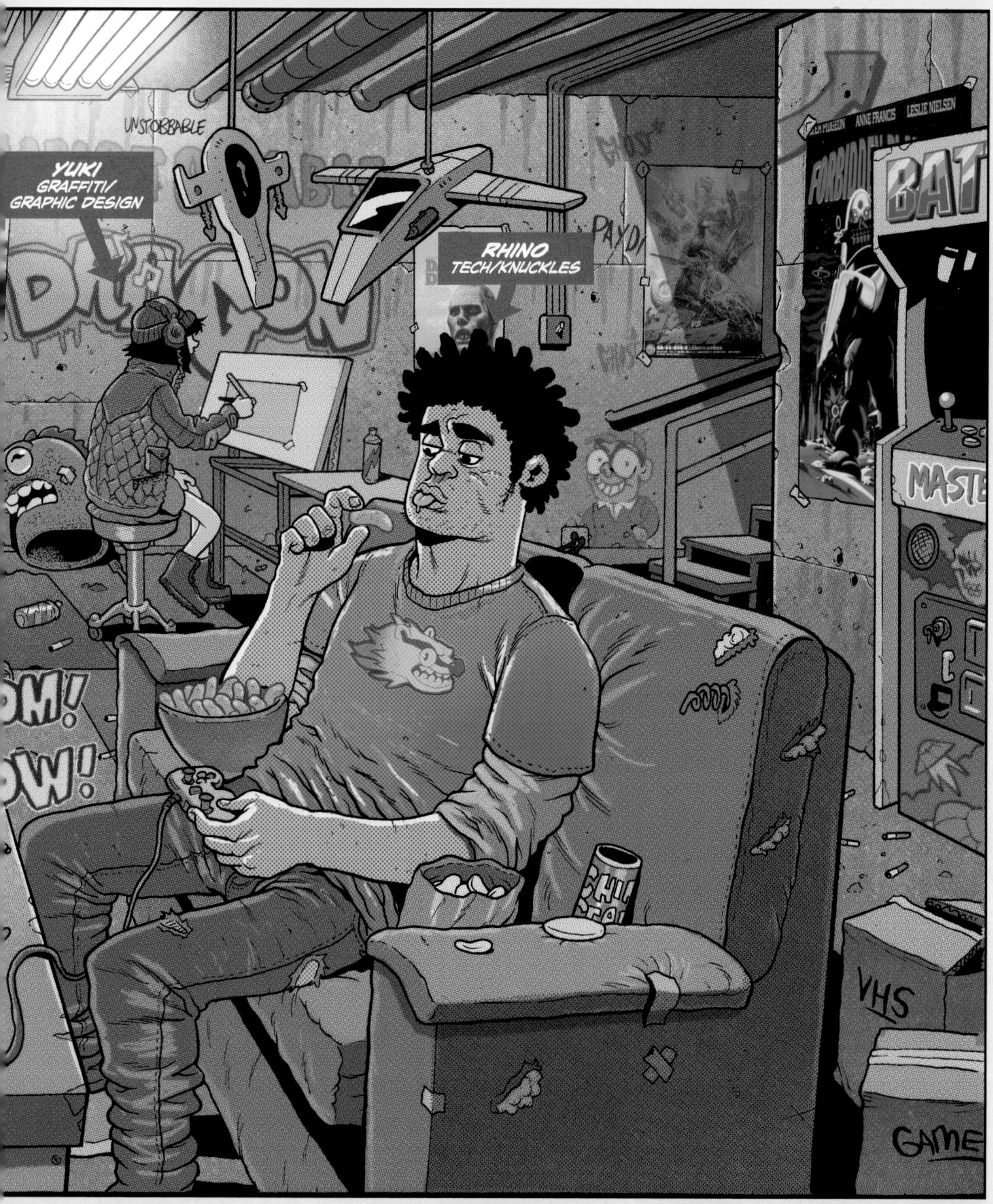
YUKI
GRAFFITI/
GRAPHIC DESIGN
RHINO
TECH/KNUCKLES
UNSTOPPABLE
VHS
GAME

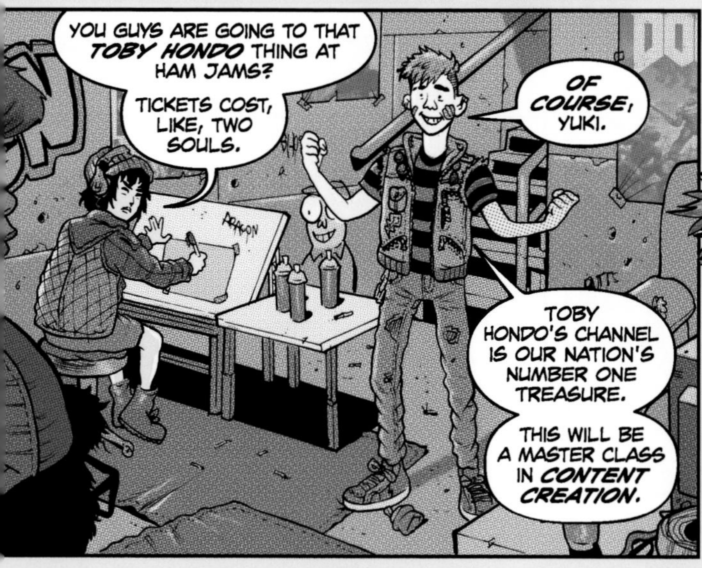
YOU GUYS ARE GOING TO THAT *TOBY HONDO* THING AT HAM JAMS?
TICKETS COST, LIKE, TWO SOULS.
OF COURSE, YUKI.
TOBY HONDO'S CHANNEL IS OUR NATION'S NUMBER ONE TREASURE.
THIS WILL BE A MASTER CLASS IN *CONTENT CREATION.*

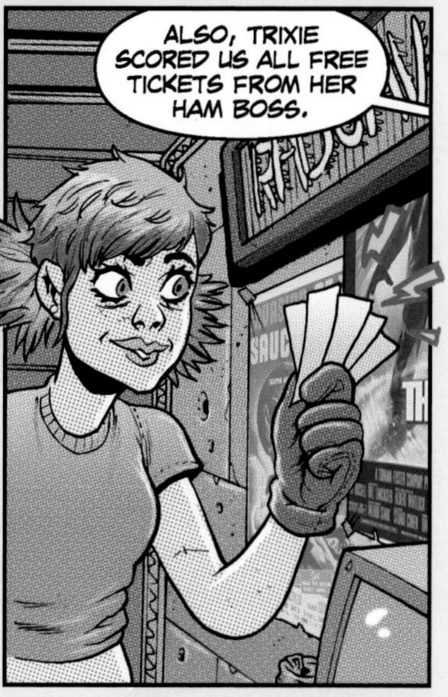
ALSO, TRIXIE SCORED US ALL FREE TICKETS FROM HER HAM BOSS.

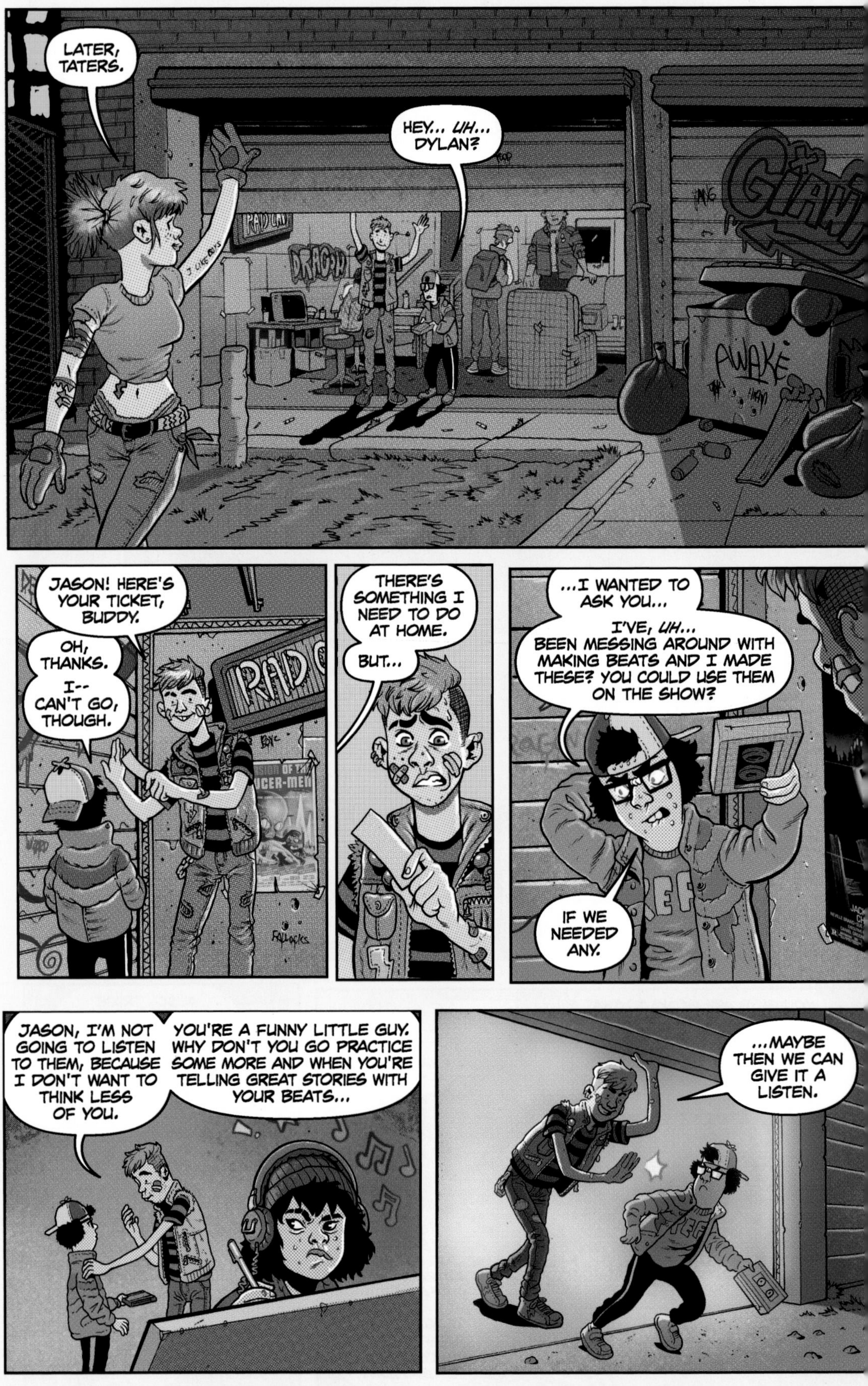
LATER, TATERS.
HEY... UH... DYLAN?
JASON! HERE'S YOUR TICKET, BUDDY.
OH, THANKS.
I-- CAN'T GO, THOUGH.
THERE'S SOMETHING I NEED TO DO AT HOME.
BUT...
...I WANTED TO ASK YOU...
I'VE, UH... BEEN MESSING AROUND WITH MAKING BEATS AND I MADE THESE? YOU COULD USE THEM ON THE SHOW?
IF WE NEEDED ANY.
JASON, I'M NOT GOING TO LISTEN TO THEM, BECAUSE I DON'T WANT TO THINK LESS OF YOU.
YOU'RE A FUNNY LITTLE GUY. WHY DON'T YOU GO PRACTICE SOME MORE AND WHEN YOU'RE TELLING GREAT STORIES WITH YOUR BEATS...
...MAYBE THEN WE CAN GIVE IT A LISTEN.

SLAM!

WELCOME TO BACK ALLEY! WE WONT BLAME YOU IF YOU LEAVE!

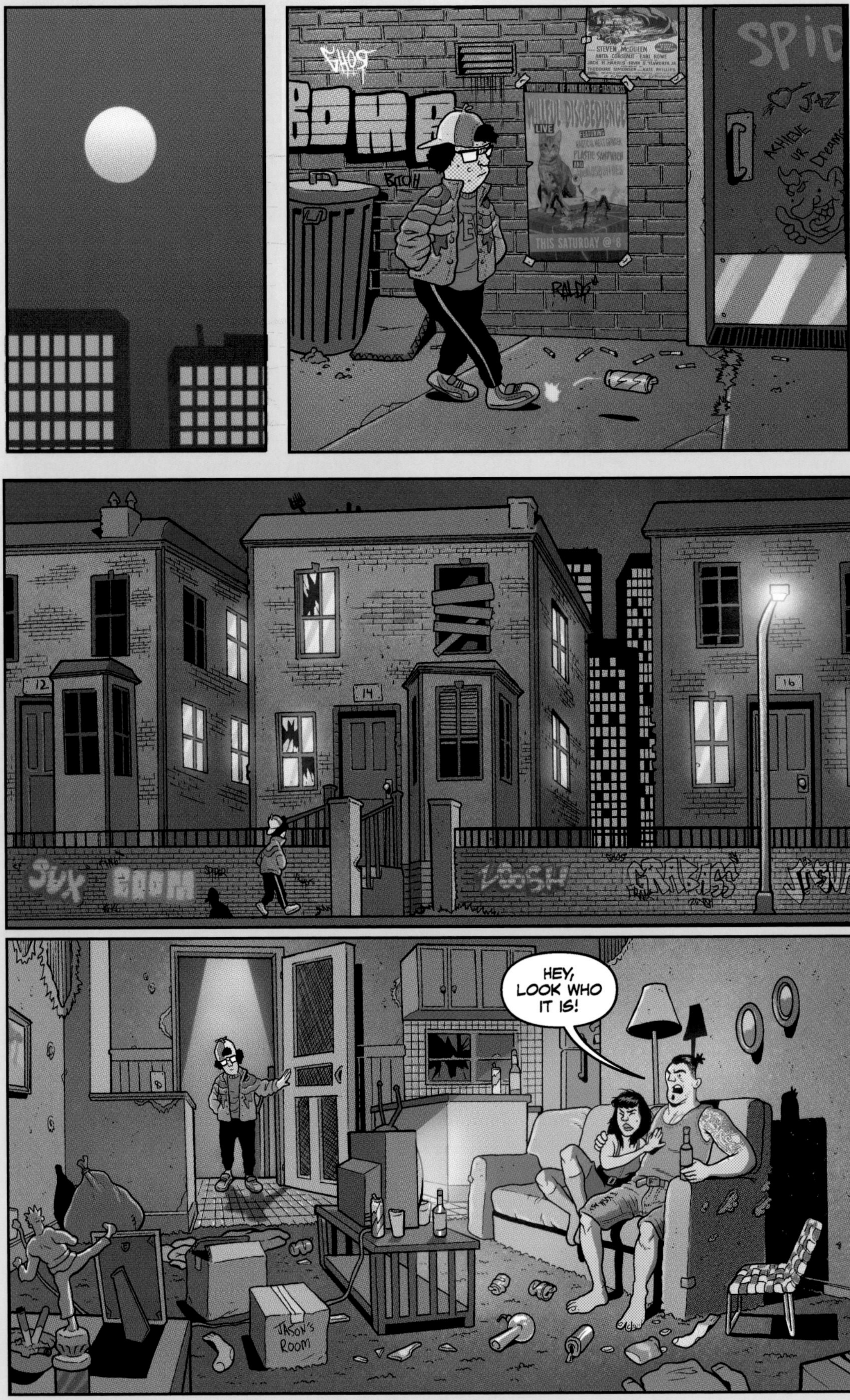
BOMB
STEVEN McQUEEN
LIVE
THIS SATURDAY @ 8
ACHIEVE UR DREAMS
12
14
16
HEY, LOOK WHO IT IS!
JASON'S ROOM

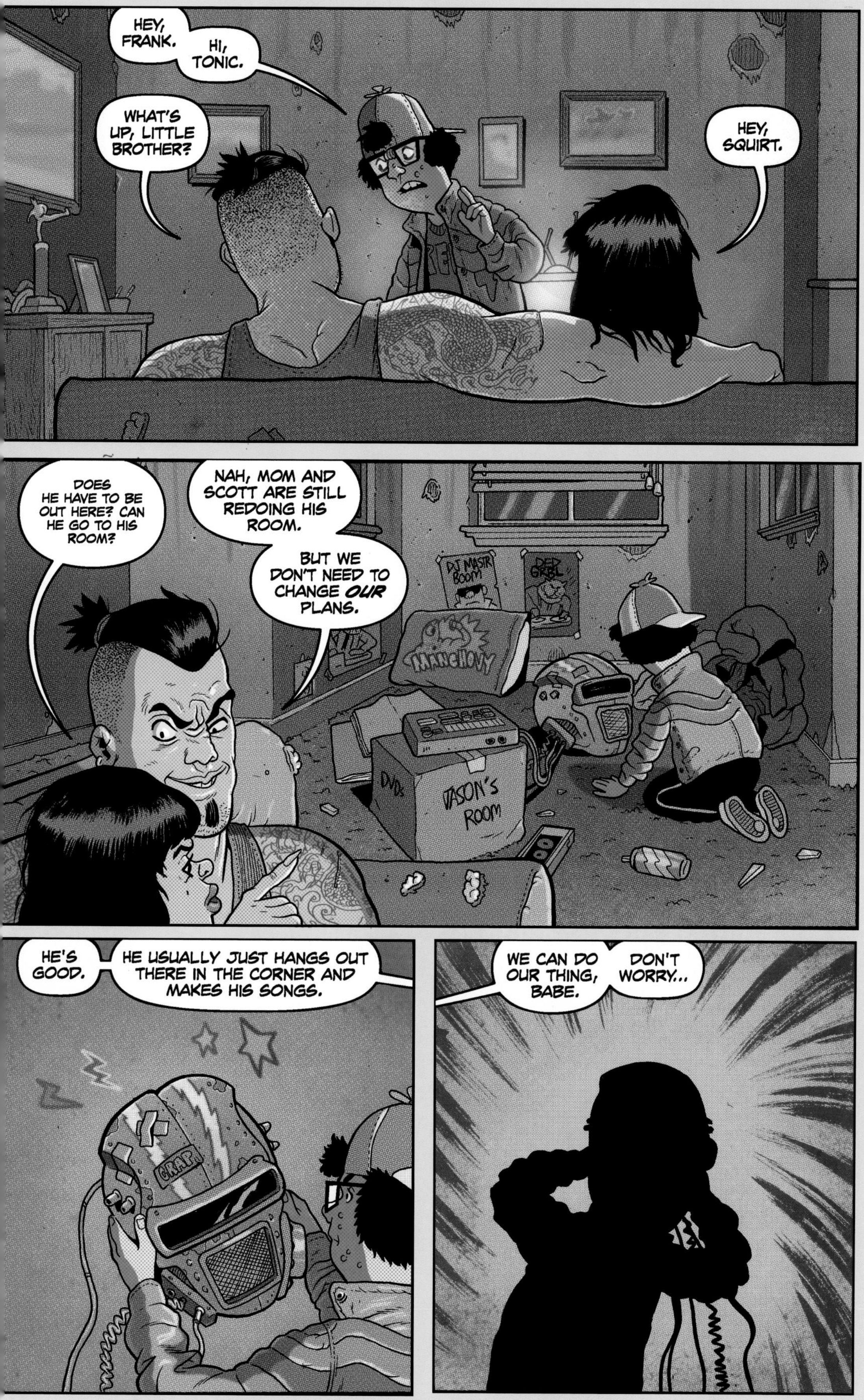
HEY, FRANK.
HI, TONIC.
WHAT'S UP, LITTLE BROTHER?
HEY, SQUIRT.
DOES HE HAVE TO BE OUT HERE? CAN HE GO TO HIS ROOM?
NAH, MOM AND SCOTT ARE STILL REDOING HIS ROOM.
BUT WE DON'T NEED TO CHANGE OUR PLANS.
DVDs
JASON'S ROOM
HE'S GOOD.
HE USUALLY JUST HANGS OUT THERE IN THE CORNER AND MAKES HIS SONGS.
WE CAN DO OUR THING, BABE.
DON'T WORRY...

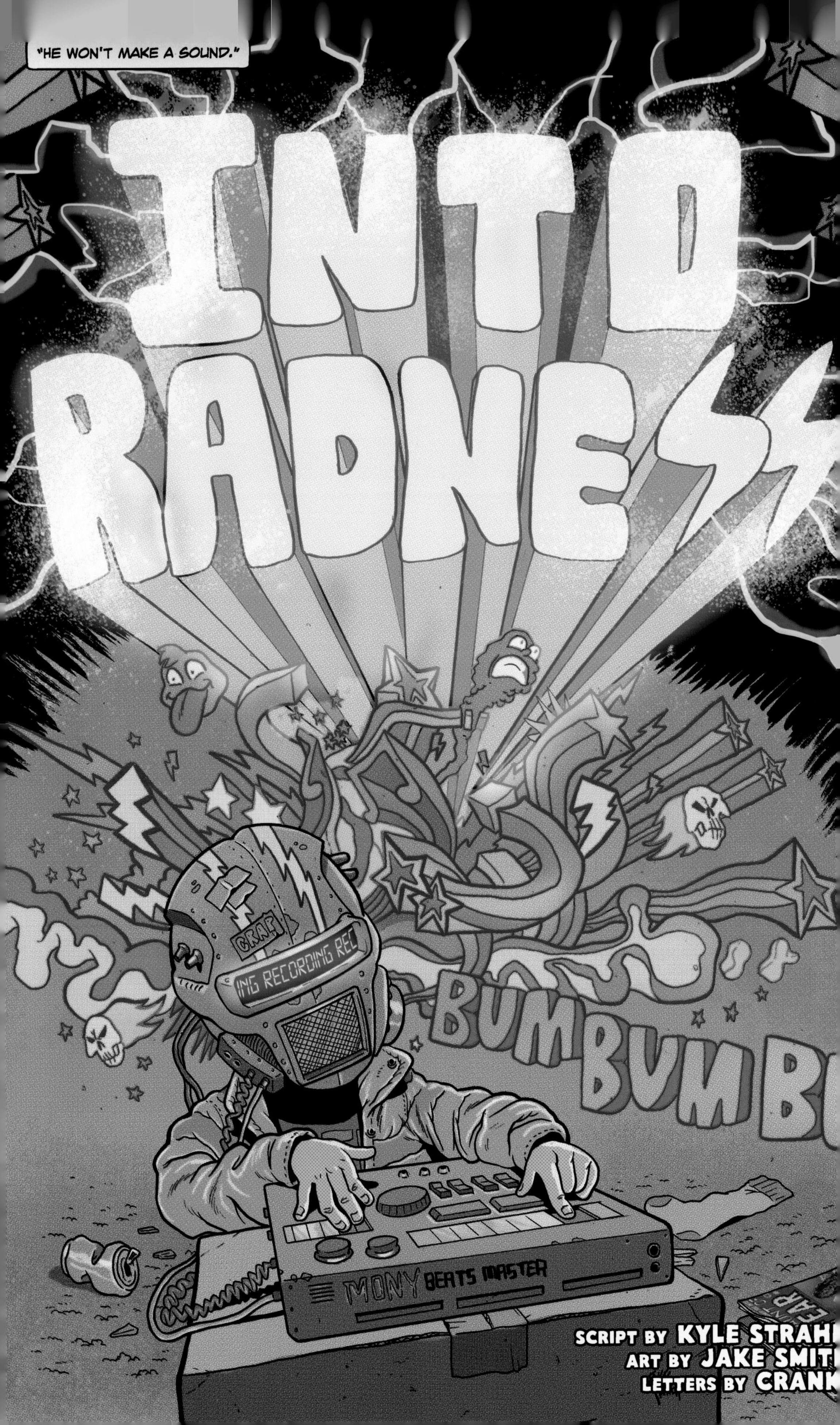

"HE WON'T MAKE A SOUND."
INTO RADNESS
CRAP
ING RECORDING REC
BUM BUM BU
MONY BEATS MASTER
SCRIPT BY KYLE STRAH
ART BY JAKE SMIT
LETTERS BY CRANK

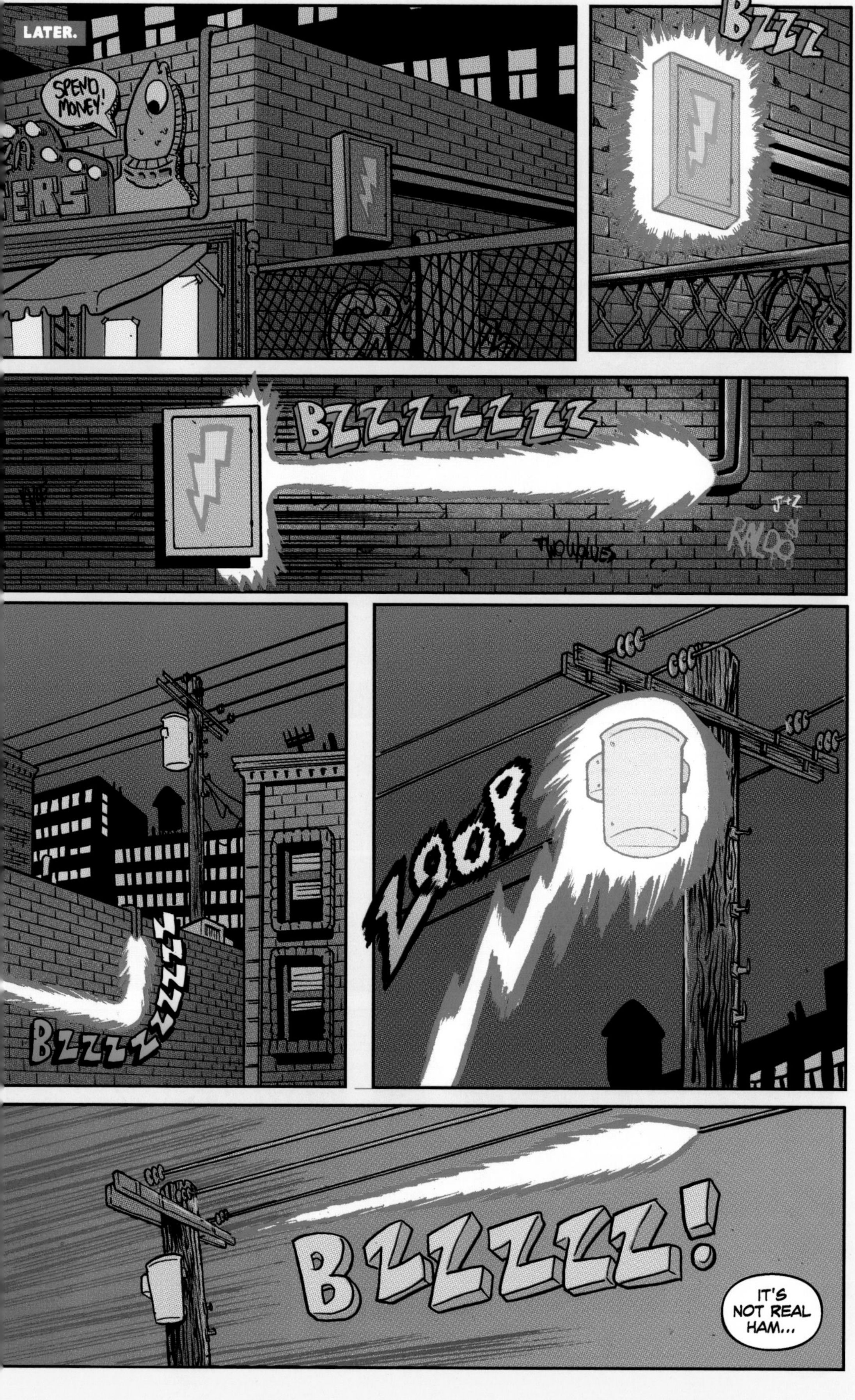
LATER.
SPEND MONEY!
BZZZ
BZZZZZZZZ
J+Z
RALDO
Bzzzzzzzzz
ZOOP
BZZZZZ!
IT'S NOT REAL HAM...

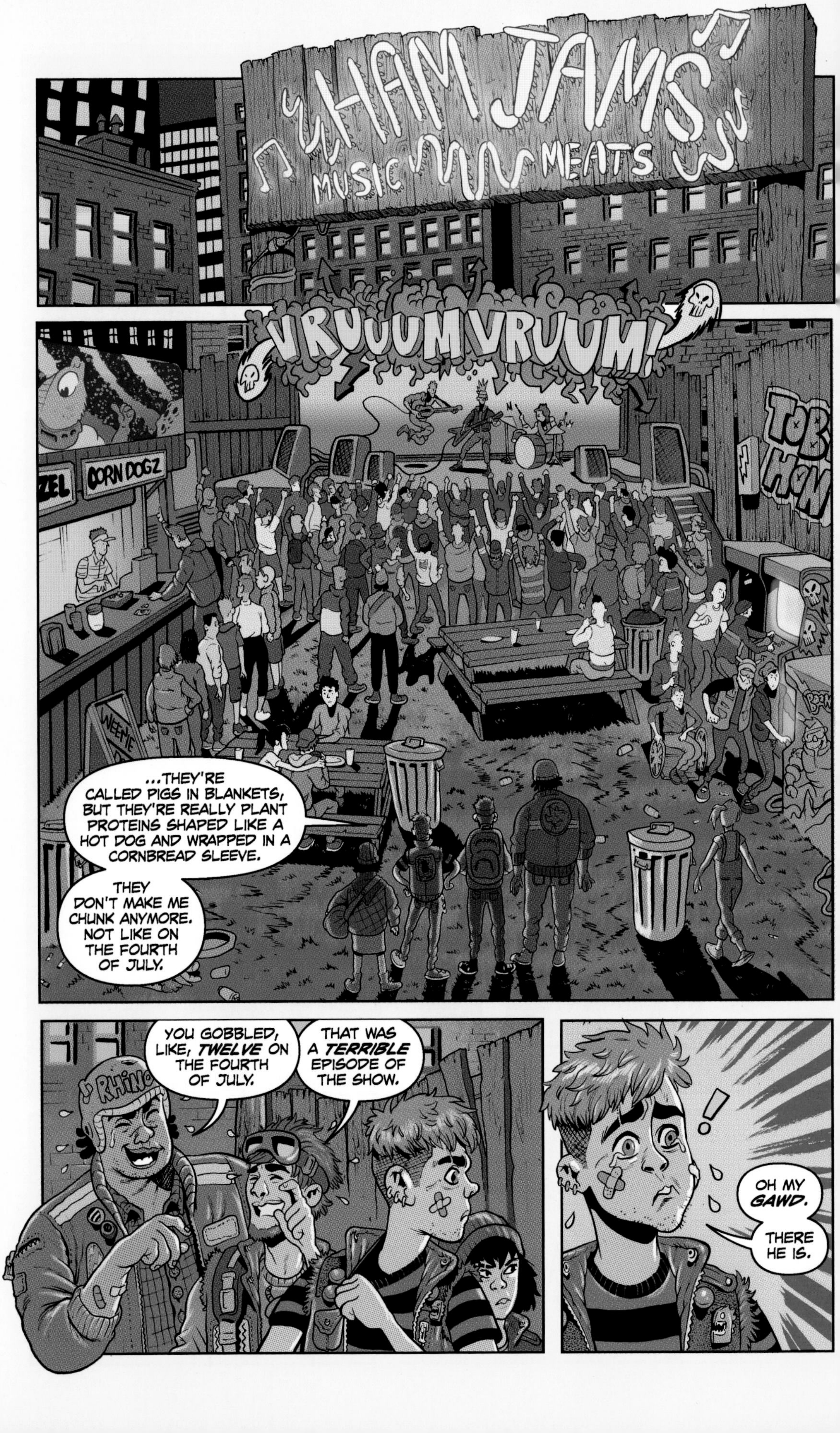
HAM JAMS
MUSIC MEATS
VRUUUM VRUUM!
CORN DOGZ
...THEY'RE CALLED PIGS IN BLANKETS, BUT THEY'RE REALLY PLANT PROTEINS SHAPED LIKE A HOT DOG AND WRAPPED IN A CORNBREAD SLEEVE.
THEY DON'T MAKE ME CHUNK ANYMORE. NOT LIKE ON THE FOURTH OF JULY.
RHINO
YOU GOBBLED, LIKE, TWELVE ON THE FOURTH OF JULY.
THAT WAS A TERRIBLE EPISODE OF THE SHOW.
!
OH MY GAWD.
THERE HE IS.

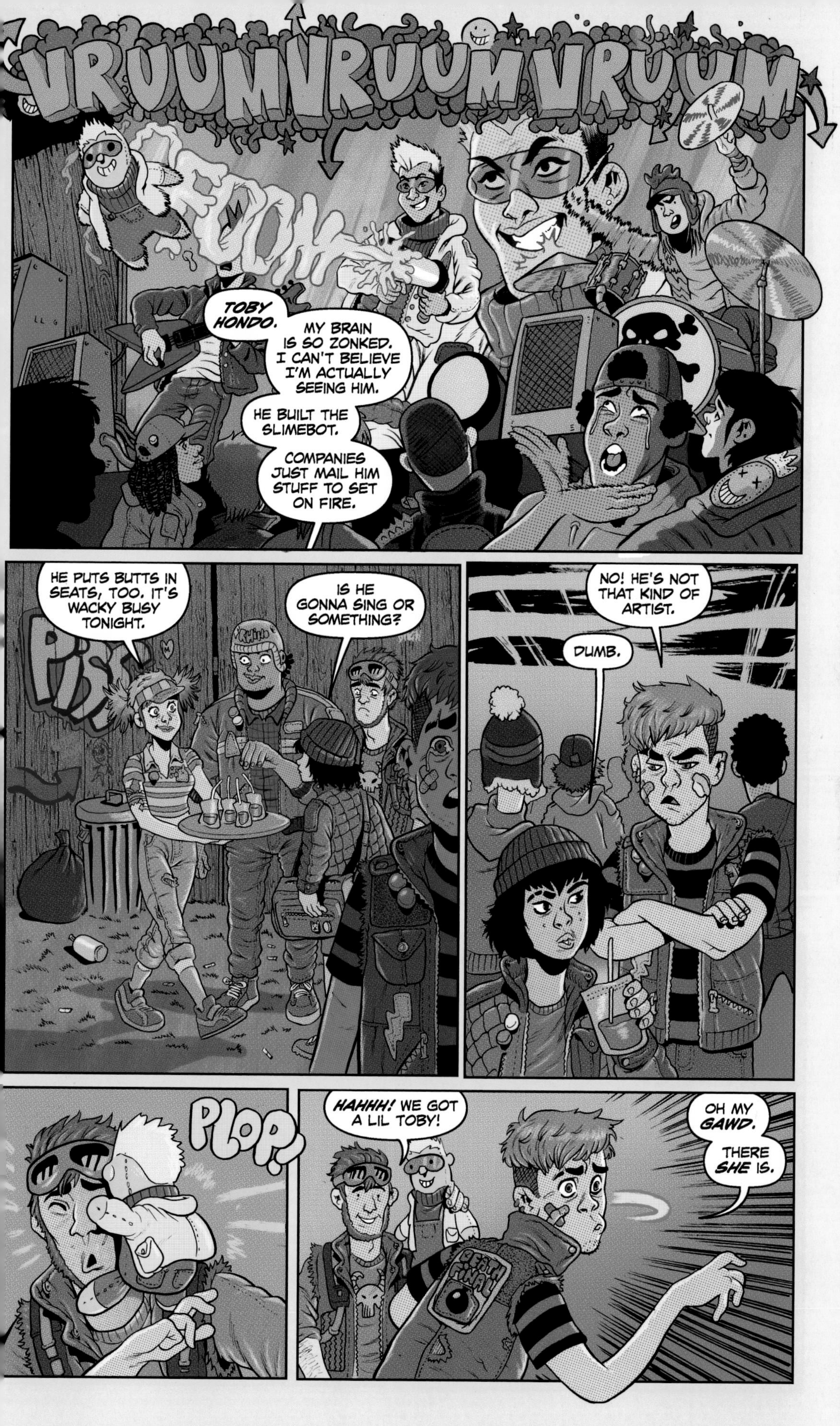
VRUUM VRUUM VRUUM
FOOM
TOBY HONDO.
MY BRAIN IS SO ZONKED. I CAN'T BELIEVE I'M ACTUALLY SEEING HIM.
HE BUILT THE SLIMEBOT.
COMPANIES JUST MAIL HIM STUFF TO SET ON FIRE.
HE PUTS BUTTS IN SEATS, TOO. IT'S WACKY BUSY TONIGHT.
IS HE GONNA SING OR SOMETHING?
NO! HE'S NOT THAT KIND OF ARTIST.
DUMB.
PLOP!
HAHHH! WE GOT A LIL TOBY!
OH MY GAWD.
THERE SHE IS.

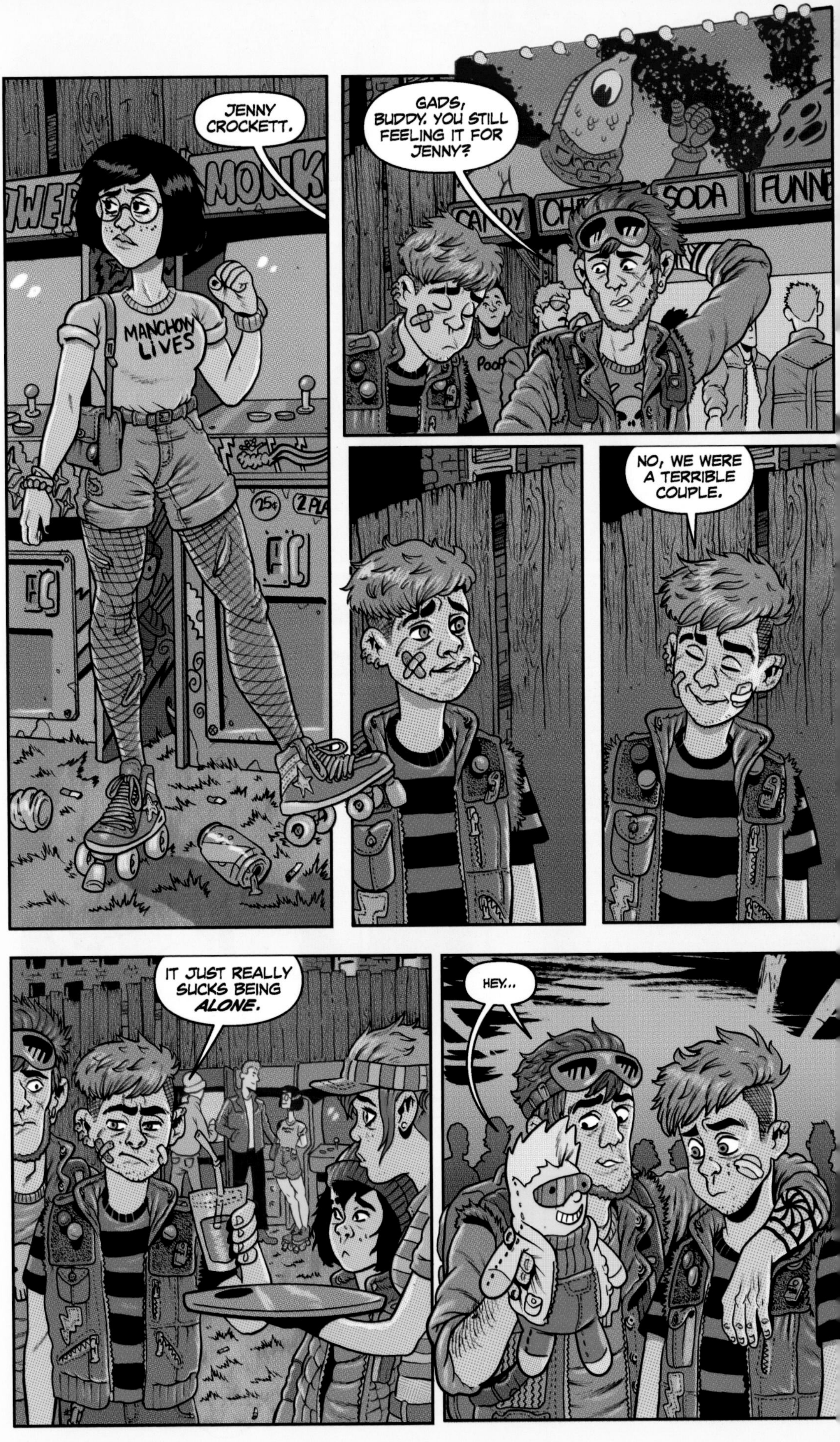
JENNY CROCKETT.
MANCHOW LIVES
GADS, BUDDY. YOU STILL FEELING IT FOR JENNY?
SODA
NO, WE WERE A TERRIBLE COUPLE.
IT JUST REALLY SUCKS BEING *ALONE*.
HEY...

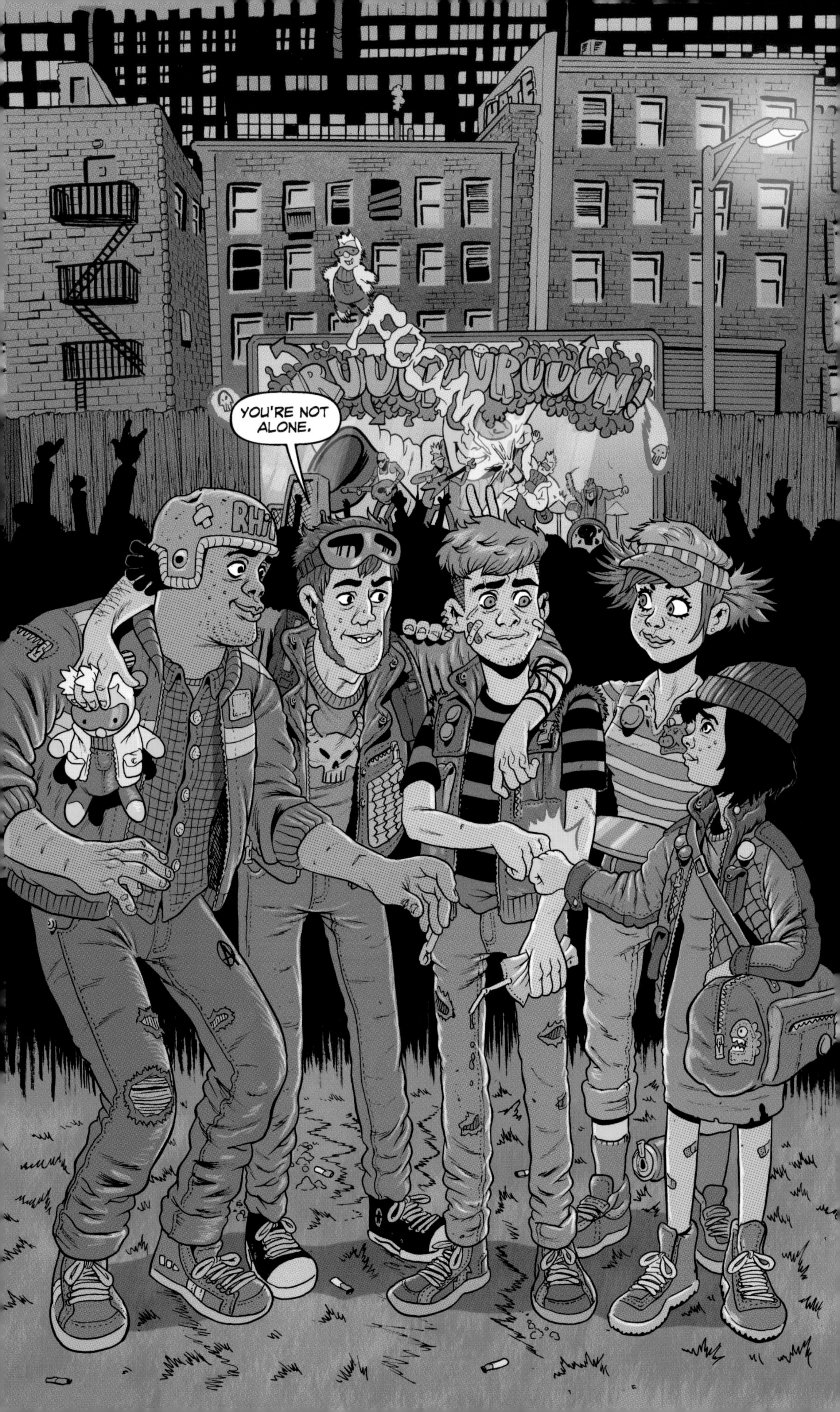
YOU'RE NOT ALONE.

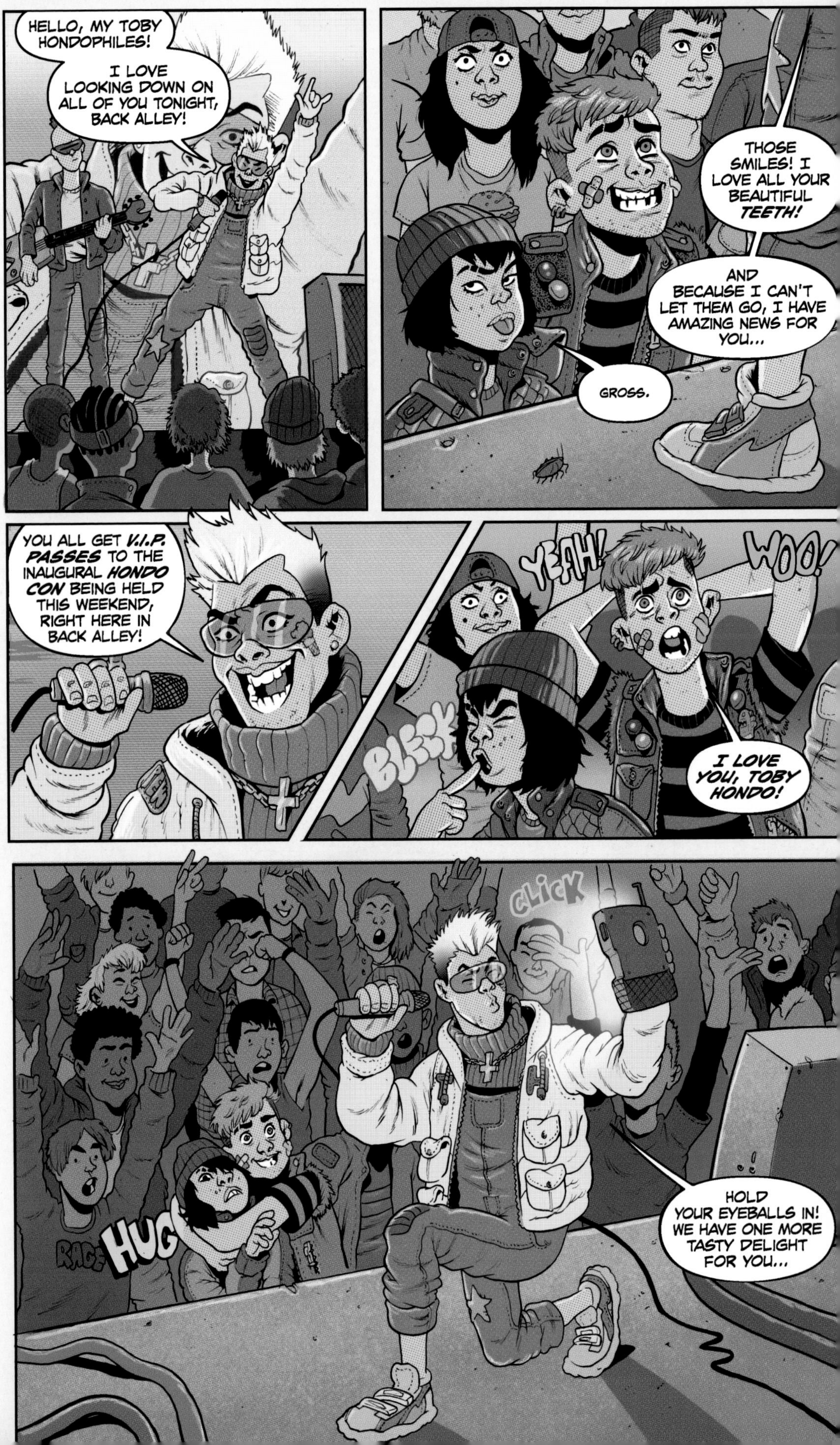
HELLO, MY TOBY HONDOPHILES!
I LOVE LOOKING DOWN ON ALL OF YOU TONIGHT, BACK ALLEY!
THOSE SMILES! I LOVE ALL YOUR BEAUTIFUL TEETH!
AND BECAUSE I CAN'T LET THEM GO, I HAVE AMAZING NEWS FOR YOU...
GROSS.
YOU ALL GET V.I.P. PASSES TO THE INAUGURAL HONDO CON BEING HELD THIS WEEKEND, RIGHT HERE IN BACK ALLEY!
YEAH!
WOO!
BLECK
I LOVE YOU, TOBY HONDO!
CLICK
HOLD YOUR EYEBALLS IN! WE HAVE ONE MORE TASTY DELIGHT FOR YOU...
RAGE
HUG

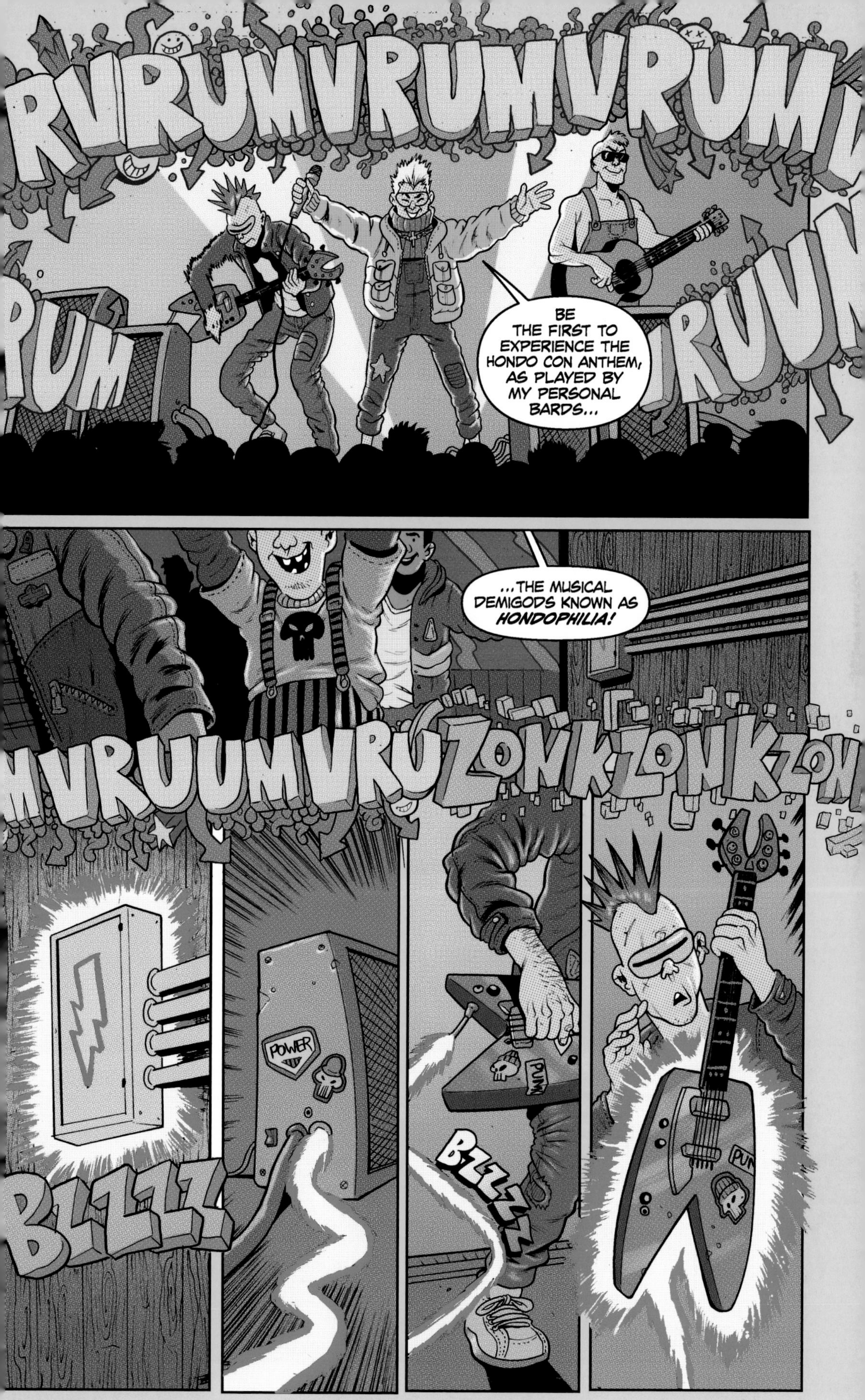
VRUMVRUMVRUMVRUM
RUM
RUUN
BE THE FIRST TO EXPERIENCE THE HONDO CON ANTHEM, AS PLAYED BY MY PERSONAL BARDS...
...THE MUSICAL DEMIGODS KNOWN AS *HONDOPHILIA!*
MVRUUMVRUZONKZONKZON
POWER
PUNK
BZZZZ
BZZZZ
PUN

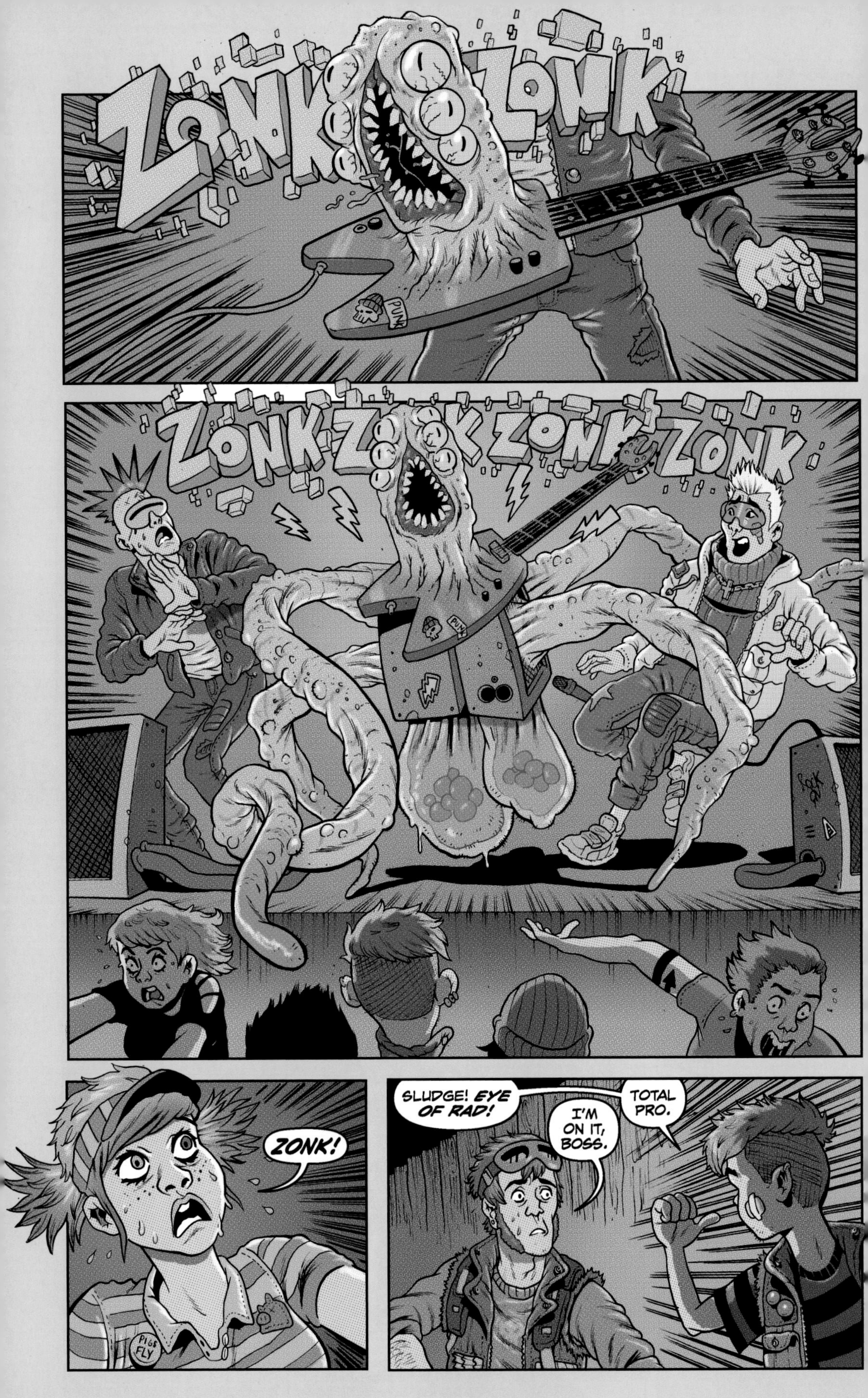
ZONK ZONK
PUNK
ZONK ZONK ZONK ZONK
PUNK
ZONK!
SLUDGE! EYE OF RAD!
TOTAL PRO.
I'M ON IT, BOSS.
PIGS FLY

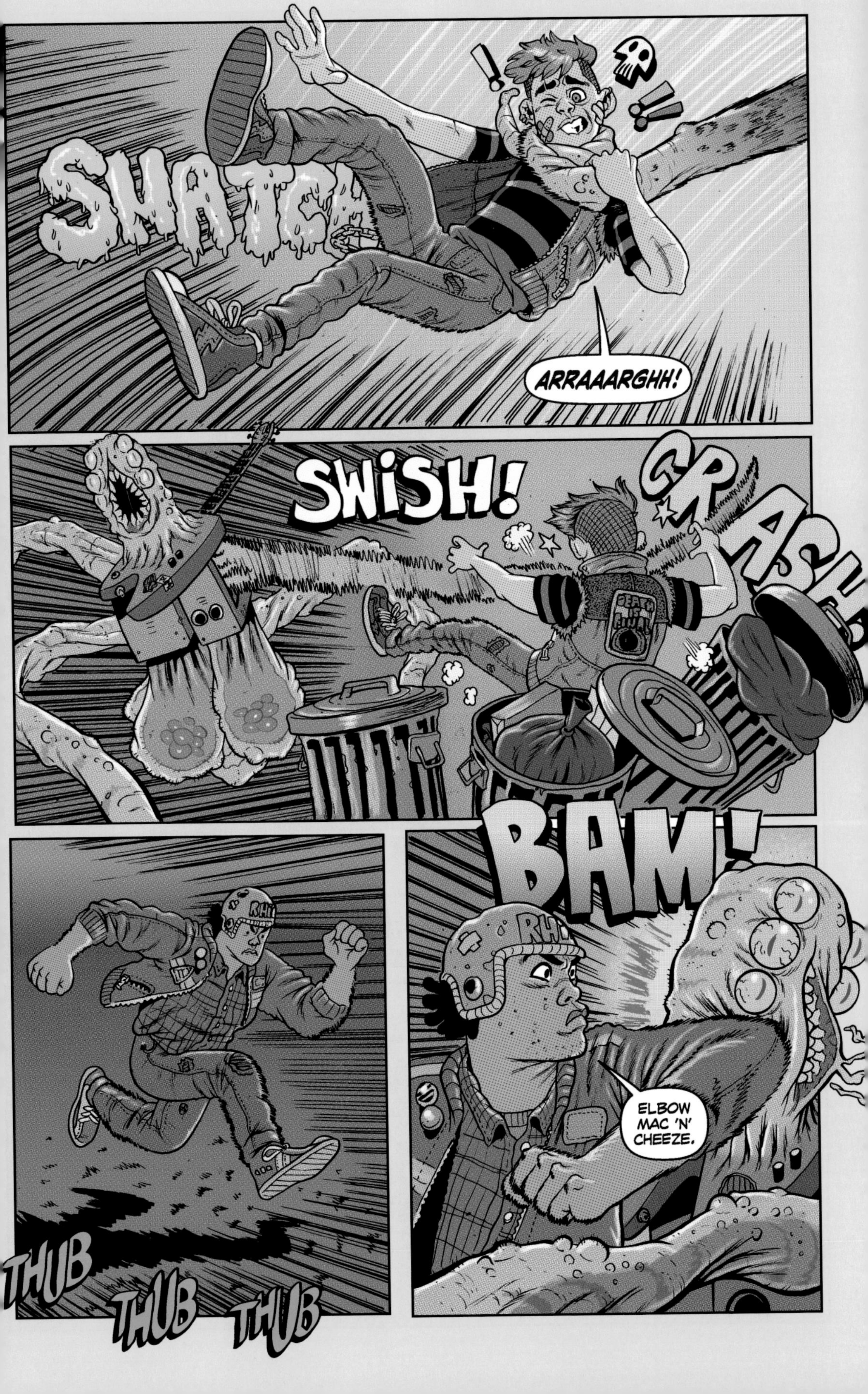
SNATCH
ARRAAARGHH!
SWISH!
CRASH
BAM!
THUB
THUB
THUB
ELBOW MAC 'N' CHEEZE.

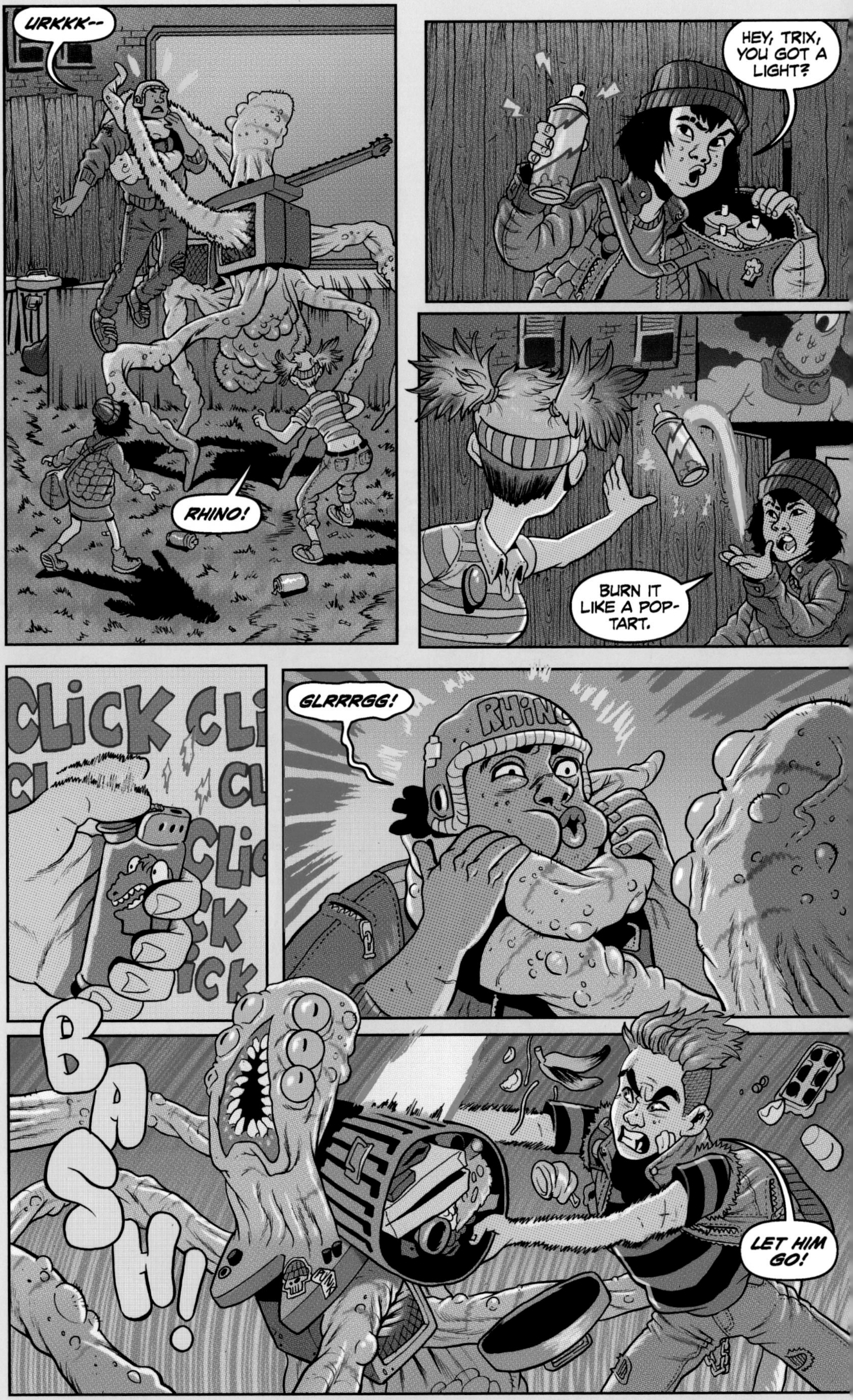
URKKK--
RHINO!
HEY, TRIX, YOU GOT A LIGHT?
BURN IT LIKE A POP-TART.
CLICK CLICK
CLICK
GLRRRGG!
RHINO
BASH!
LET HIM GO!
PUNK

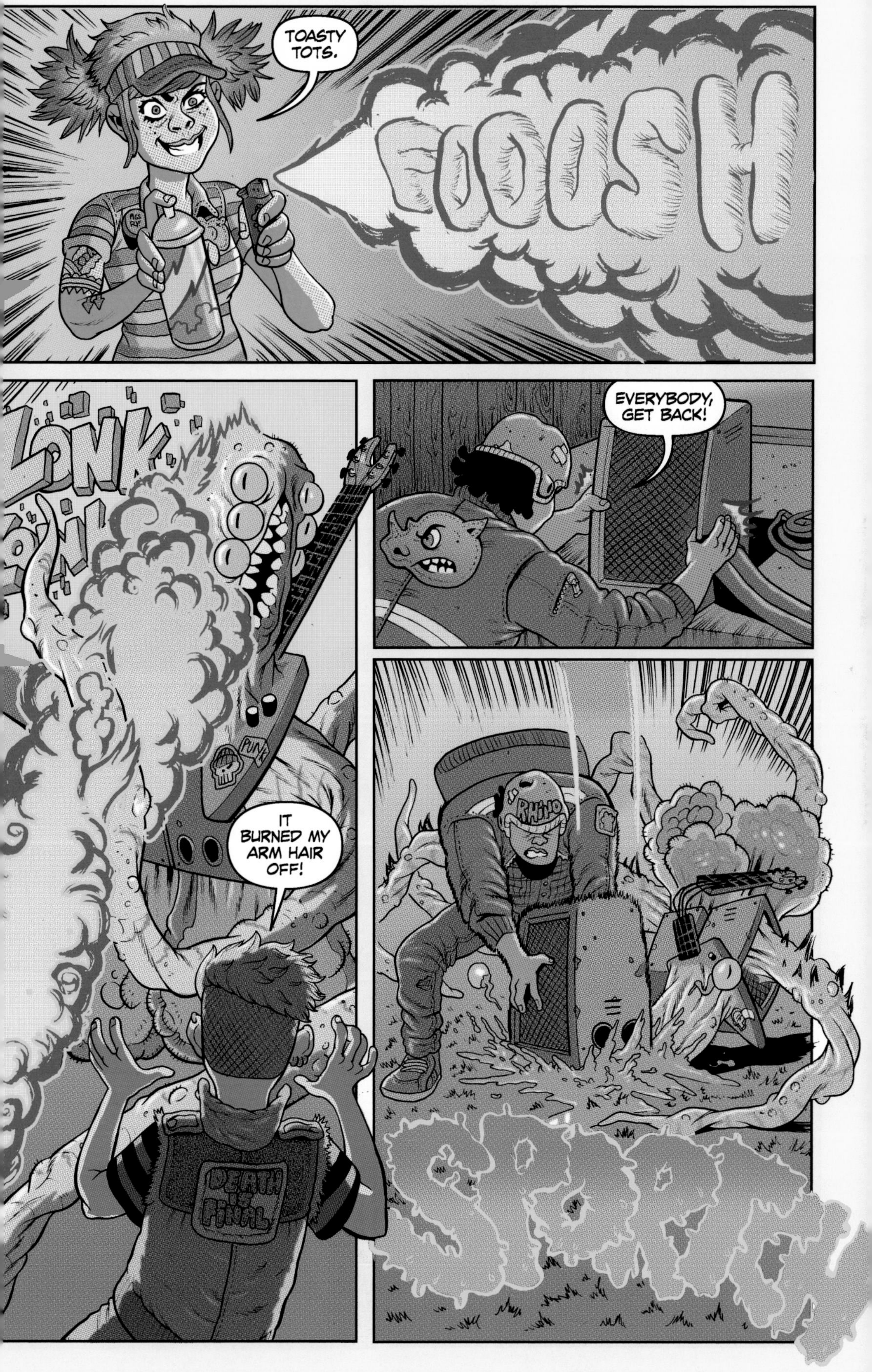
TOASTY TOTS.
FOOOSH
IT BURNED MY ARM HAIR OFF!
DEATH IS FINAL
EVERYBODY, GET BACK!
RHINO

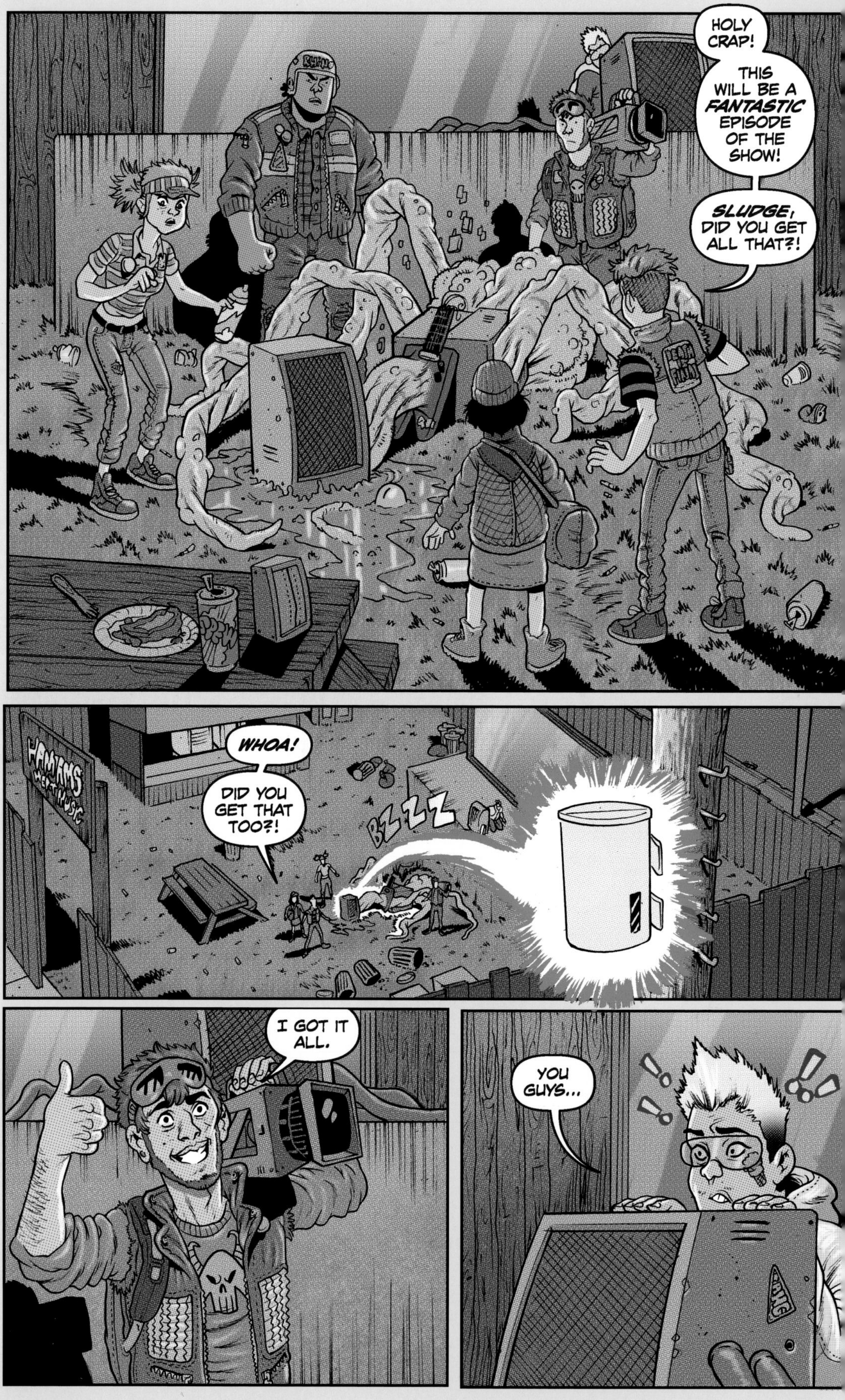
HOLY CRAP!
THIS WILL BE A *FANTASTIC* EPISODE OF THE SHOW!
SLUDGE, DID YOU GET ALL THAT?!
WHOA!
DID YOU GET THAT TOO?!
BZZZ
I GOT IT ALL.
YOU GUYS...

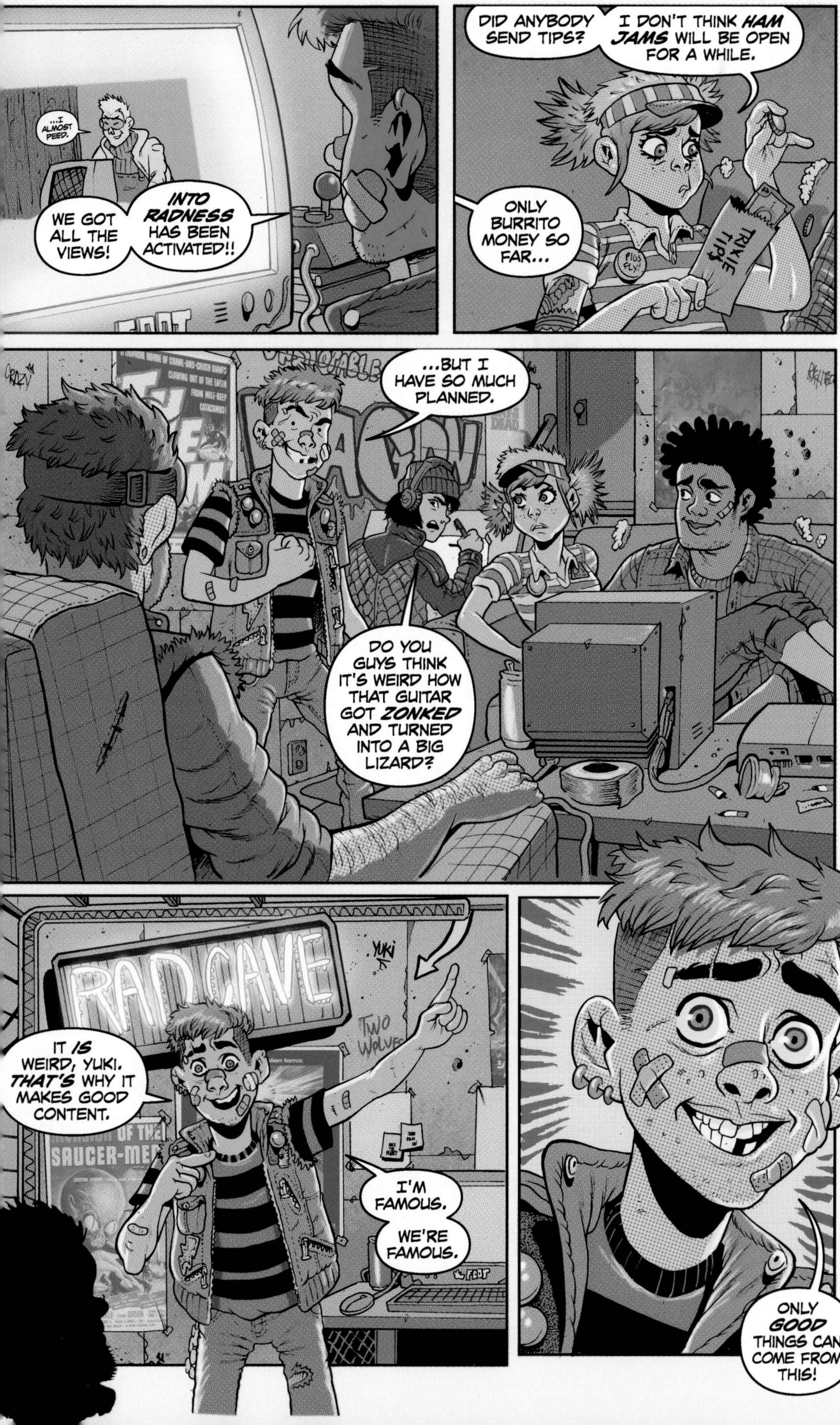
...I ALMOST PEED.
WE GOT ALL THE VIEWS!
INTO RADNESS HAS BEEN ACTIVATED!!
DID ANYBODY SEND TIPS?
I DON'T THINK HAM JAMS WILL BE OPEN FOR A WHILE.
ONLY BURRITO MONEY SO FAR...
TRIXIE TIPS
...BUT I HAVE SO MUCH PLANNED.
DO YOU GUYS THINK IT'S WEIRD HOW THAT GUITAR GOT ZONKED AND TURNED INTO A BIG LIZARD?
RAD CAVE
YUKI
TWO WOLVES
IT IS WEIRD, YUKI. THAT'S WHY IT MAKES GOOD CONTENT.
SAUCER-MEN
I'M FAMOUS.
WE'RE FAMOUS.
ONLY GOOD THINGS CAN COME FROM THIS!

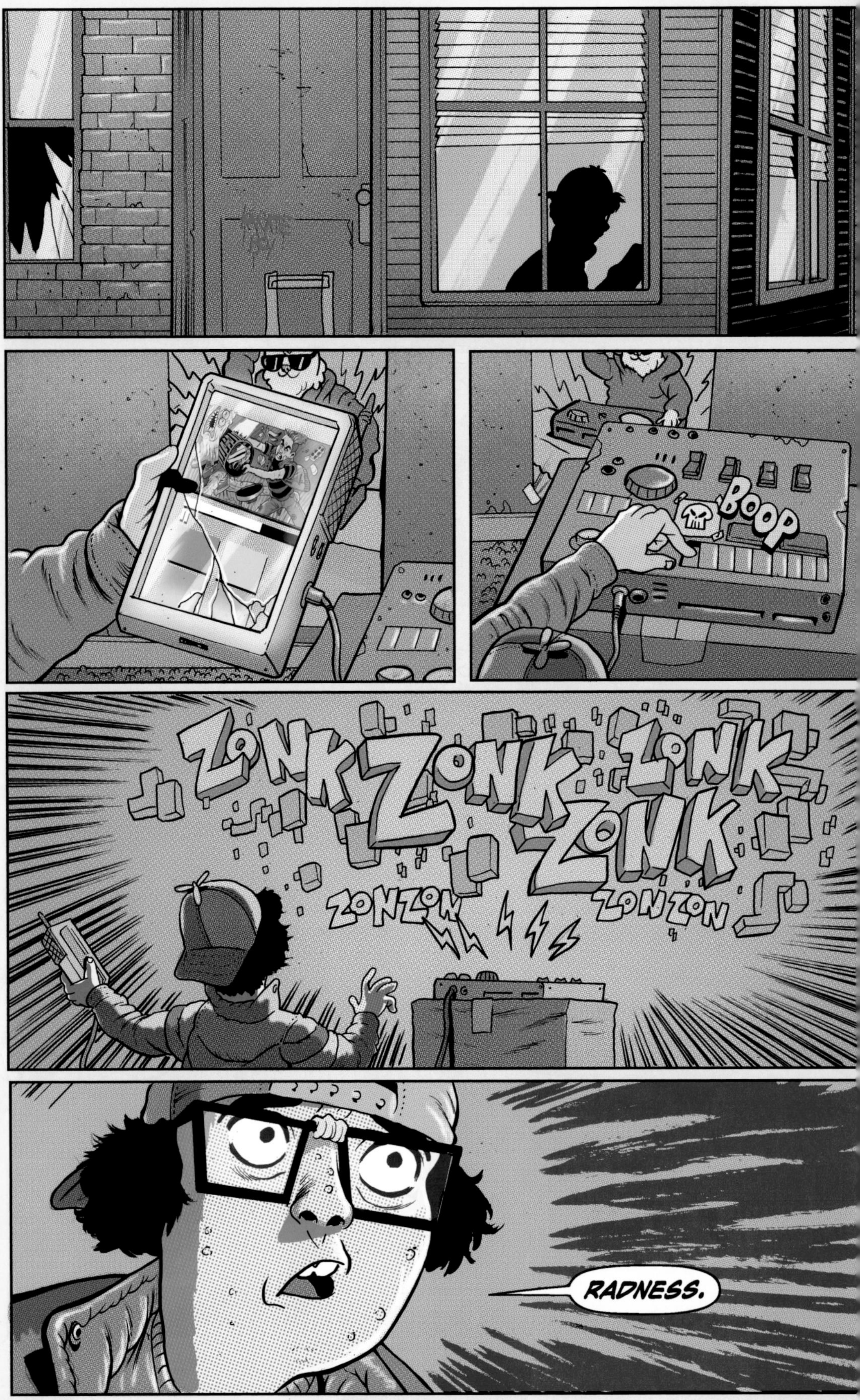
BOOP
ZONK ZONK ZONK ZONK
ZONZON
ZONZON
RADNESS.

CHAPTER TWO

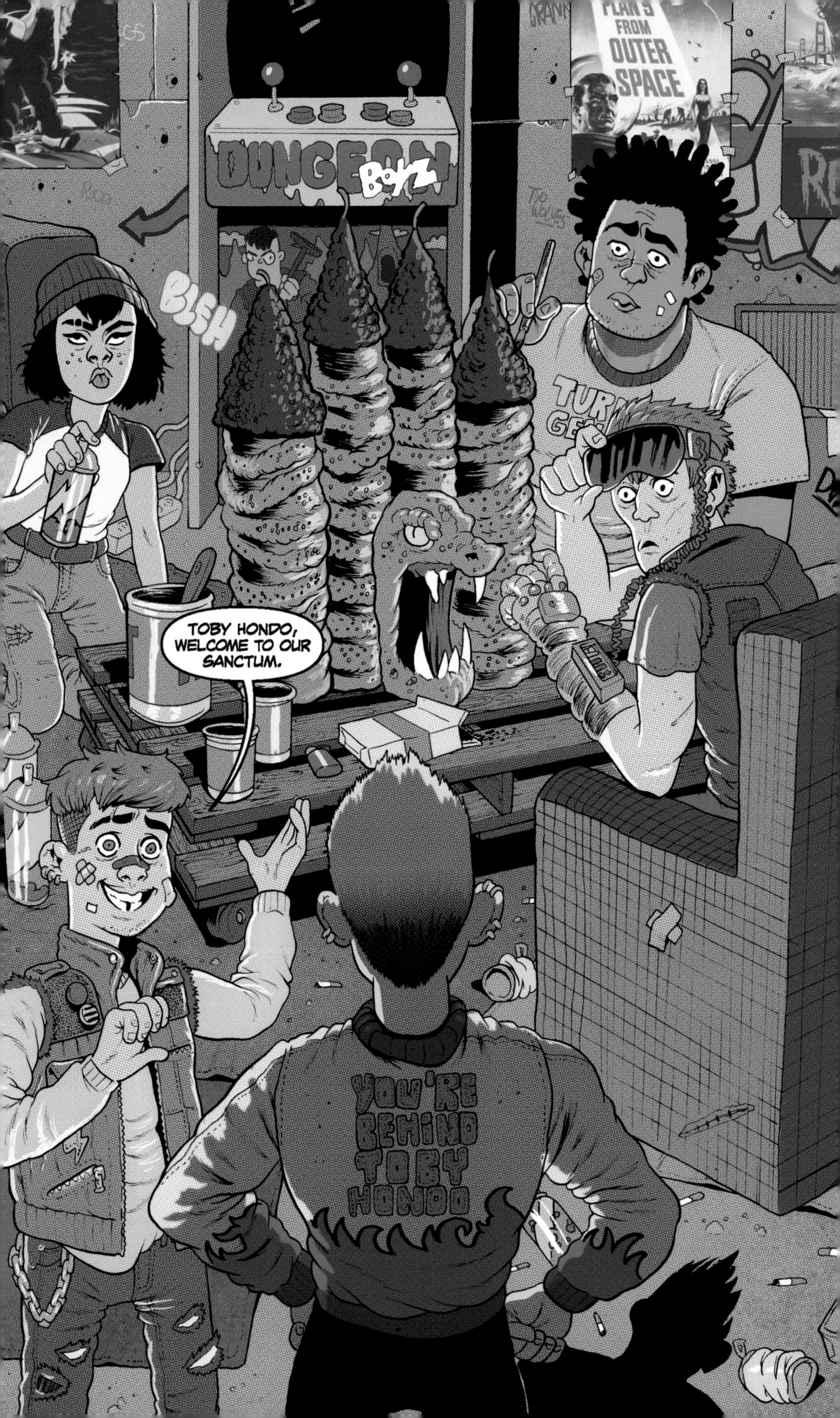
DUNGEON Boyz
FROM OUTER SPACE
BLEH
TOBY HONDO, WELCOME TO OUR SANCTUM.
YOU'RE BEHIND TOBY HONDO

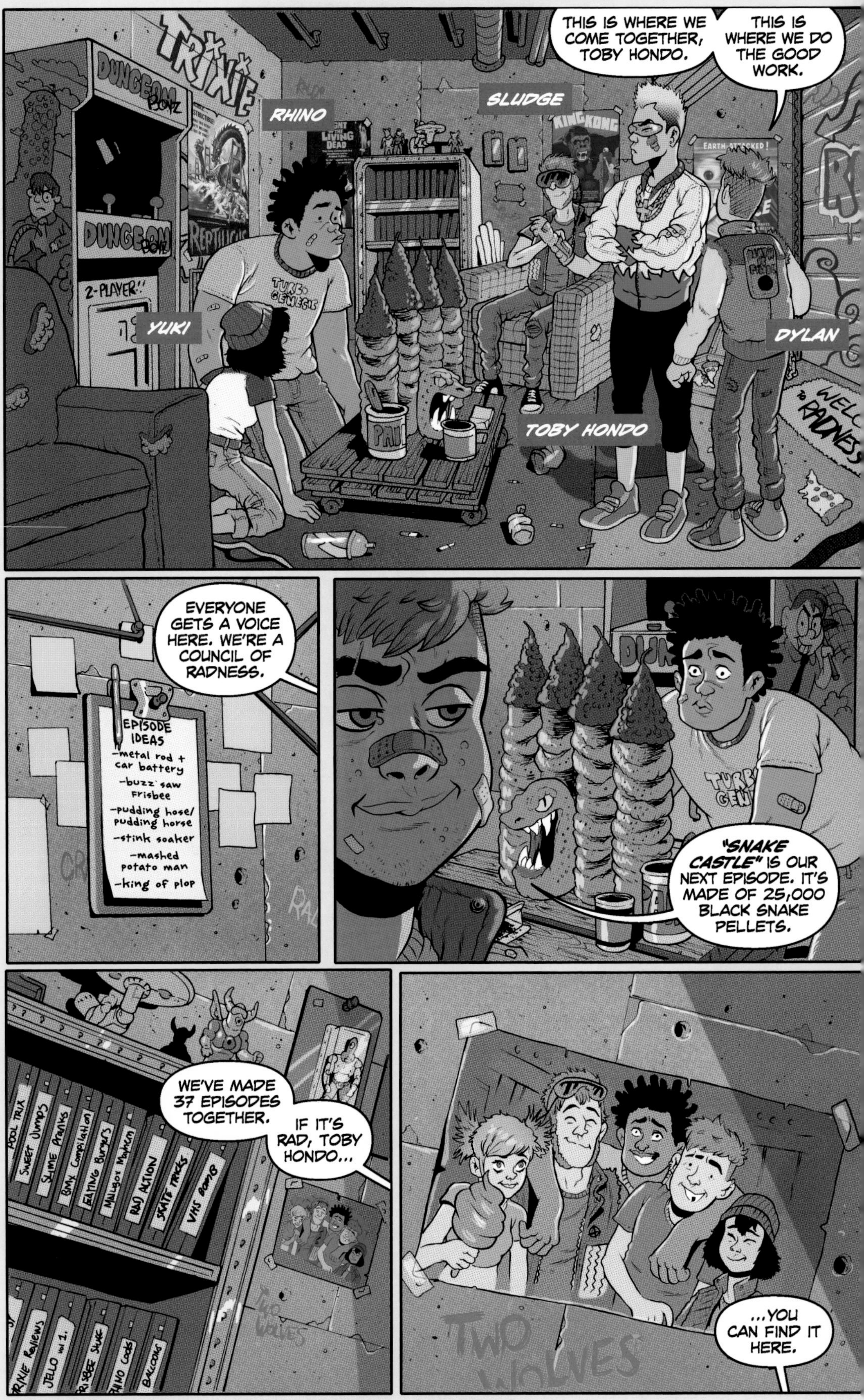
TRIXIE
DUNGEON BONZ
RHINO
SLUDGE
KING KONG
THIS IS WHERE WE COME TOGETHER, TOBY HONDO.
THIS IS WHERE WE DO THE GOOD WORK.
YUKI
DYLAN
TOBY HONDO
2-PLAYER!!
WELCOME TO RADNESS
EVERYONE GETS A VOICE HERE. WE'RE A COUNCIL OF RADNESS.
EPISODE IDEAS
-metal rod + car battery
-buzz saw Frisbee
-pudding hose/ pudding horse
-stink soaker
-mashed potato man
-king of plop
"SNAKE CASTLE" IS OUR NEXT EPISODE. IT'S MADE OF 25,000 BLACK SNAKE PELLETS.
WE'VE MADE 37 EPISODES TOGETHER.
IF IT'S RAD, TOBY HONDO...
POOL TRIX
SWEET JUMPS
SLIME PRANKS
BMX COMPILATION
EATING BURGERS
MALLGOER MAYHEM
RAD ACTION
SKATE TRICKS
VHS BOMB
TRIXIE REVIEWS
JELLO vol 1.
FRISBEE STUFF
RHINO CARDS
BALLOONS
...YOU CAN FIND IT HERE.
TWO WOLVES

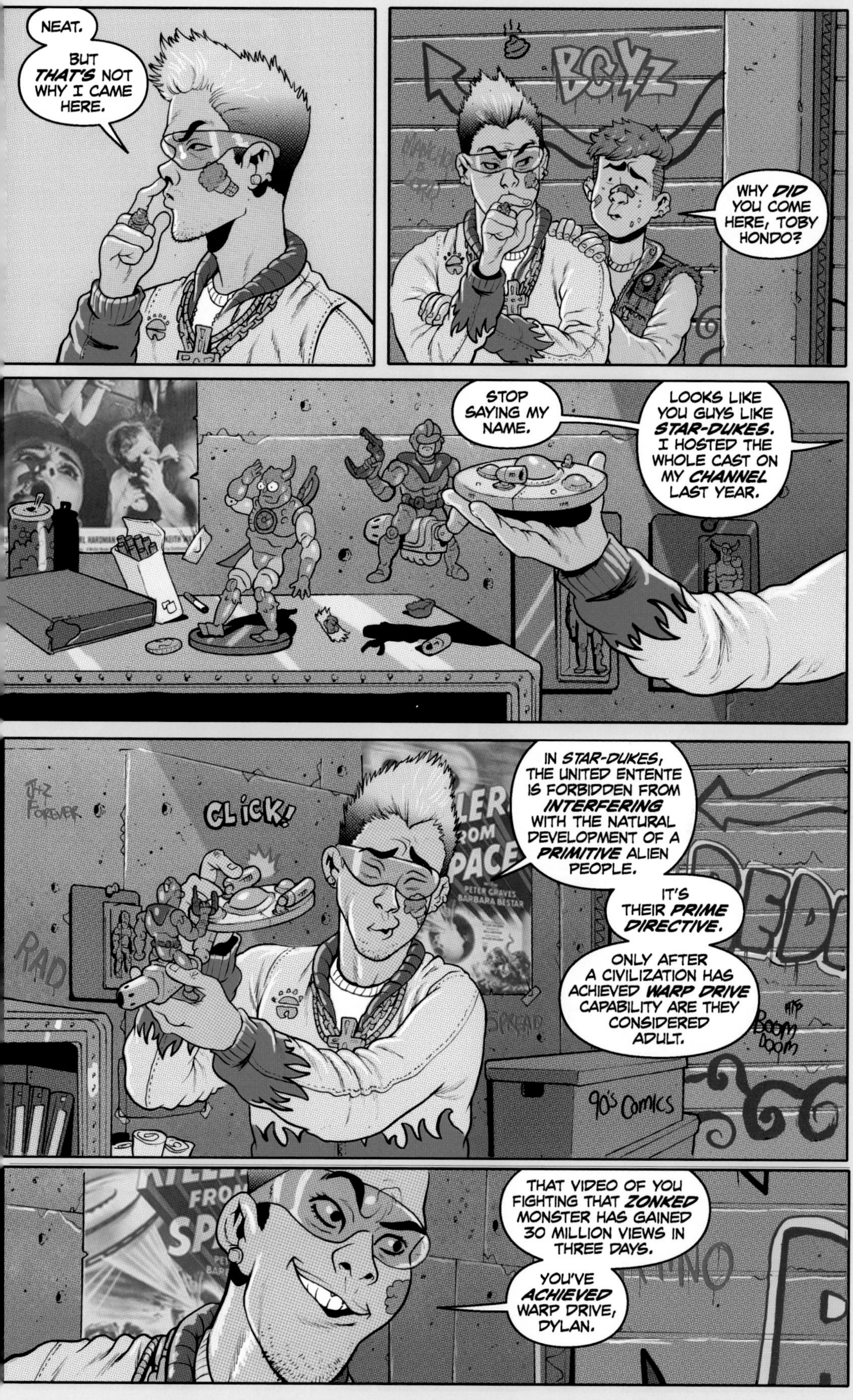
NEAT.
BUT *THAT'S* NOT WHY I CAME HERE.
WHY *DID* YOU COME HERE, TOBY HONDO?
STOP SAYING MY NAME.
LOOKS LIKE YOU GUYS LIKE *STAR-DUKES*. I HOSTED THE WHOLE CAST ON MY *CHANNEL* LAST YEAR.
CLICK!
IN *STAR-DUKES*, THE UNITED ENTENTE IS FORBIDDEN FROM *INTERFERING* WITH THE NATURAL DEVELOPMENT OF A *PRIMITIVE* ALIEN PEOPLE.
IT'S THEIR *PRIME DIRECTIVE*.
ONLY AFTER A CIVILIZATION HAS ACHIEVED *WARP DRIVE* CAPABILITY ARE THEY CONSIDERED ADULT.
90's Comics
THAT VIDEO OF YOU FIGHTING THAT *ZONKED* MONSTER HAS GAINED 30 MILLION VIEWS IN THREE DAYS.
YOU'VE *ACHIEVED* WARP DRIVE, DYLAN.

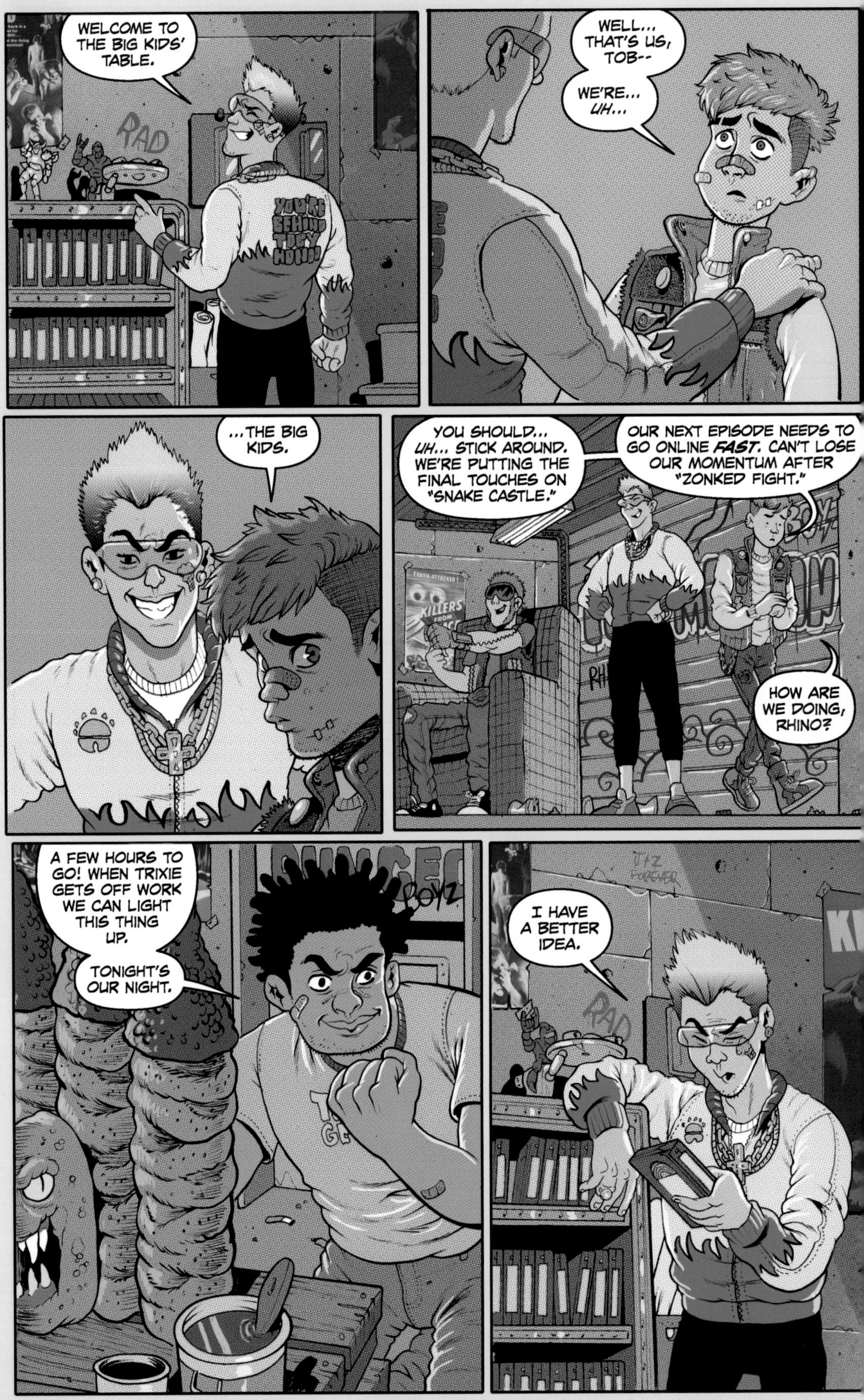

WELCOME TO THE BIG KIDS' TABLE.
RAD
WELL... THAT'S US, TOB--
WE'RE... UH...
...THE BIG KIDS.
YOU SHOULD... UH... STICK AROUND. WE'RE PUTTING THE FINAL TOUCHES ON "SNAKE CASTLE."
OUR NEXT EPISODE NEEDS TO GO ONLINE FAST. CAN'T LOSE OUR MOMENTUM AFTER "ZONKED FIGHT."
EARTH ATTACKED!
KILLERS
HOW ARE WE DOING, RHINO?
A FEW HOURS TO GO! WHEN TRIXIE GETS OFF WORK WE CAN LIGHT THIS THING UP.
TONIGHT'S OUR NIGHT.
BOYZ
I HAVE A BETTER IDEA.
RAD

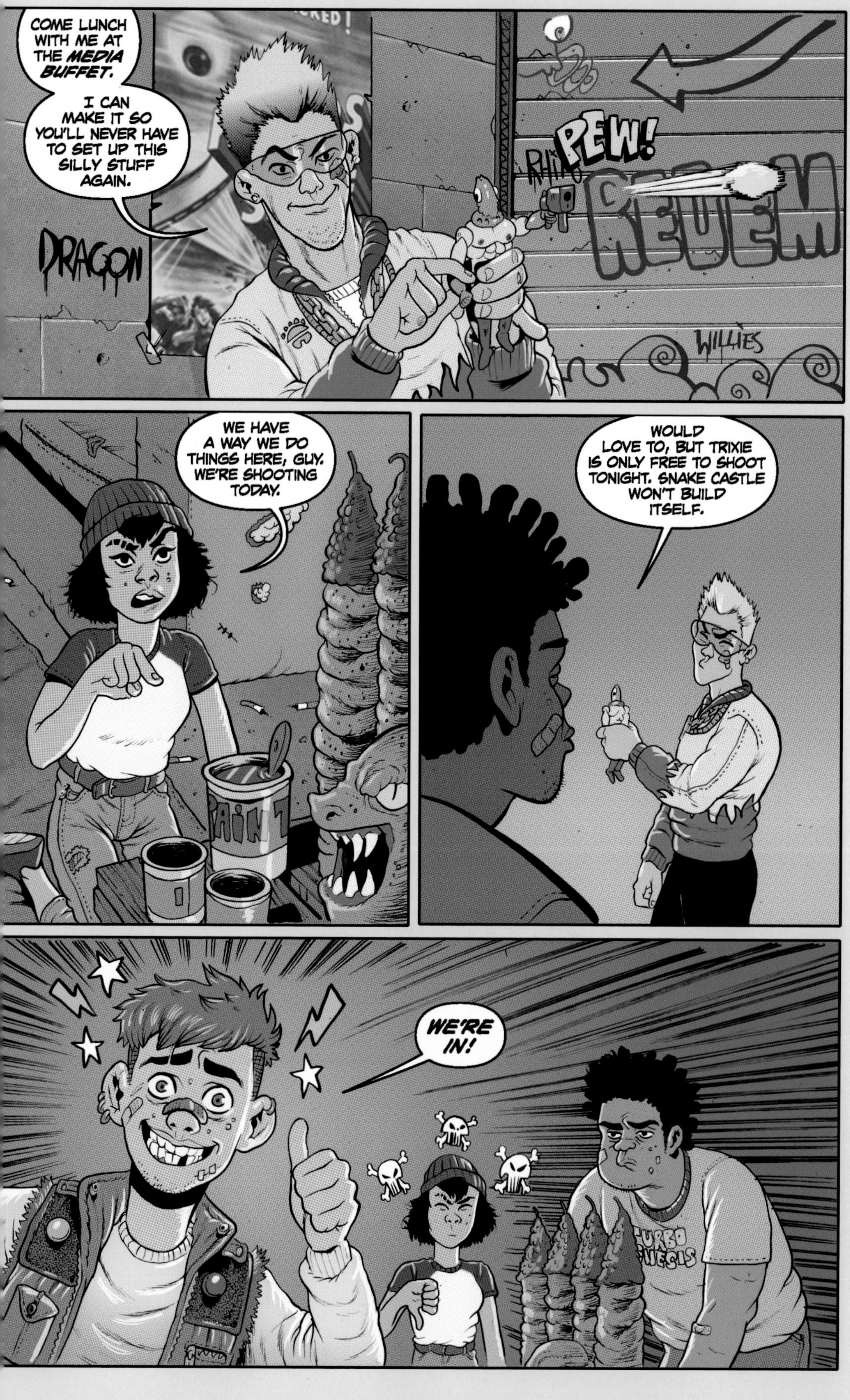
COME LUNCH WITH ME AT THE *MEDIA BUFFET*.
I CAN MAKE IT SO YOU'LL NEVER HAVE TO SET UP THIS SILLY STUFF AGAIN.
DRAGON
PEW!
RHINO
WILLIES
WE HAVE A WAY WE DO THINGS HERE, GUY. WE'RE SHOOTING TODAY.
PAINT
WOULD LOVE TO, BUT TRIXIE IS ONLY FREE TO SHOOT TONIGHT. SNAKE CASTLE WON'T BUILD ITSELF.
WE'RE IN!

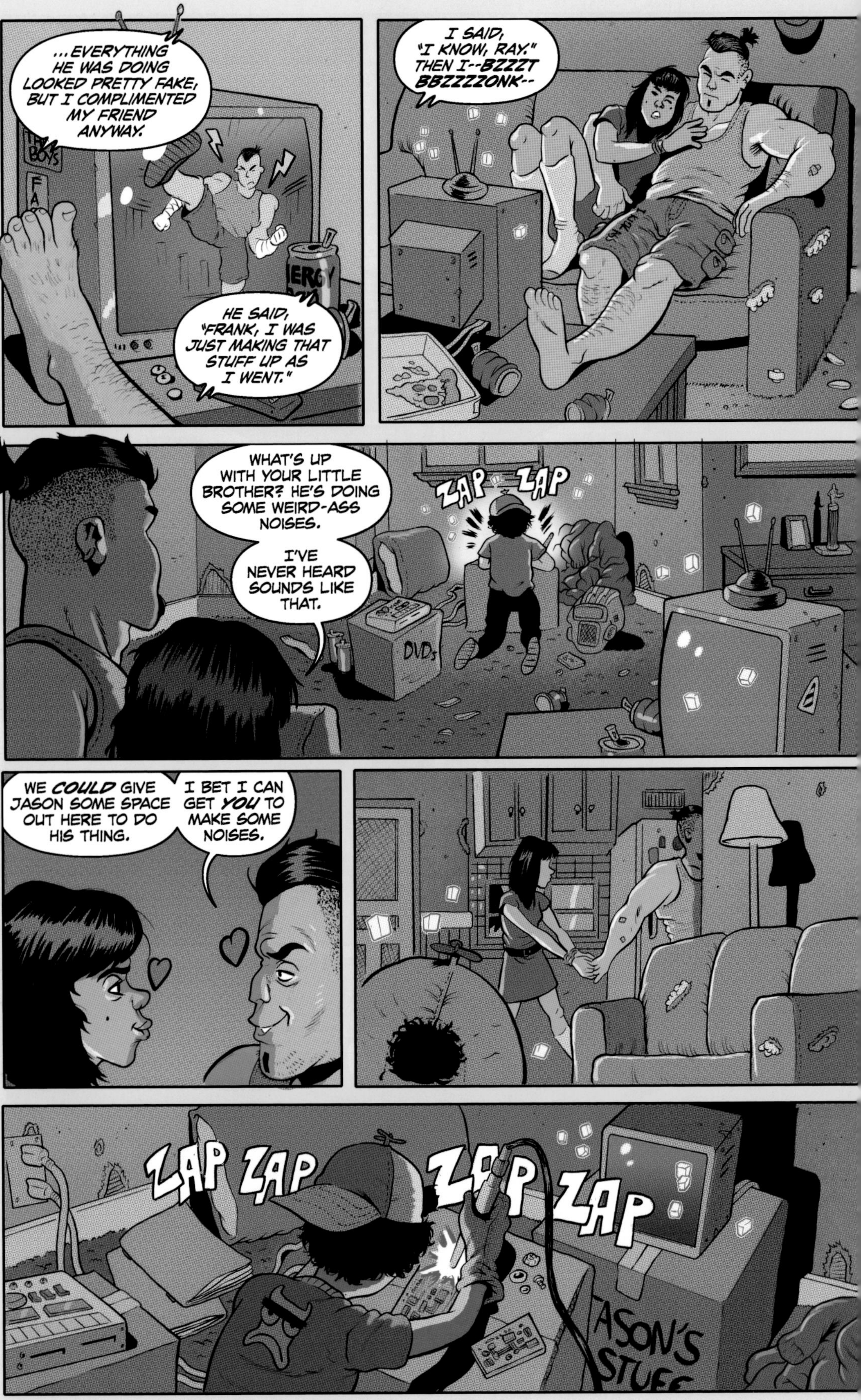
...EVERYTHING HE WAS DOING LOOKED PRETTY FAKE; BUT I COMPLIMENTED MY FRIEND ANYWAY.
HE SAID, "FRANK, I WAS JUST MAKING THAT STUFF UP AS I WENT."
I SAID, "I KNOW, RAY." THEN I--BZZZT BBZZZZZONK--
WHAT'S UP WITH YOUR LITTLE BROTHER? HE'S DOING SOME WEIRD-ASS NOISES.
I'VE NEVER HEARD SOUNDS LIKE THAT.
ZAP ZAP
DVDs
WE COULD GIVE JASON SOME SPACE OUT HERE TO DO HIS THING.
I BET I CAN GET YOU TO MAKE SOME NOISES.
ZAP ZAP ZAP ZAP
JASON'S STUFF

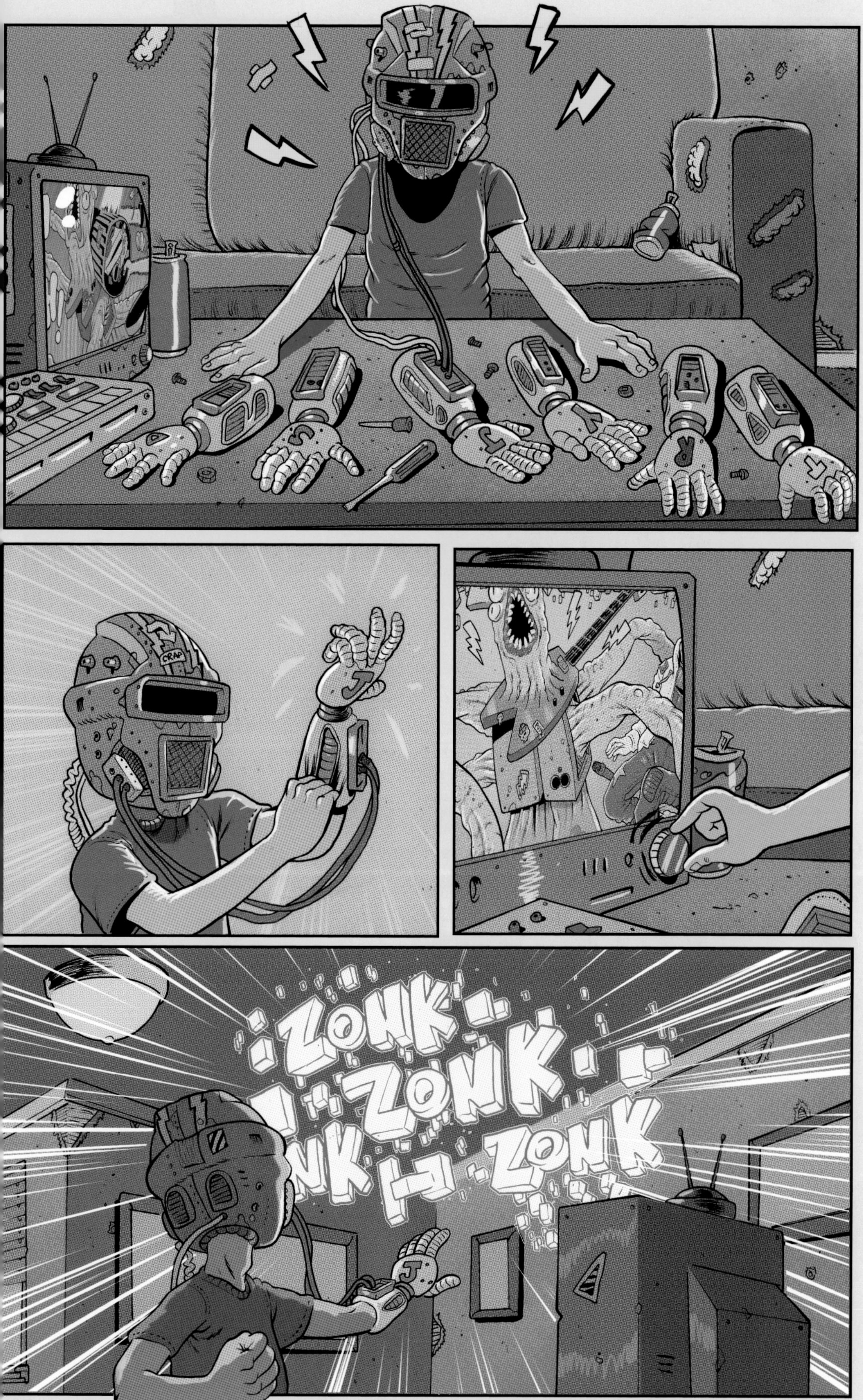
CRAP
ZONK
ZONK
NK
ZONK

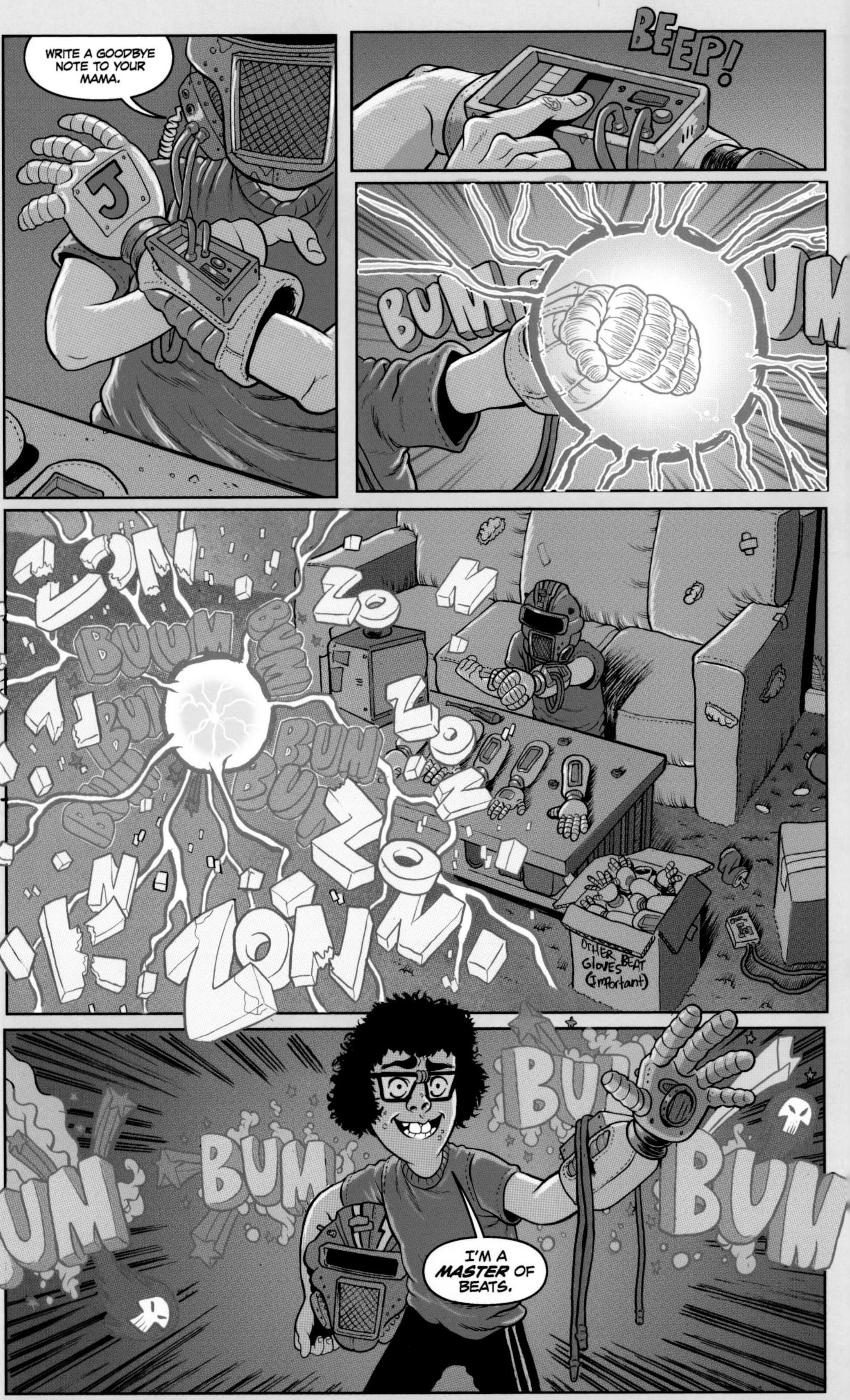
WRITE A GOODBYE NOTE TO YOUR MAMA.
BEEP!
BUM BUM
ZON ZON
OTHER BEAT GLOVES (Important)
BUM BUM BUM
I'M A MASTER OF BEATS.

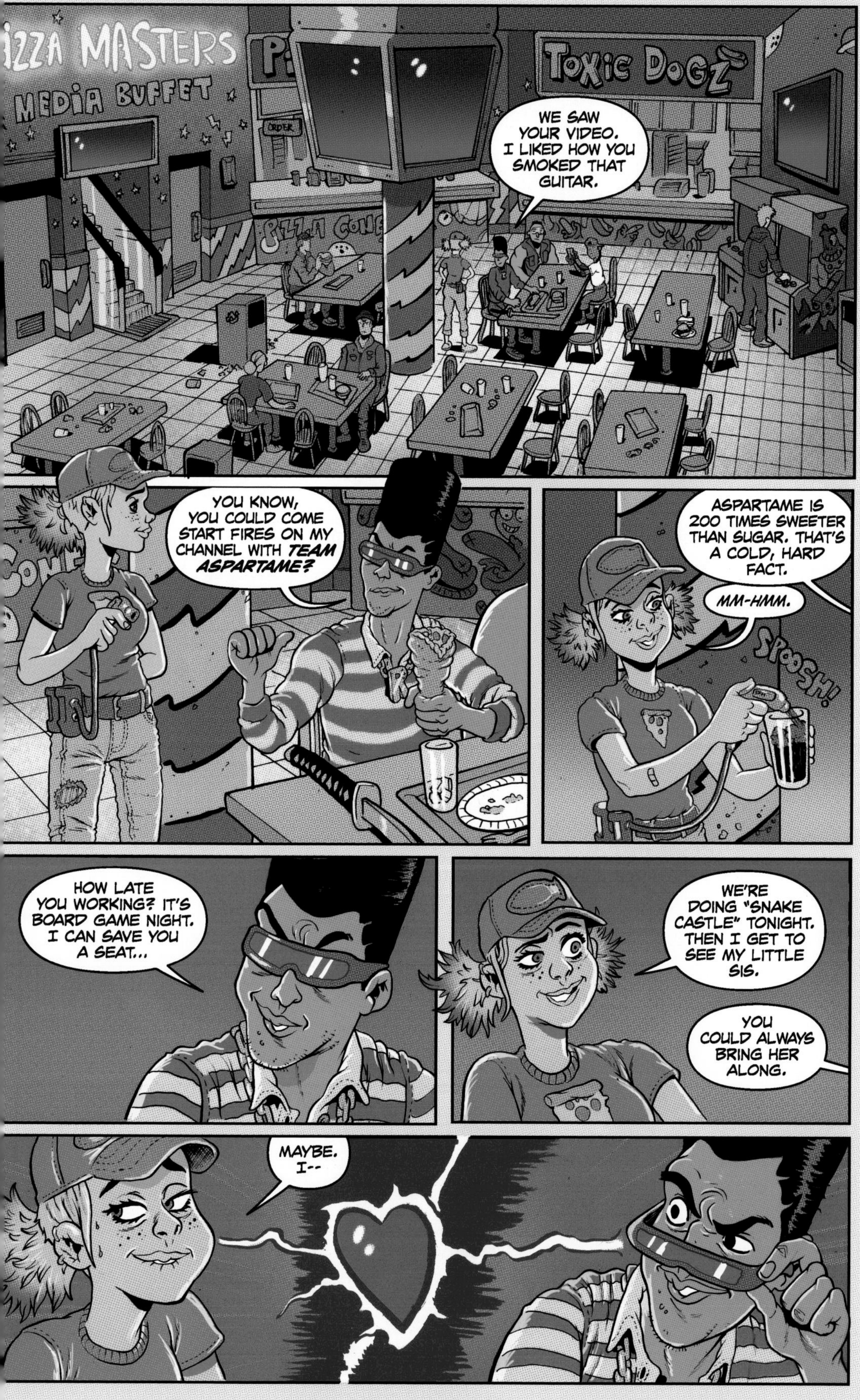
PIZZA MASTERS
MEDIA BUFFET
TOXIC DOGZ
ORDER
PIZZA CONE
WE SAW YOUR VIDEO. I LIKED HOW YOU SMOKED THAT GUITAR.
YOU KNOW, YOU COULD COME START FIRES ON MY CHANNEL WITH *TEAM ASPARTAME?*
ASPARTAME IS 200 TIMES SWEETER THAN SUGAR. THAT'S A COLD, HARD FACT.
MM-HMM.
SPOOSH!
HOW LATE YOU WORKING? IT'S BOARD GAME NIGHT. I CAN SAVE YOU A SEAT...
WE'RE DOING "SNAKE CASTLE" TONIGHT. THEN I GET TO SEE MY LITTLE SIS.
YOU COULD ALWAYS BRING HER ALONG.
MAYBE. I--

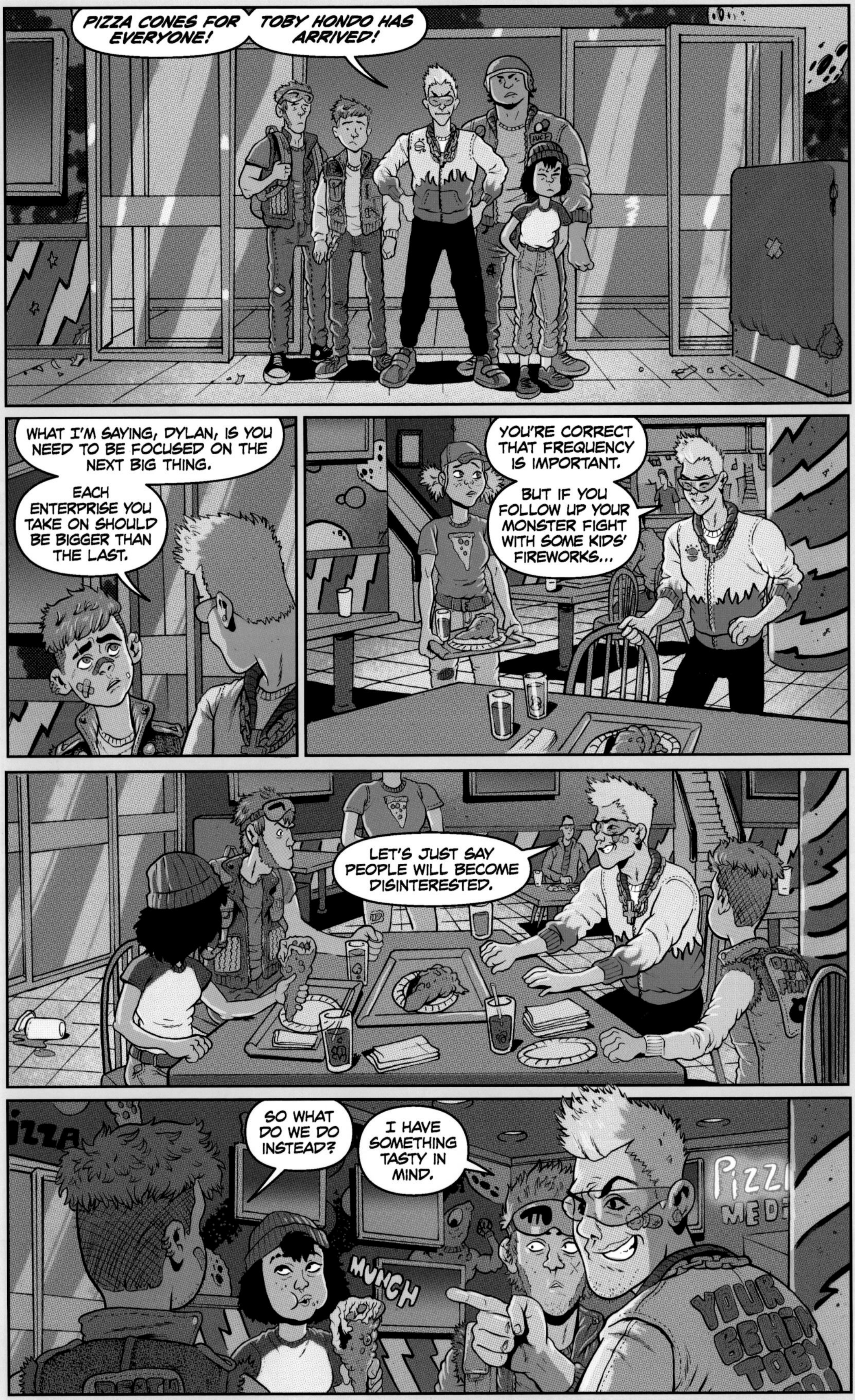

PIZZA CONES FOR EVERYONE!
TOBY HONDO HAS ARRIVED!
WHAT I'M SAYING, DYLAN, IS YOU NEED TO BE FOCUSED ON THE NEXT BIG THING.
EACH ENTERPRISE YOU TAKE ON SHOULD BE BIGGER THAN THE LAST.
YOU'RE CORRECT THAT FREQUENCY IS IMPORTANT.
BUT IF YOU FOLLOW UP YOUR MONSTER FIGHT WITH SOME KIDS' FIREWORKS...
LET'S JUST SAY PEOPLE WILL BECOME DISINTERESTED.
SO WHAT DO WE DO INSTEAD?
I HAVE SOMETHING TASTY IN MIND.
MUNCH

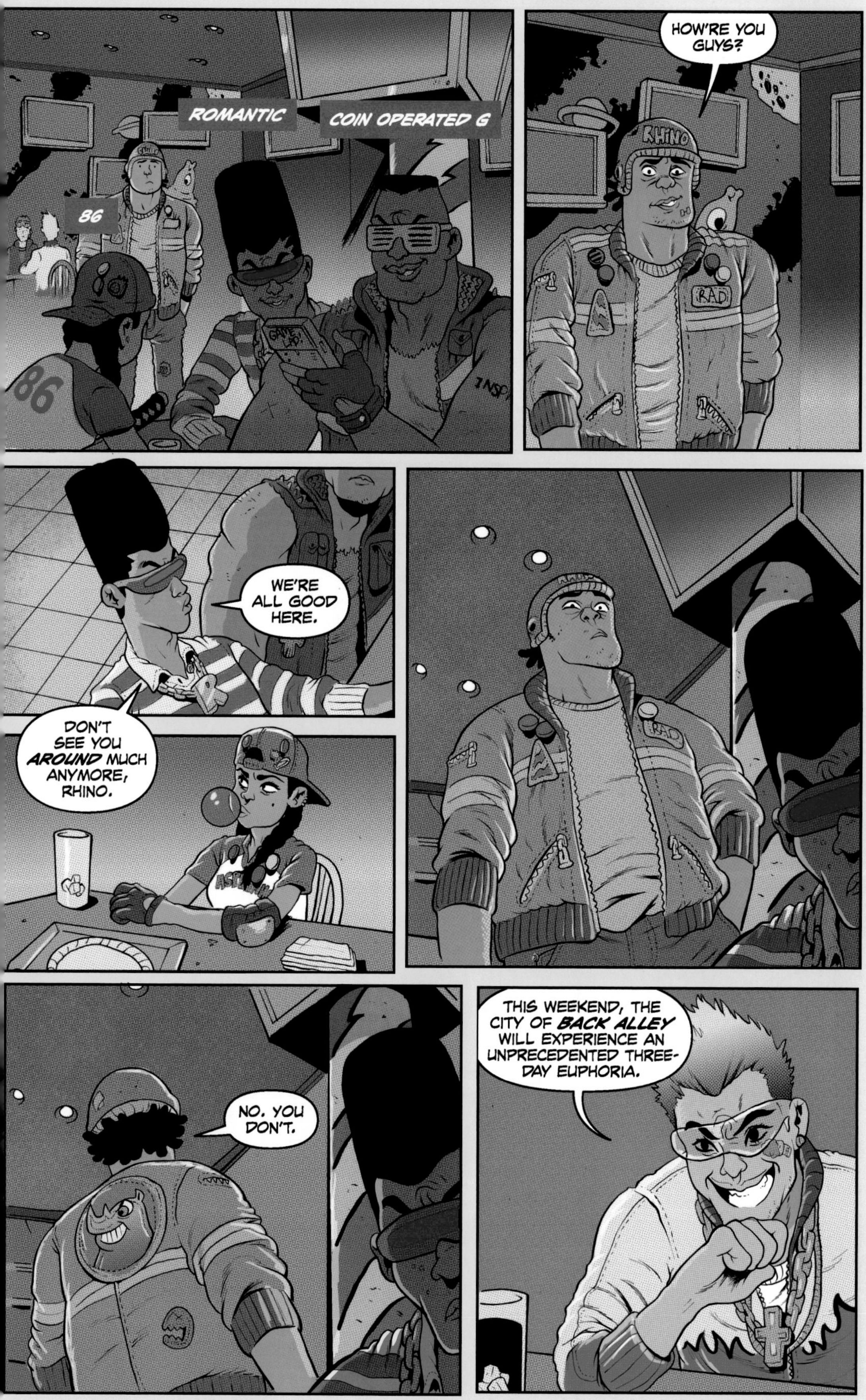
ROMANTIC
COIN OPERATED G
86
HOW'RE YOU GUYS?
RHINO
RAD
WE'RE ALL GOOD HERE.
DON'T SEE YOU AROUND MUCH ANYMORE, RHINO.
NO. YOU DON'T.
THIS WEEKEND, THE CITY OF BACK ALLEY WILL EXPERIENCE AN UNPRECEDENTED THREE-DAY EUPHORIA.

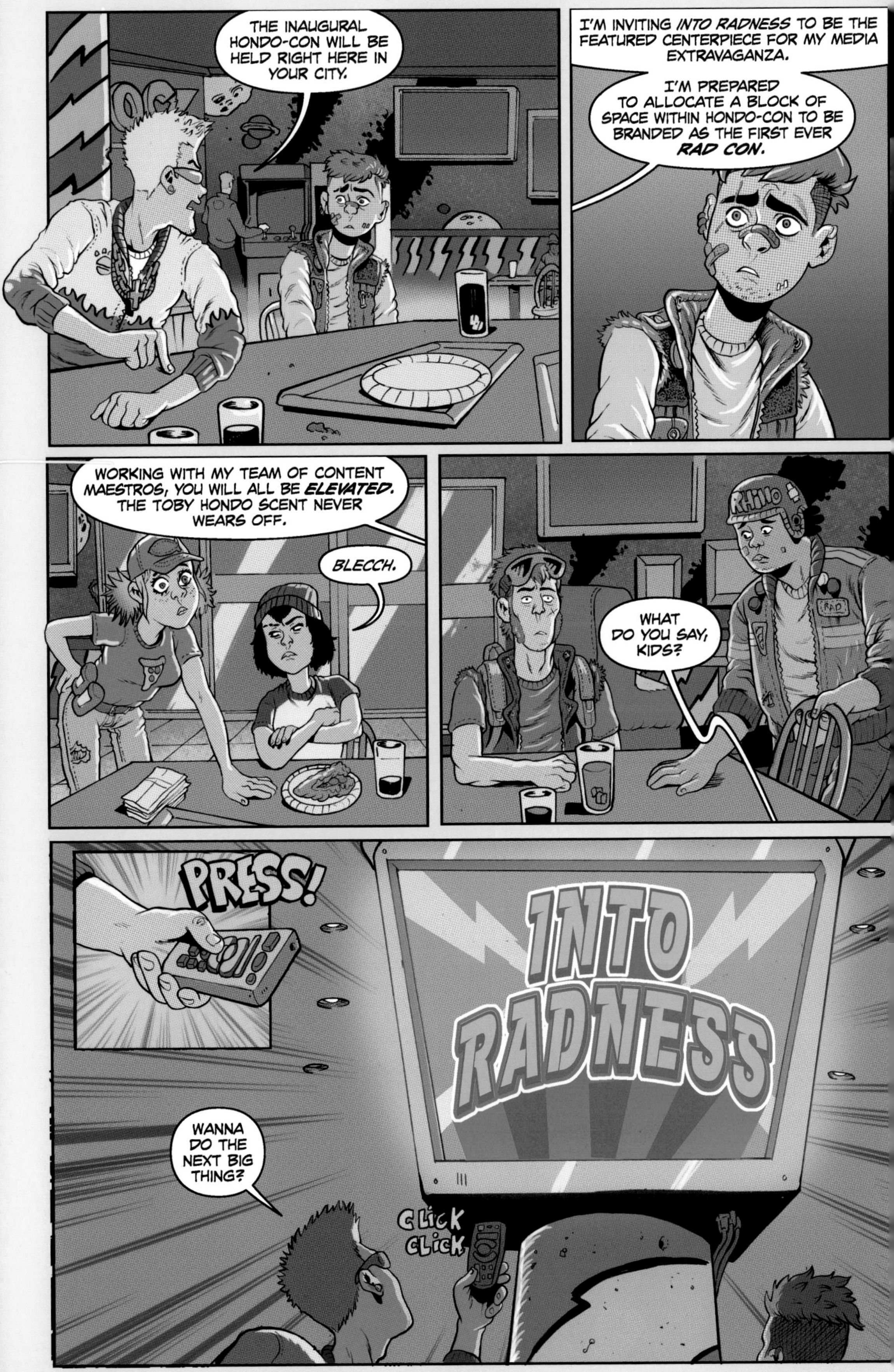
THE INAUGURAL HONDO-CON WILL BE HELD RIGHT HERE IN YOUR CITY.
I'M INVITING INTO RADNESS TO BE THE FEATURED CENTERPIECE FOR MY MEDIA EXTRAVAGANZA.
I'M PREPARED TO ALLOCATE A BLOCK OF SPACE WITHIN HONDO-CON TO BE BRANDED AS THE FIRST EVER RAD CON.
WORKING WITH MY TEAM OF CONTENT MAESTROS, YOU WILL ALL BE ELEVATED. THE TOBY HONDO SCENT NEVER WEARS OFF.
BLECCH.
RHINO
RAD
WHAT DO YOU SAY, KIDS?
PRESS!
INTO RADNESS
WANNA DO THE NEXT BIG THING?
CLICK CLICK

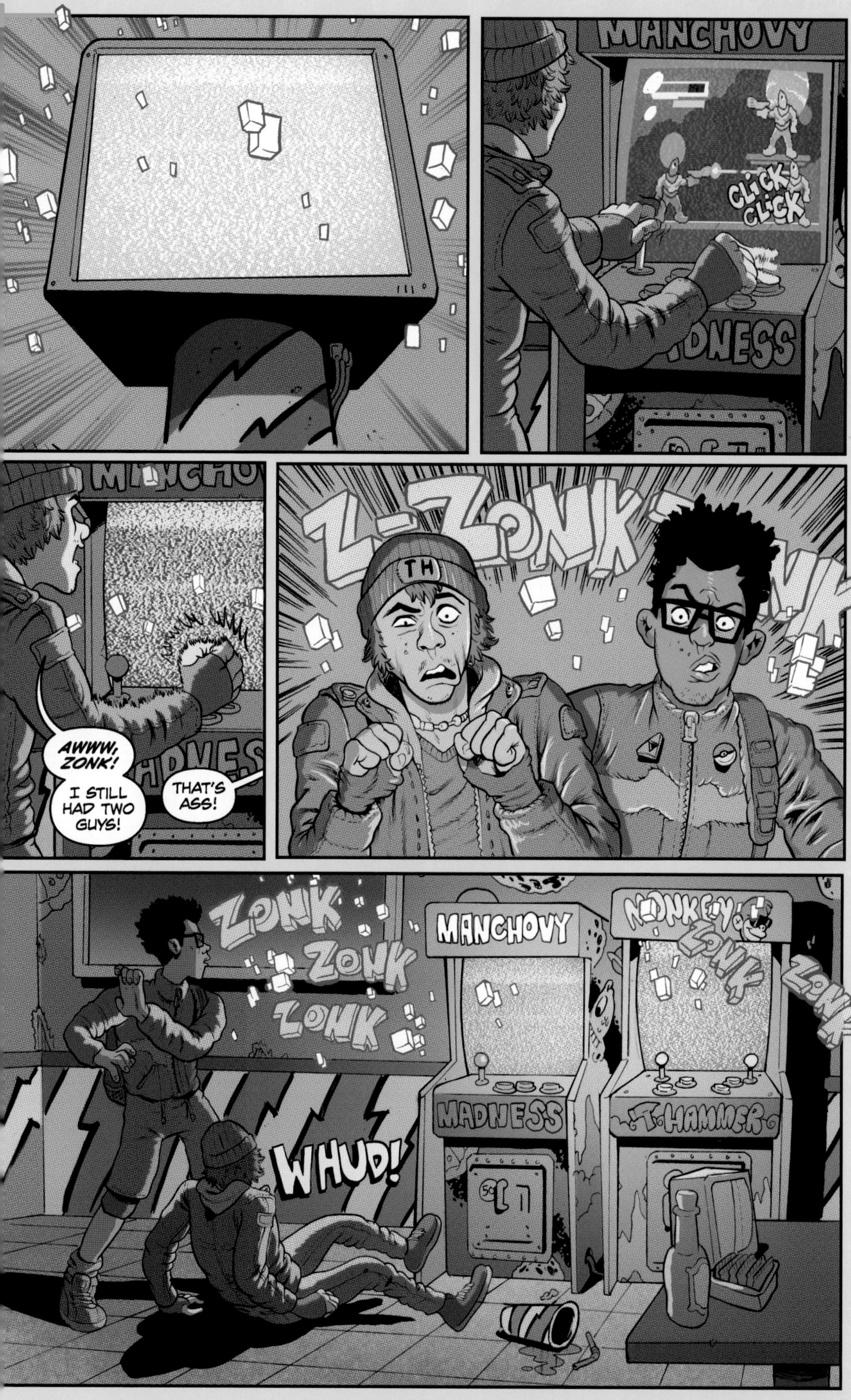
MANCHOVY
CLICK CLICK
MADNESS
AWWW, ZONK!
I STILL HAD TWO GUYS!
THAT'S ASS!
Z-ZONK
ZONK
ZONK
ZONK
MANCHOVY
MADNESS
T-HAMMER
ZONK
ZONK
WHUD!

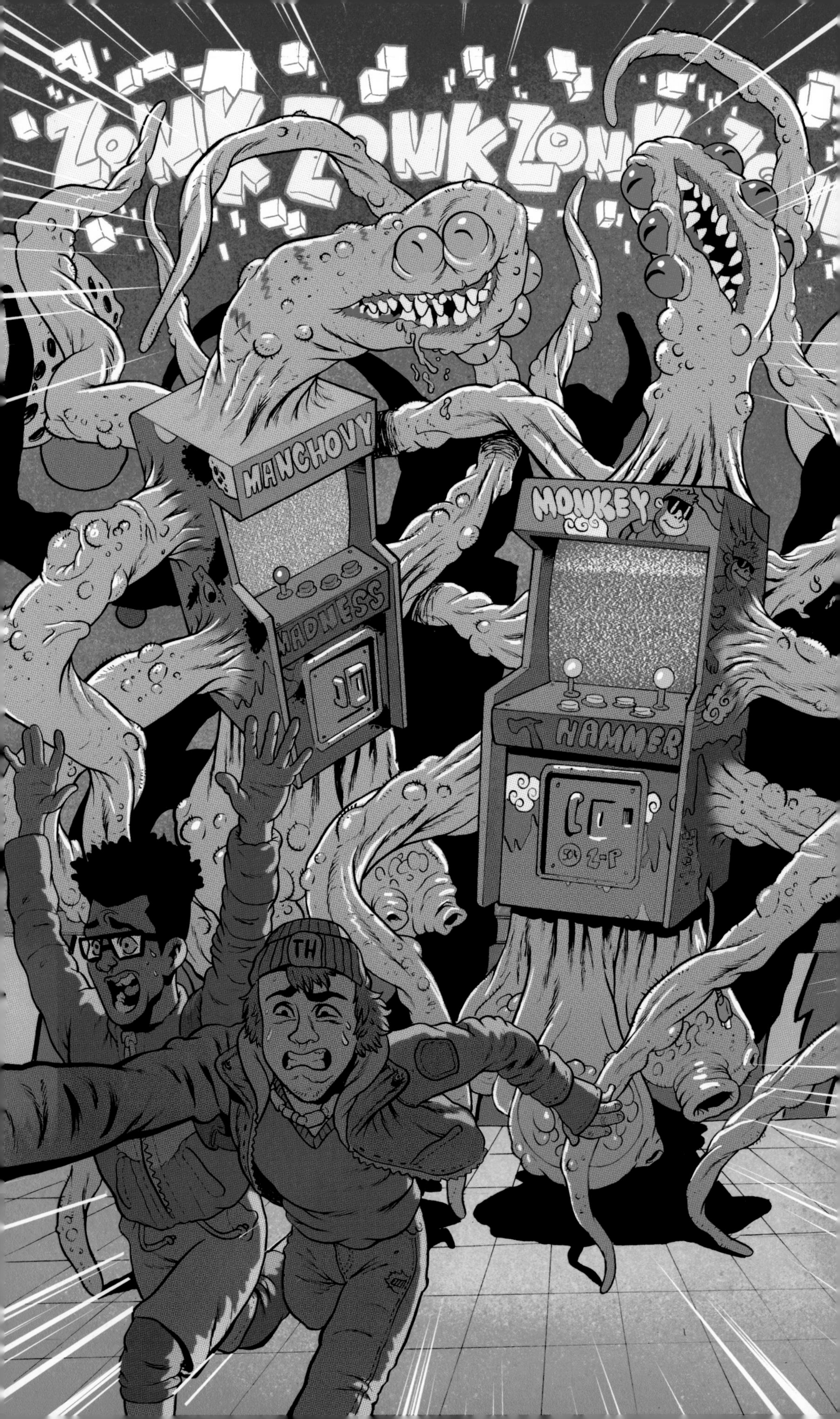
ZONK ZONK ZONK
MANCHOVY
MADNESS
MONKEY
HAMMER
TH

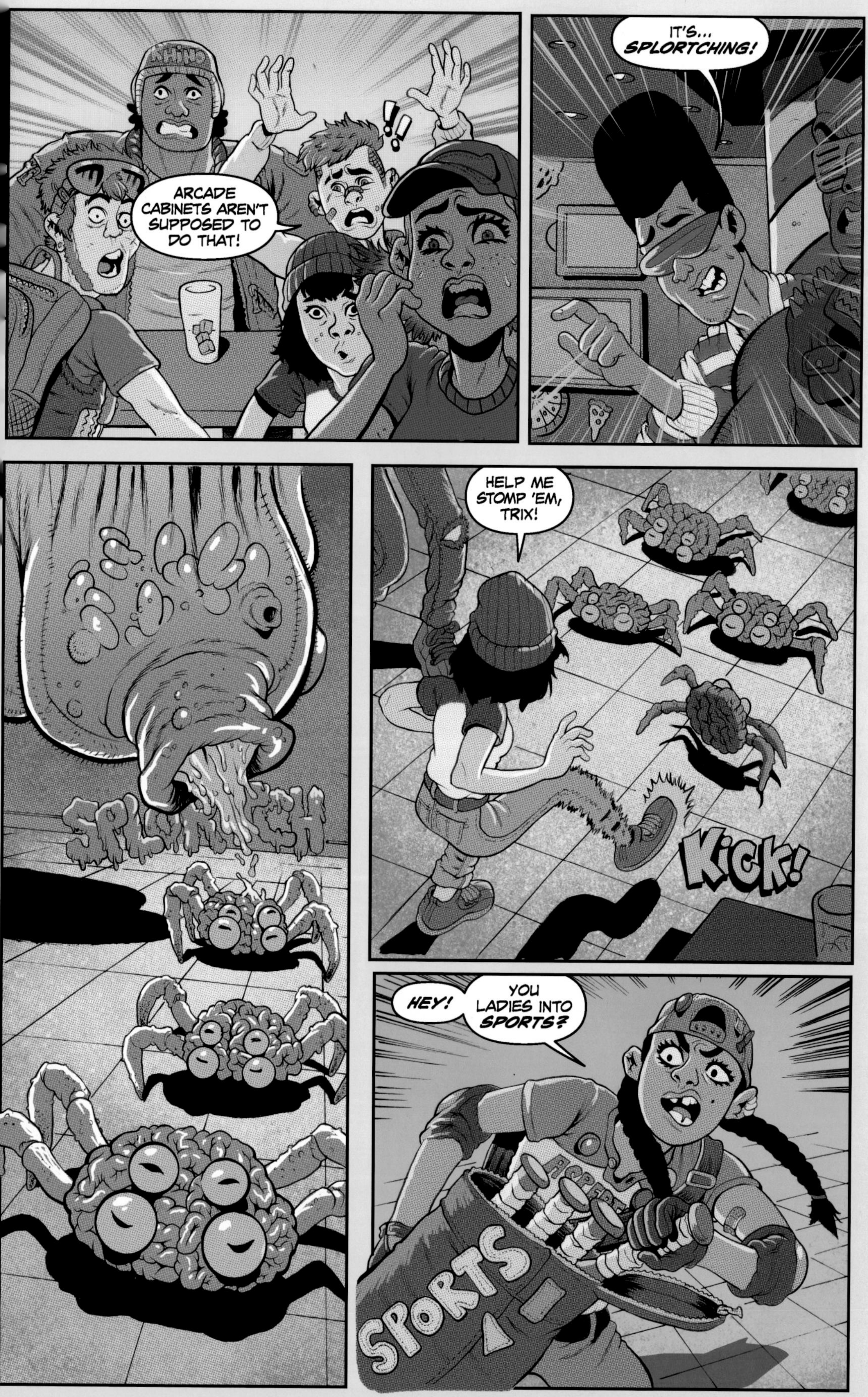

!!
ARCADE CABINETS AREN'T SUPPOSED TO DO THAT!
IT'S... SPLORTCHING!
SPLORTCH
HELP ME STOMP 'EM, TRIX!
KICK!
HEY!
YOU LADIES INTO SPORTS?
SPORTS

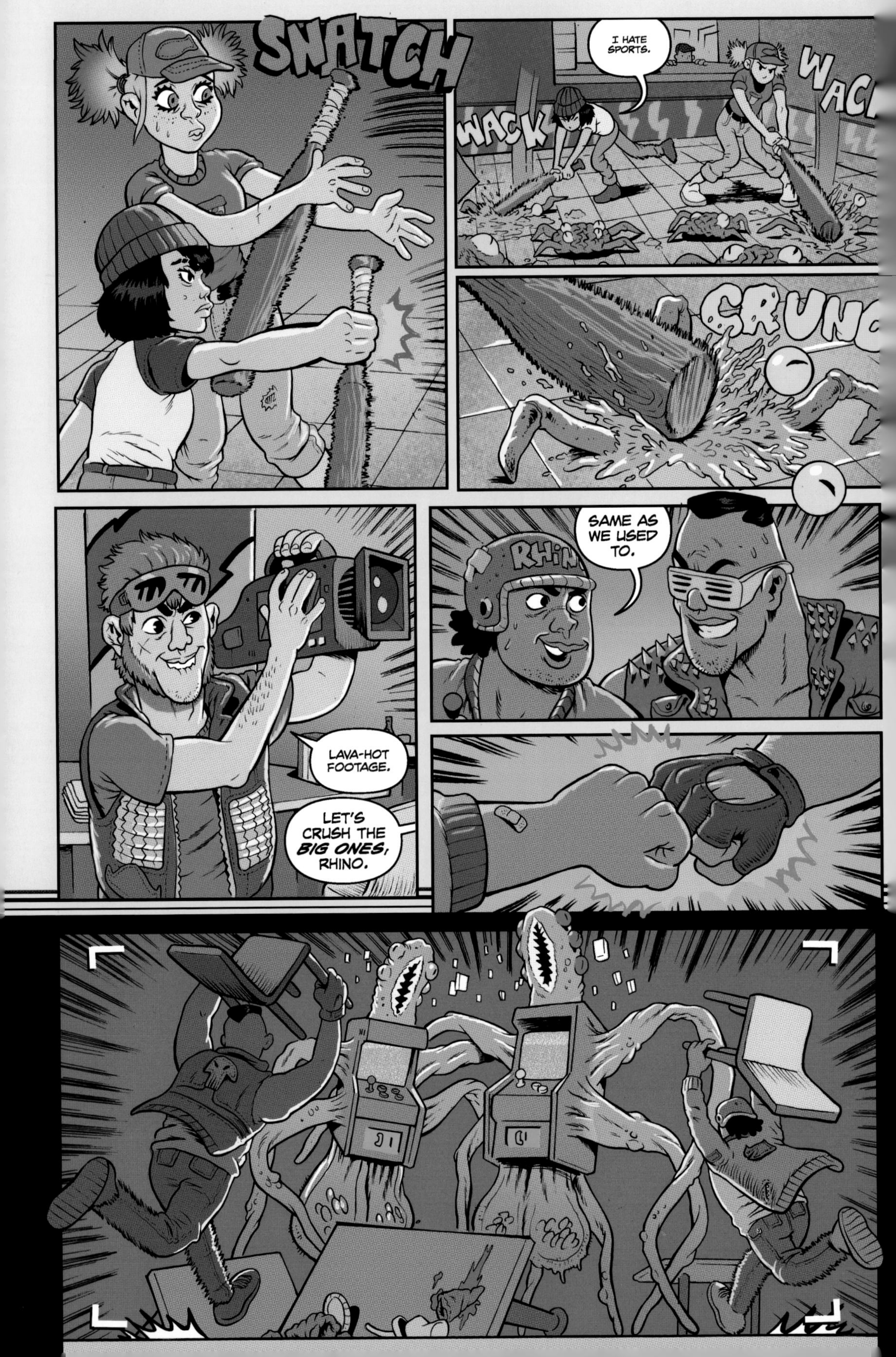

SNATCH
I HATE SPORTS.
WACK
WACK
GRUNC
LAVA-HOT FOOTAGE.
LET'S CRUSH THE BIG ONES, RHINO.
SAME AS WE USED TO.

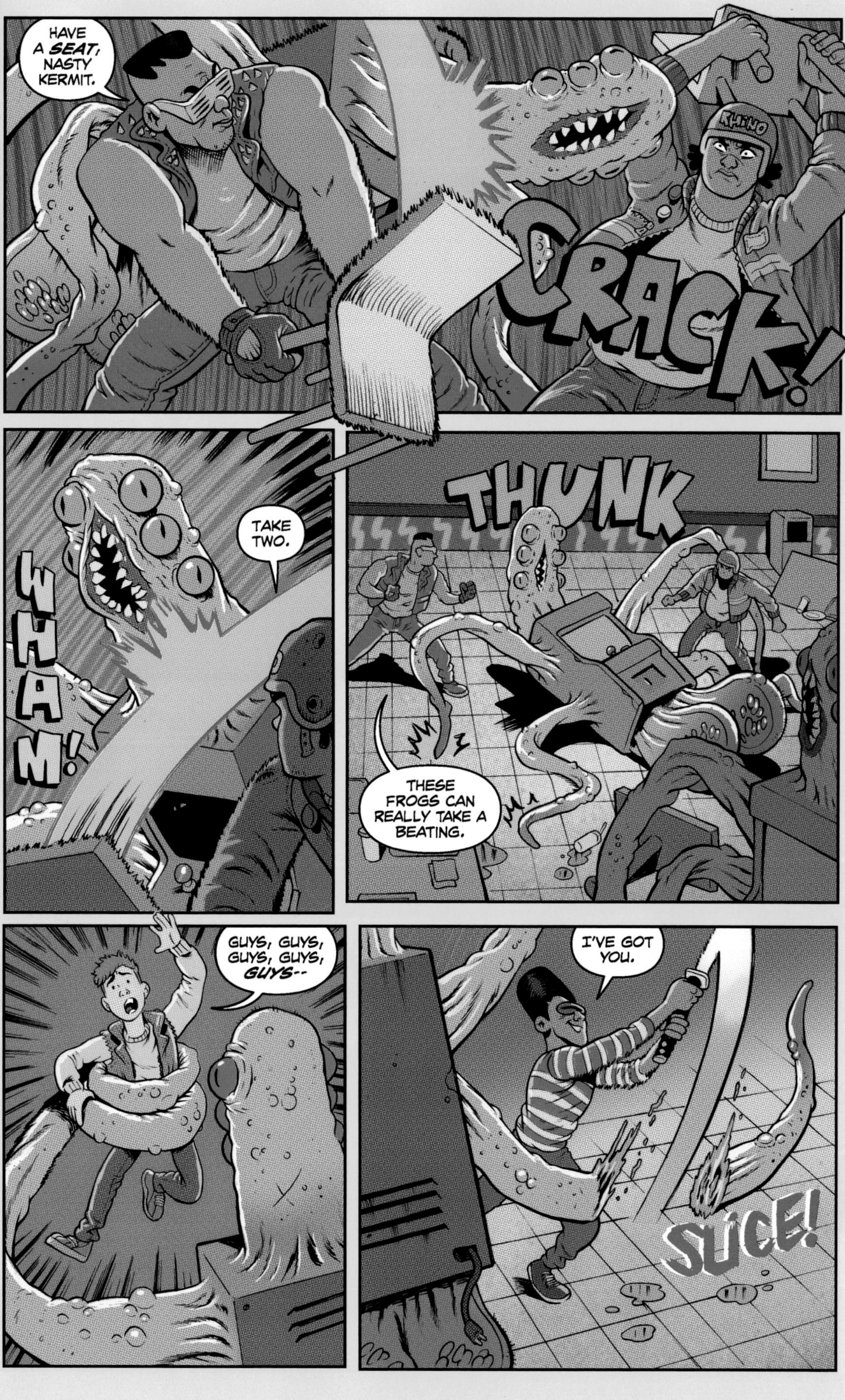
HAVE A SEAT, NASTY KERMIT.
RHINO
CRACK!
TAKE TWO.
WHAM!
THUNK
THESE FROGS CAN REALLY TAKE A BEATING.
GUYS, GUYS, GUYS, GUYS, GUYS--
I'VE GOT YOU.
SLICE!

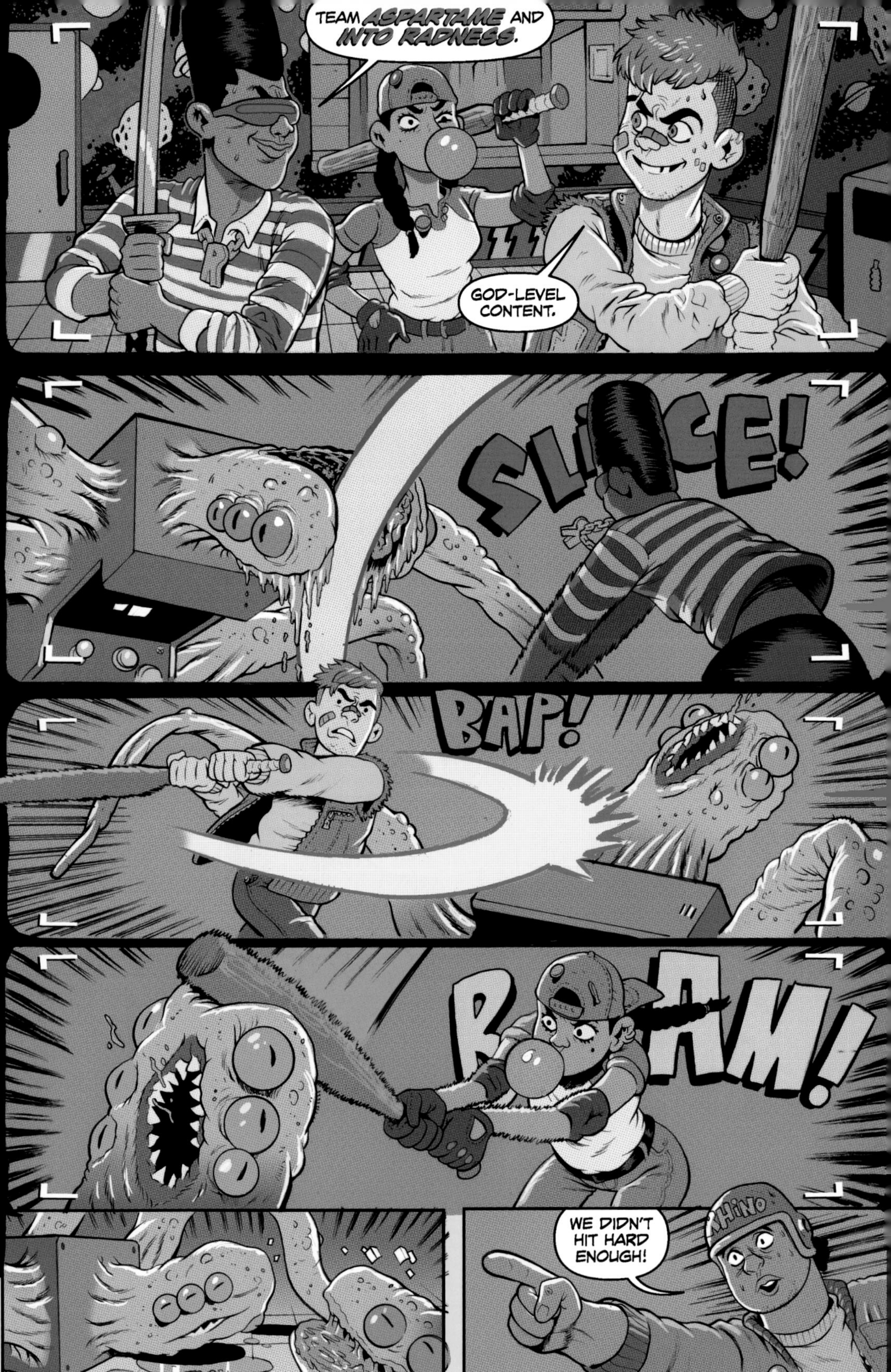
TEAM ASPARTAME AND INTO RADNESS.
GOD-LEVEL CONTENT.
SLICE!
BAP!
BAM!
WE DIDN'T HIT HARD ENOUGH!
RHINO

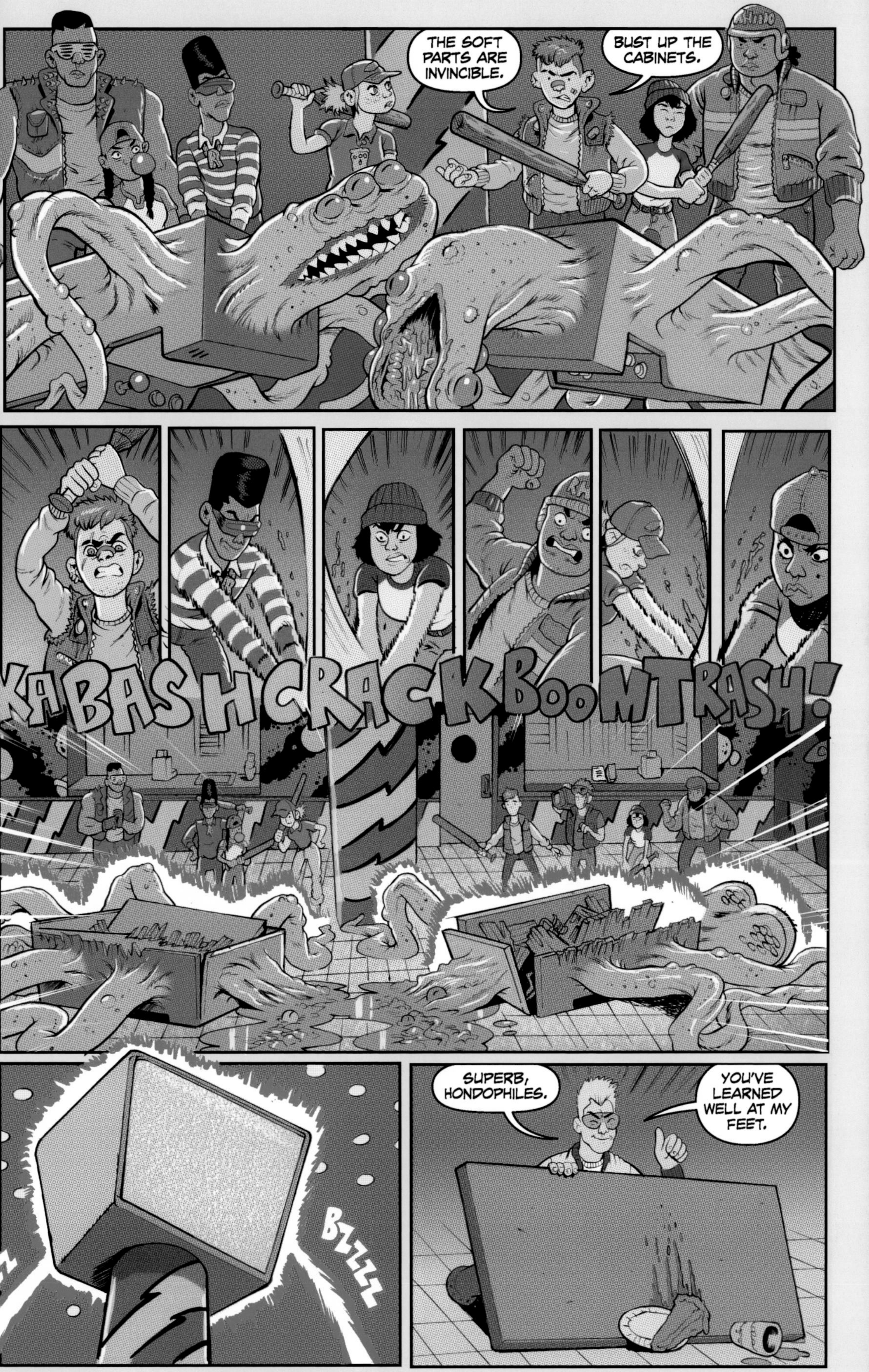
THE SOFT PARTS ARE INVINCIBLE.
BUST UP THE CABINETS.
KABASHCRACKBOOMTRASH!
BZZZZ
SUPERB, HONDOPHILES.
YOU'VE LEARNED WELL AT MY FEET.

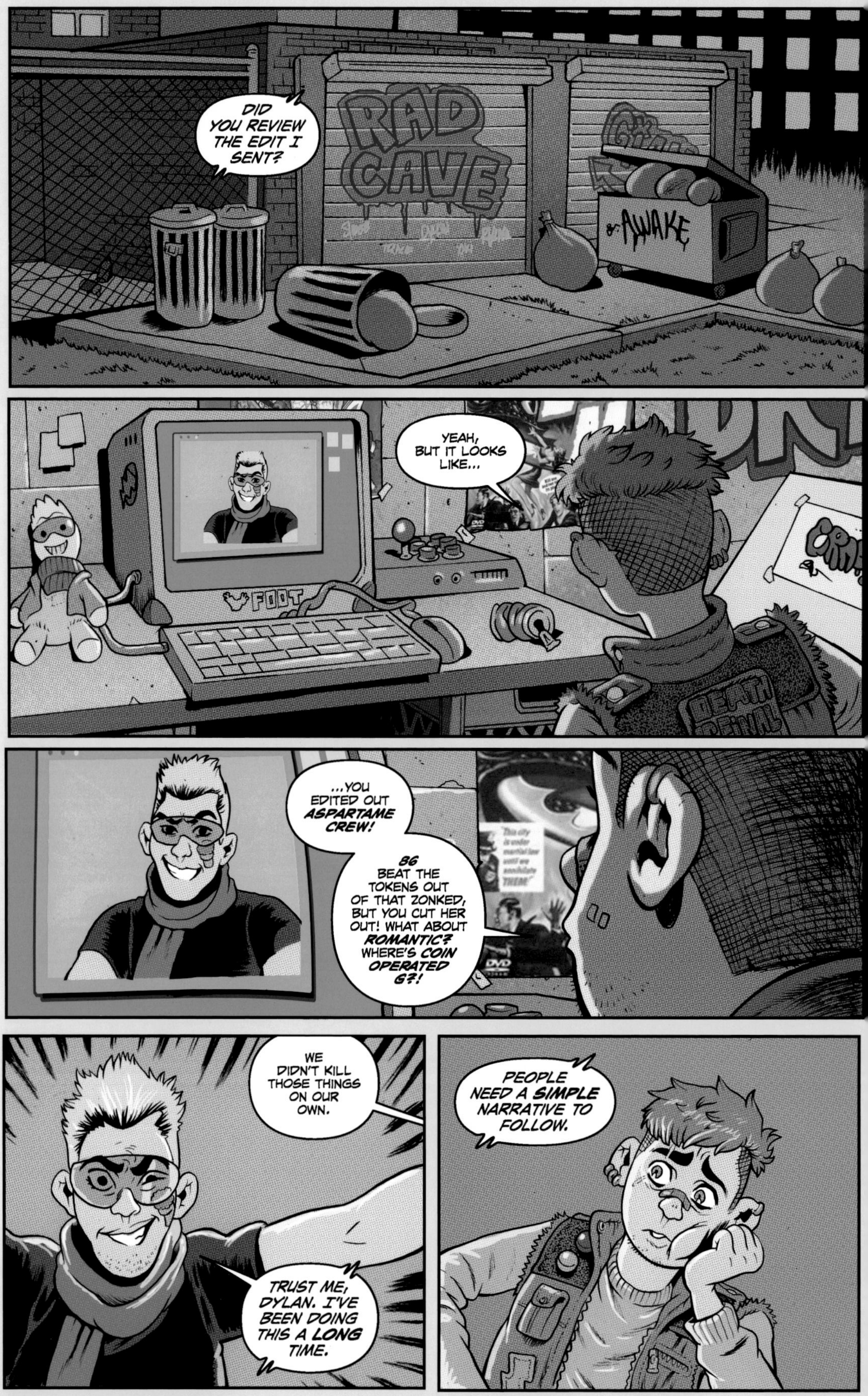
DID YOU REVIEW THE EDIT I SENT?
RAD CAVE
AWAKE
YEAH, BUT IT LOOKS LIKE...
FOOT
...YOU EDITED OUT ASPARTAME CREW!
86 BEAT THE TOKENS OUT OF THAT ZONKED, BUT YOU CUT HER OUT! WHAT ABOUT ROMANTIC? WHERE'S COIN OPERATED G?!
WE DIDN'T KILL THOSE THINGS ON OUR OWN.
TRUST ME, DYLAN. I'VE BEEN DOING THIS A LONG TIME.
PEOPLE NEED A SIMPLE NARRATIVE TO FOLLOW.

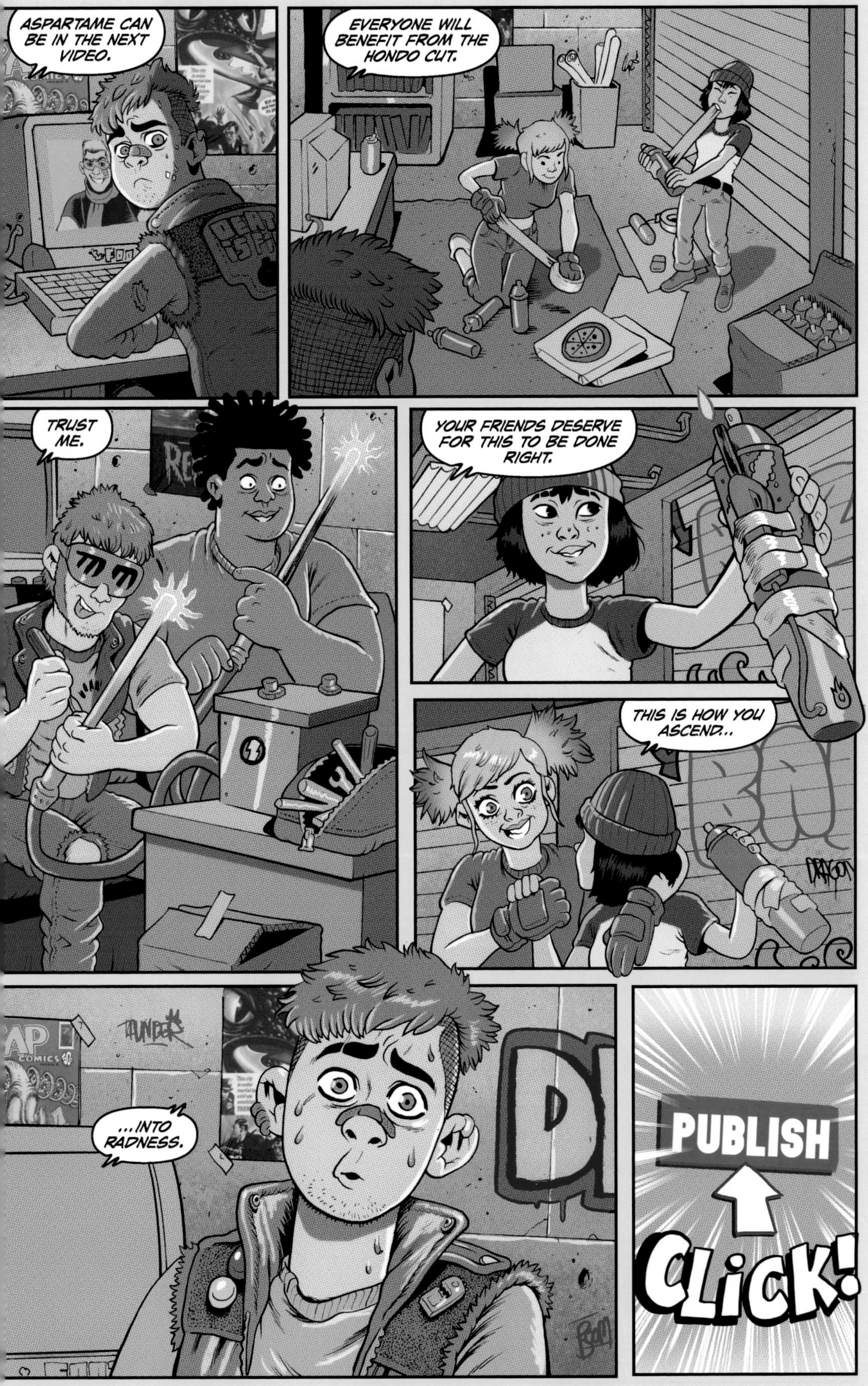
ASPARTAME CAN BE IN THE NEXT VIDEO.
EVERYONE WILL BENEFIT FROM THE HONDO CUT.
TRUST ME.
YOUR FRIENDS DESERVE FOR THIS TO BE DONE RIGHT.
THIS IS HOW YOU ASCEND...
...INTO RADNESS.
PUBLISH
CLICK!

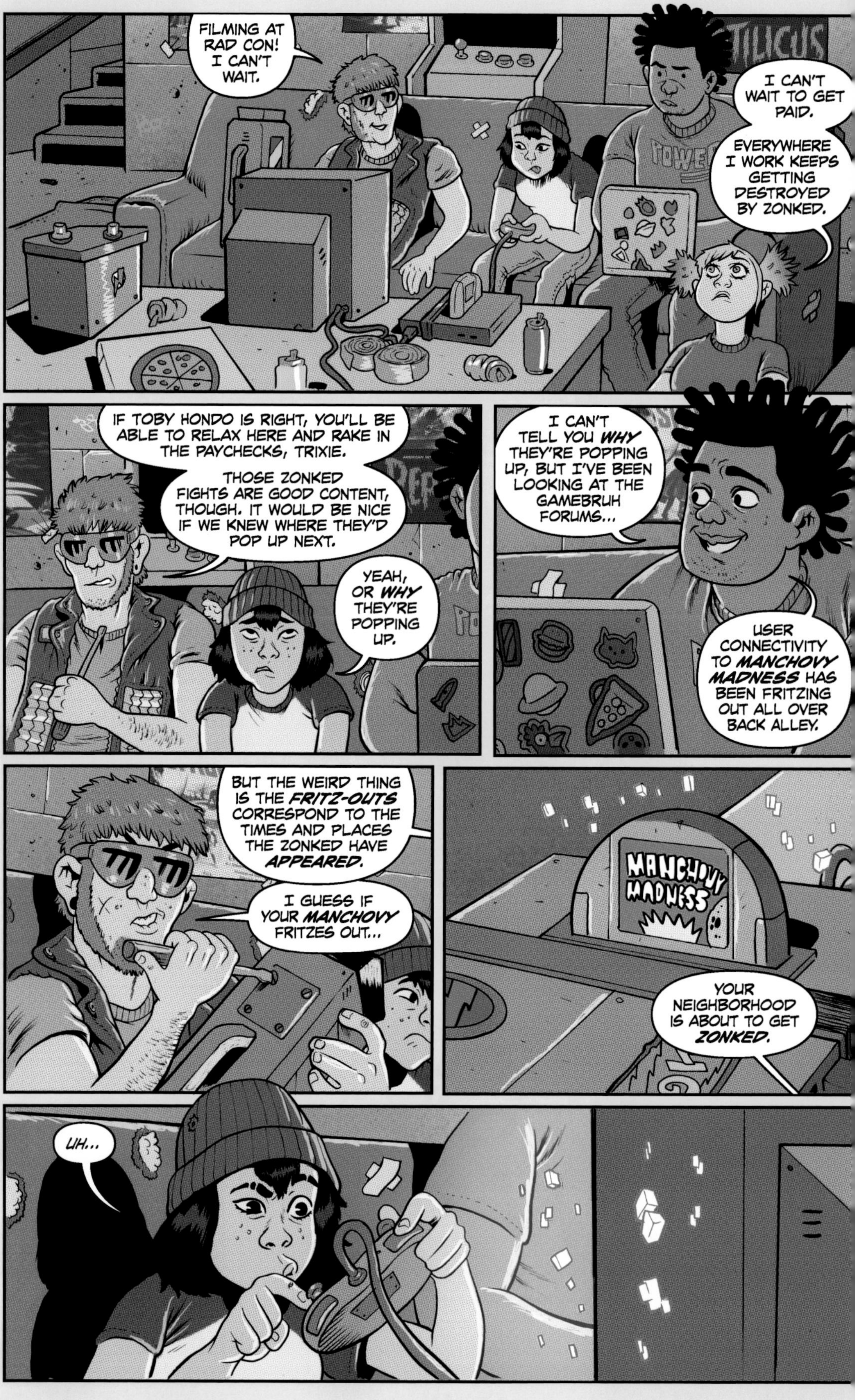
FILMING AT RAD CON! I CAN'T WAIT.
I CAN'T WAIT TO GET PAID.
EVERYWHERE I WORK KEEPS GETTING DESTROYED BY ZONKED.
IF TOBY HONDO IS RIGHT, YOU'LL BE ABLE TO RELAX HERE AND RAKE IN THE PAYCHECKS, TRIXIE.
THOSE ZONKED FIGHTS ARE GOOD CONTENT, THOUGH. IT WOULD BE NICE IF WE KNEW WHERE THEY'D POP UP NEXT.
YEAH, OR *WHY* THEY'RE POPPING UP.
I CAN'T TELL YOU *WHY* THEY'RE POPPING UP, BUT I'VE BEEN LOOKING AT THE GAMEBRUH FORUMS...
USER CONNECTIVITY TO *MANCHOVY MADNESS* HAS BEEN FRITZING OUT ALL OVER BACK ALLEY.
BUT THE WEIRD THING IS THE *FRITZ-OUTS* CORRESPOND TO THE TIMES AND PLACES THE ZONKED HAVE *APPEARED.*
I GUESS IF YOUR *MANCHOVY* FRITZES OUT...
MANCHOVY MADNESS
YOUR NEIGHBORHOOD IS ABOUT TO GET *ZONKED.*
UH...

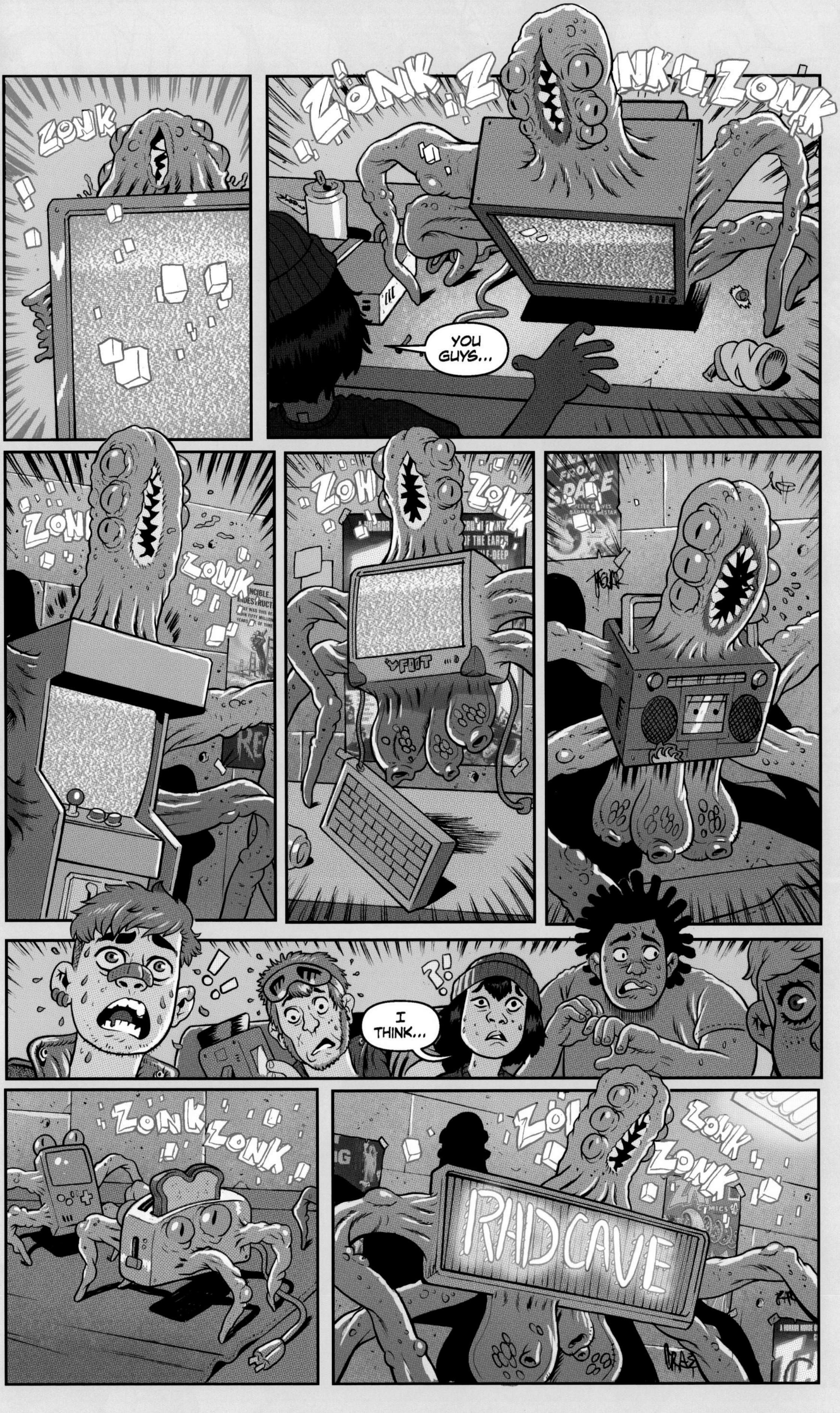
ZONK
ZONK ZONK ZONK ZONK
YOU GUYS...
ZONK
ZONK
ZONK
ZONK
I THINK...
ZONK ZONK
ZONK ZONK ZONK
RADCAVE

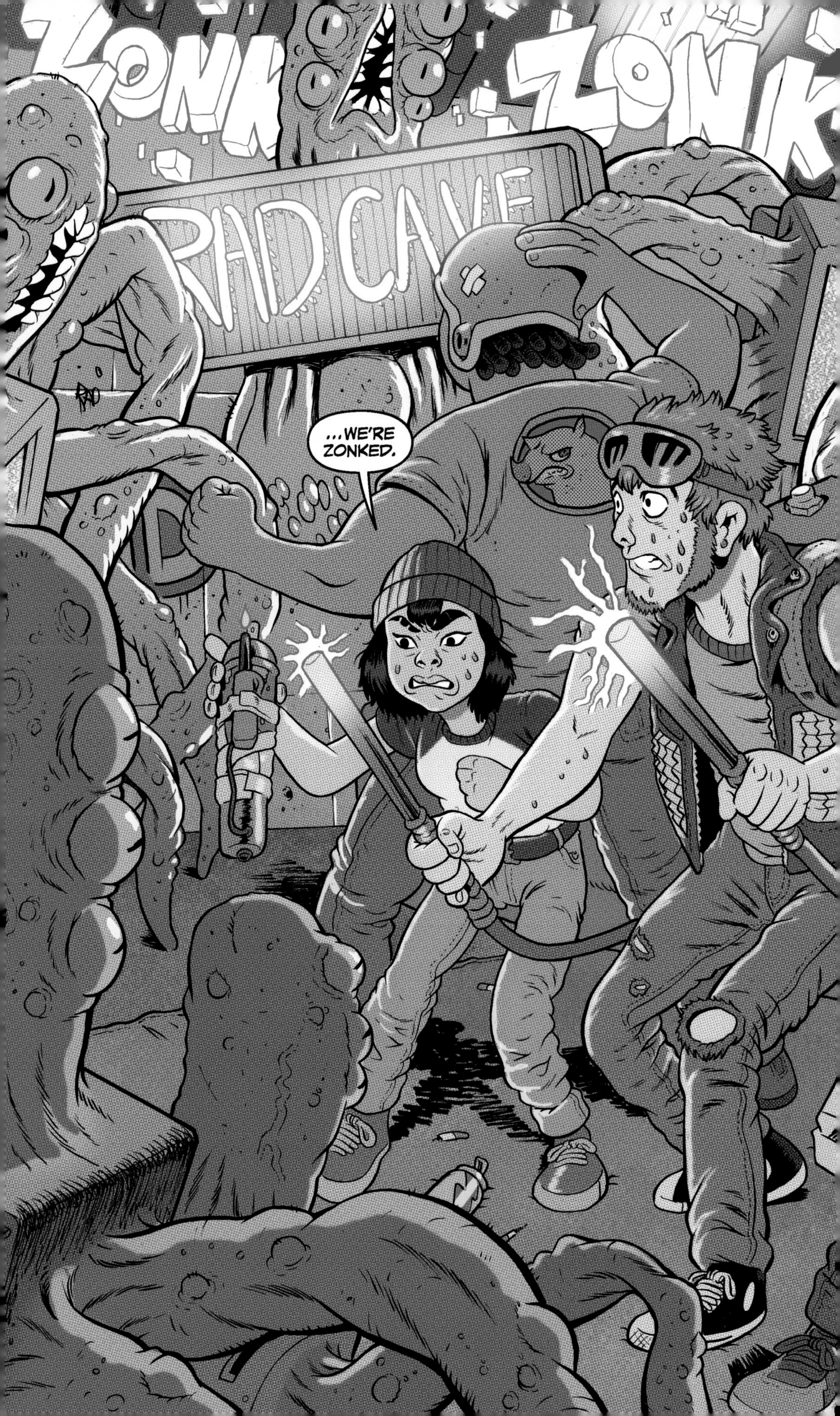
ZONK
ZONK
RAD CAVE
...WE'RE ZONKED.

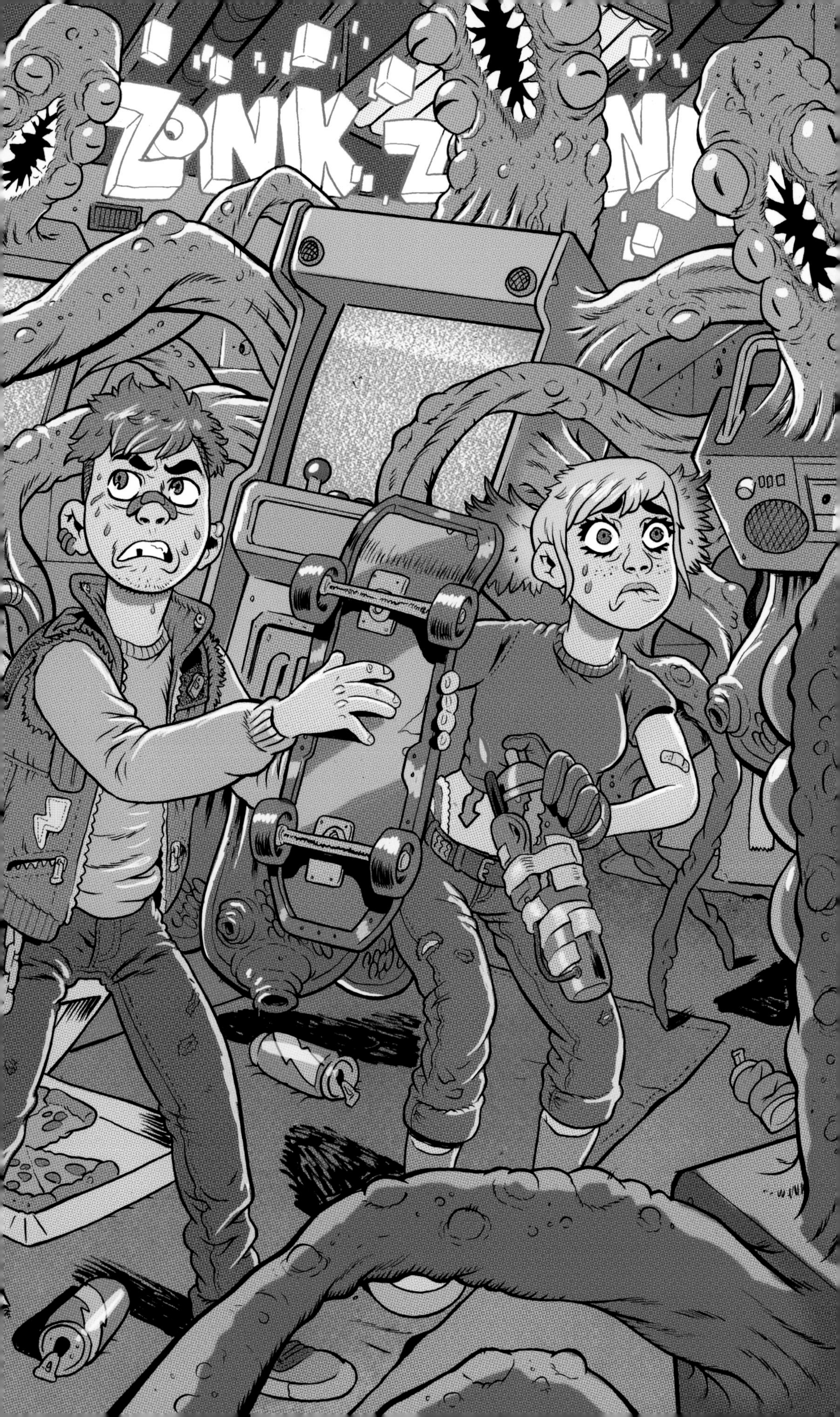

ZONK.

CHAPTER THREE

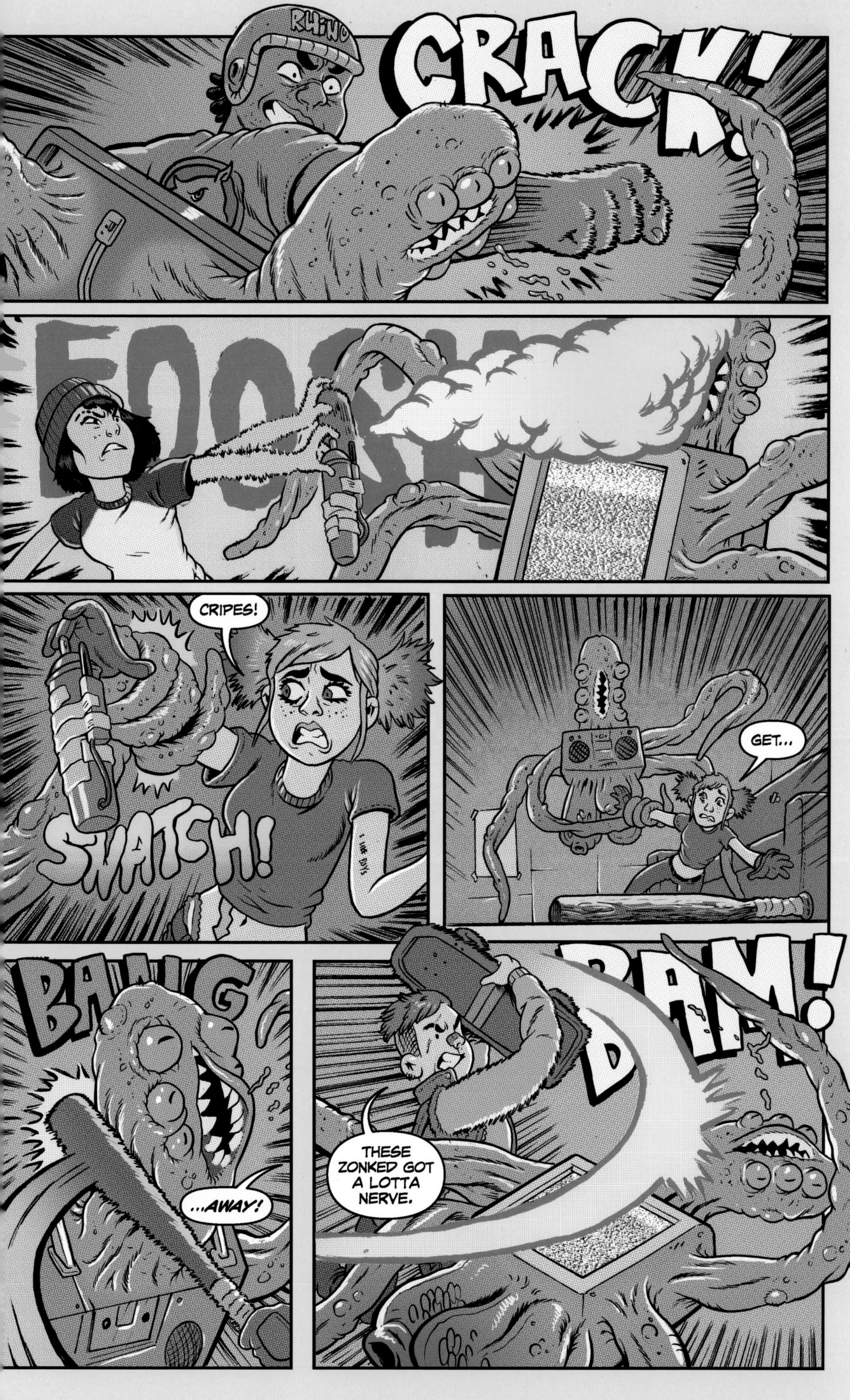
RHINO
CRACK!
FOOSH
CRIPES!
SNATCH!
GET...
BANG
...AWAY!
BAM!
THESE ZONKED GOT A LOTTA NERVE.

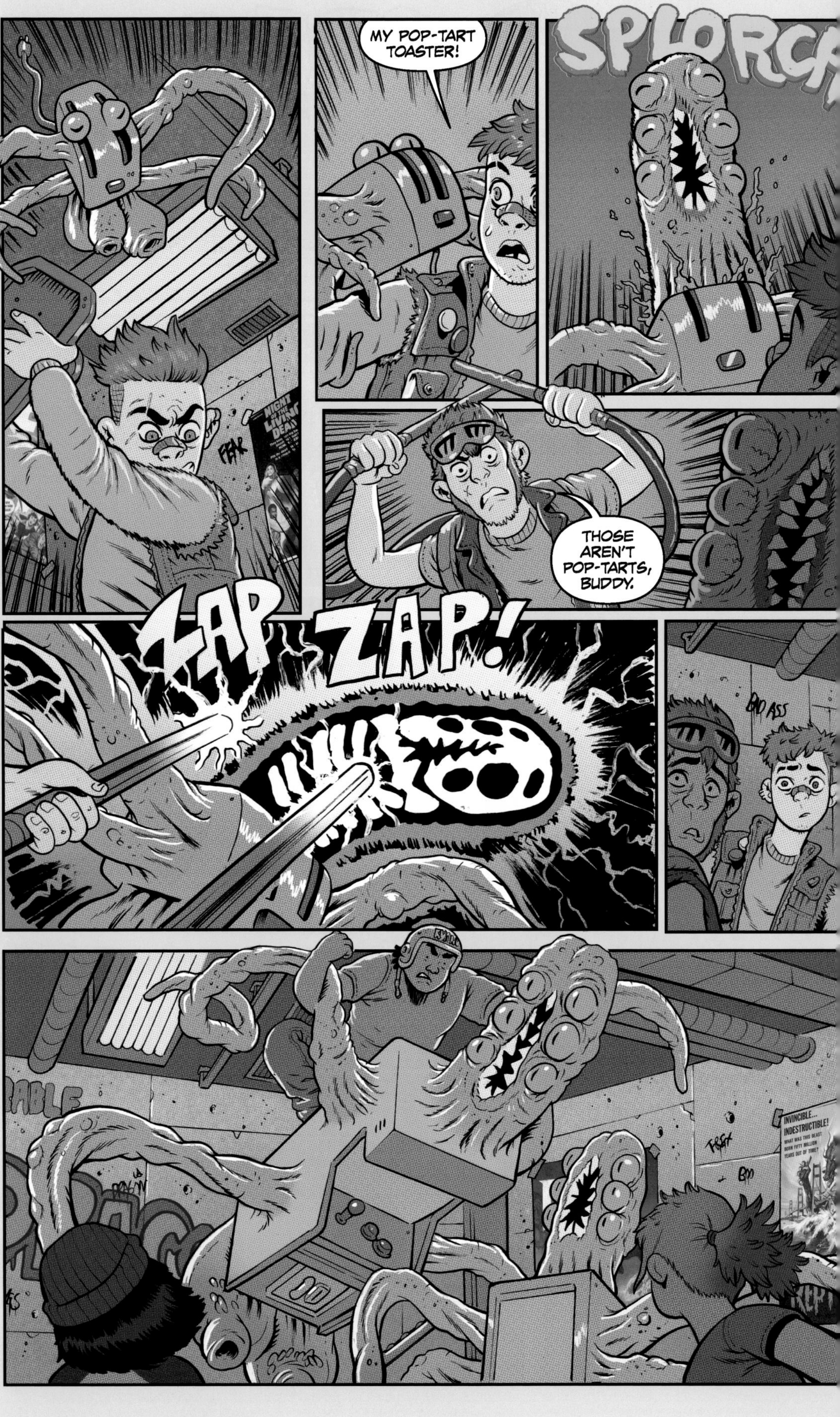

FEAR
NIGHT OF THE LIVING DEAD
MY POP-TART TOASTER!
SPLORCH
THOSE AREN'T POP-TARTS, BUDDY.
ZAP ZAP!
BAD ASS
INVINCIBLE... INDESTRUCTIBLE!
WHAT WAS THIS BEAST BORN FIFTY MILLION YEARS OUT OF TIME?

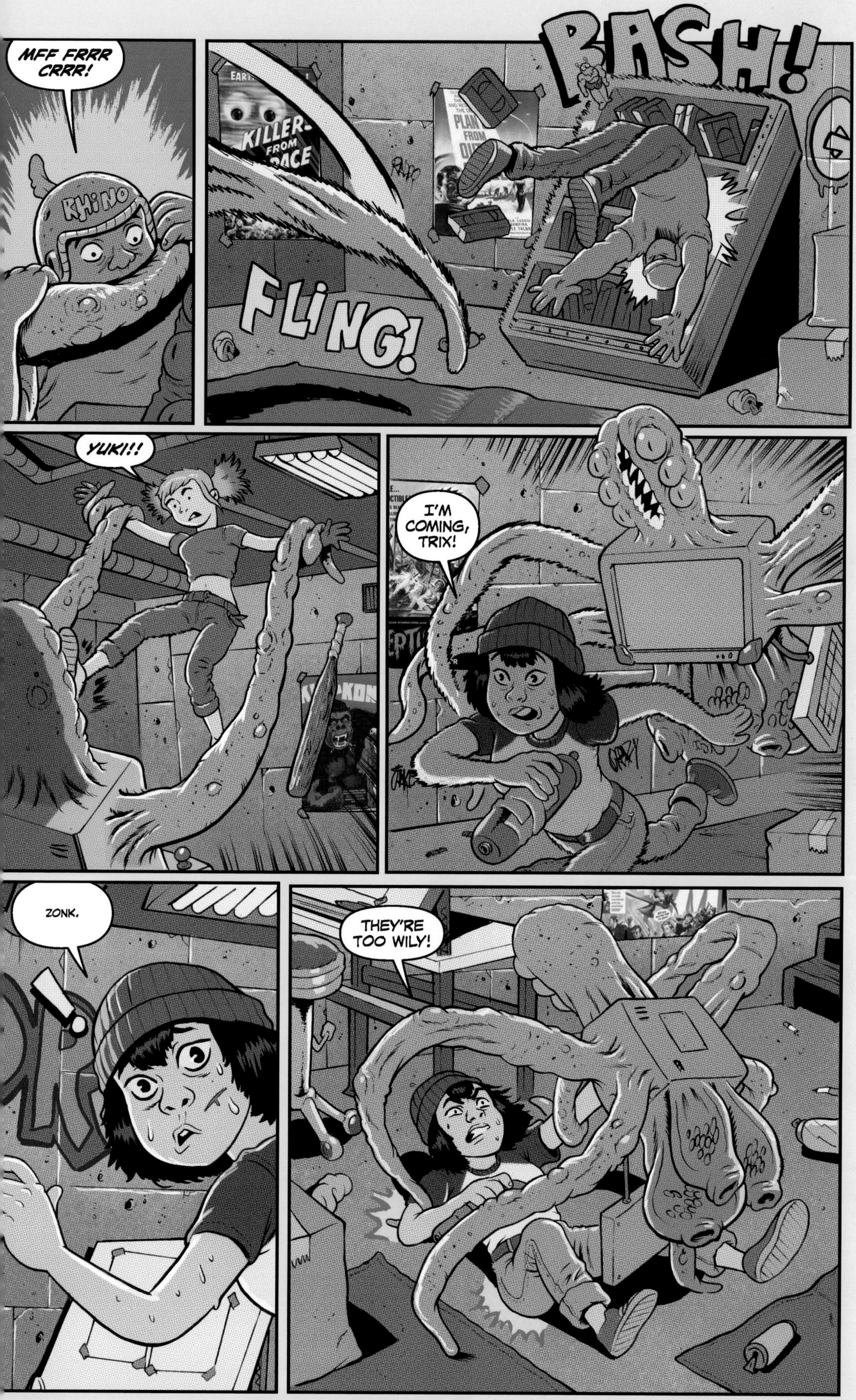
MFF FRRR CRRR!
RHINO
KILLERS
FROM
FLING!
BASH!
YUKI!!
I'M COMING, TRIX!
ZONK.
THEY'RE TOO WILY!

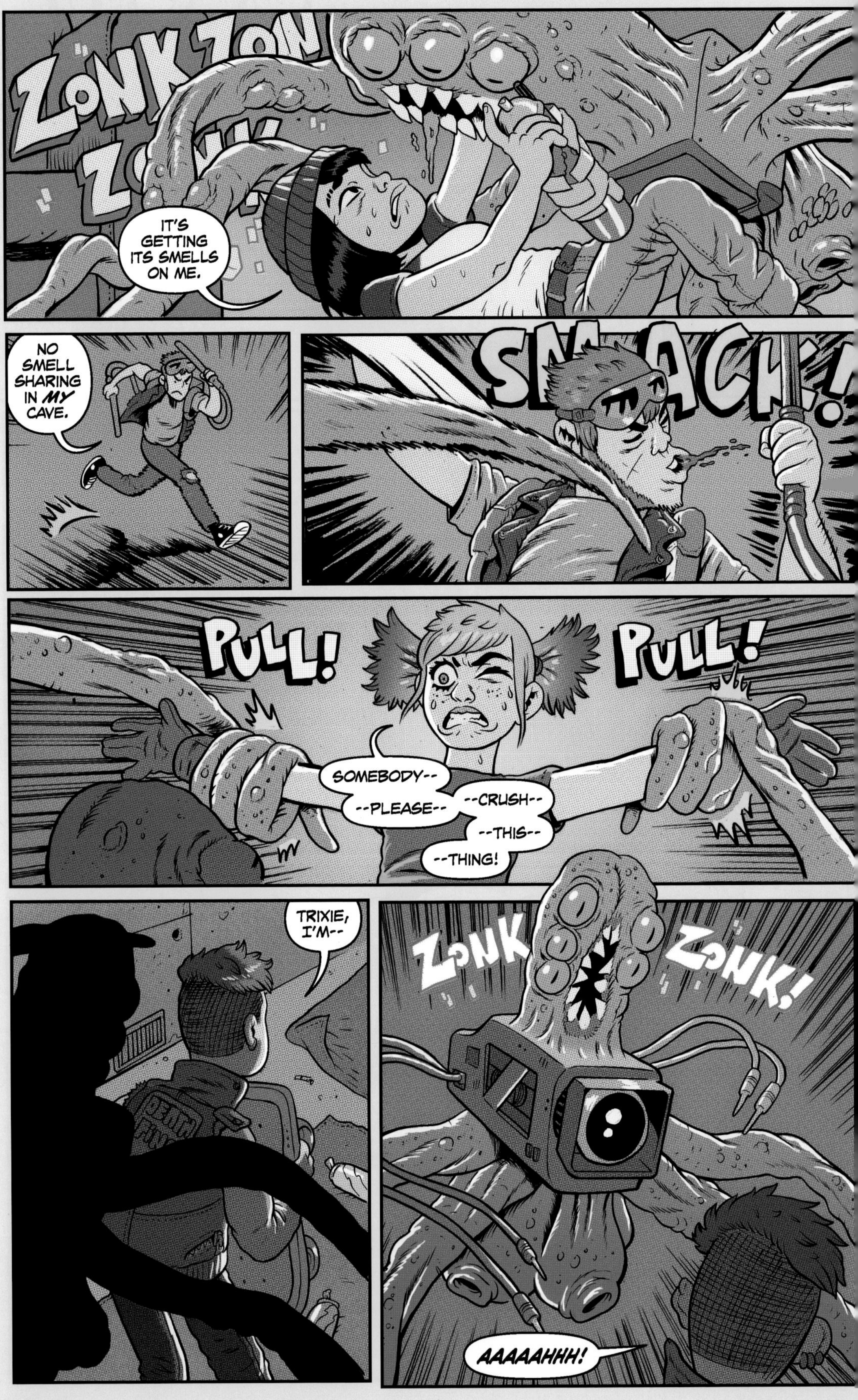
ZONK ZON
ZONK
IT'S GETTING ITS SMELLS ON ME.
NO SMELL SHARING IN *MY* CAVE.
SMACK!!
PULL! PULL!
SOMEBODY--
--PLEASE--
--CRUSH--
--THIS--
--THING!
TRIXIE, I'M--
ZONK ZONK!
AAAAAHHH!

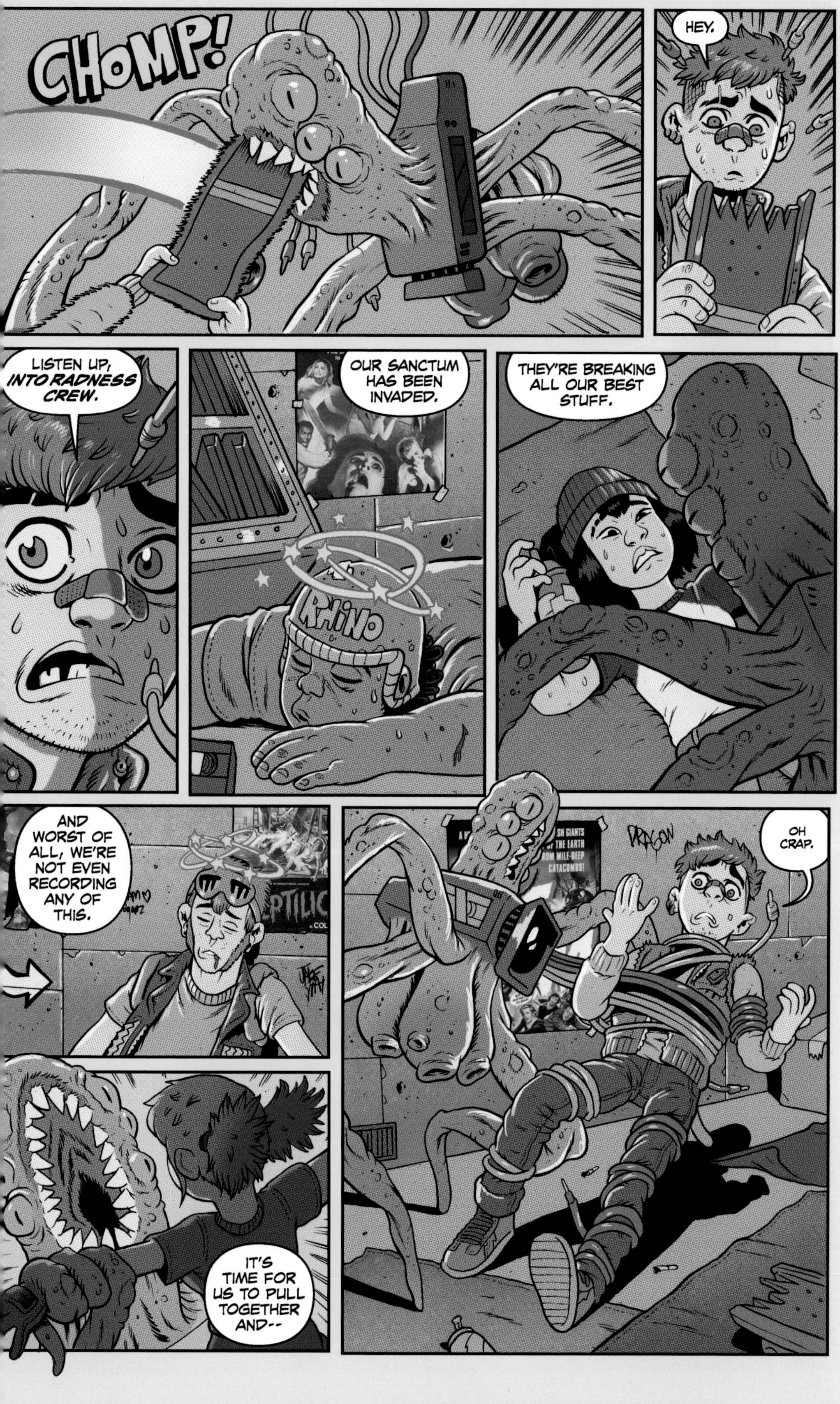
CHOMP!
HEY.
LISTEN UP, *INTO RADNESS* CREW.
OUR SANCTUM HAS BEEN INVADED.
RHINO
THEY'RE BREAKING ALL OUR BEST STUFF.
AND WORST OF ALL, WE'RE NOT EVEN RECORDING ANY OF THIS.
IT'S TIME FOR US TO PULL TOGETHER AND--
OH CRAP.

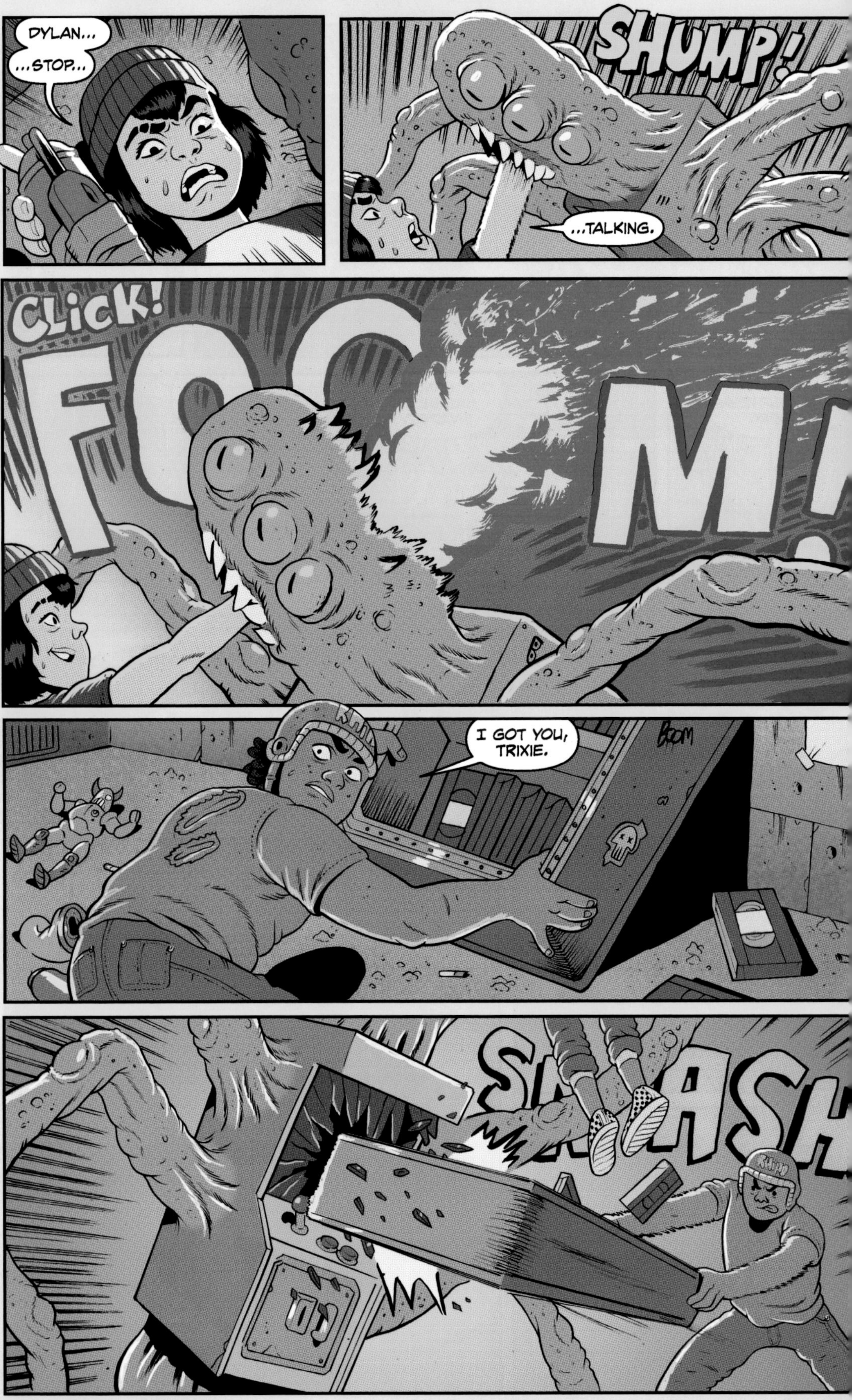

DYLAN...
...STOP...
SHUMP!
...TALKING.
CLICK!
FOOM
I GOT YOU, TRIXIE.
SMASH

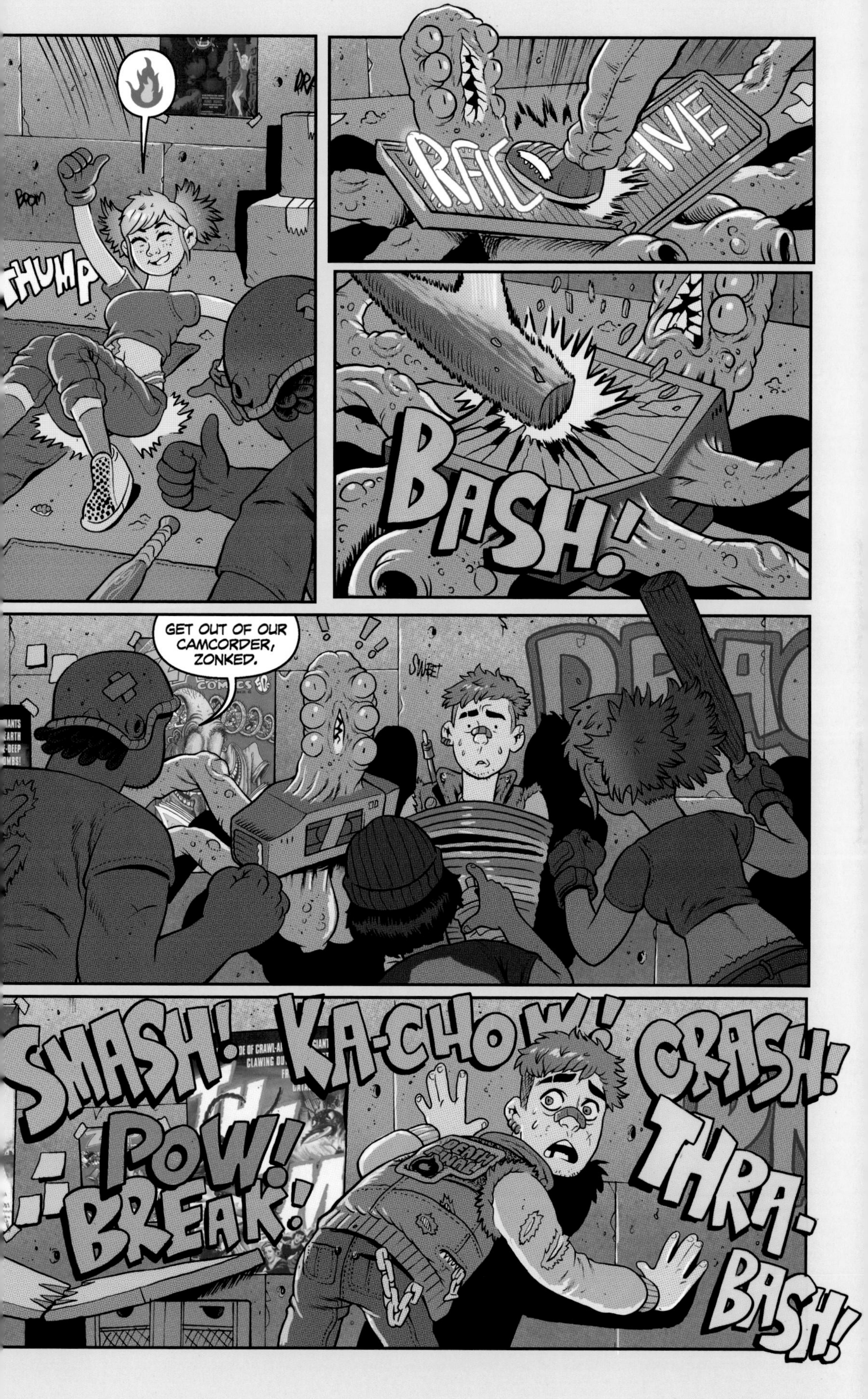
THUMP
RAC-IVE
BASH!
GET OUT OF OUR CAMCORDER, ZONKED.
SMASH!
KA-CHOW!
CRASH!
POW!
BREAK!
THRA-BASH!

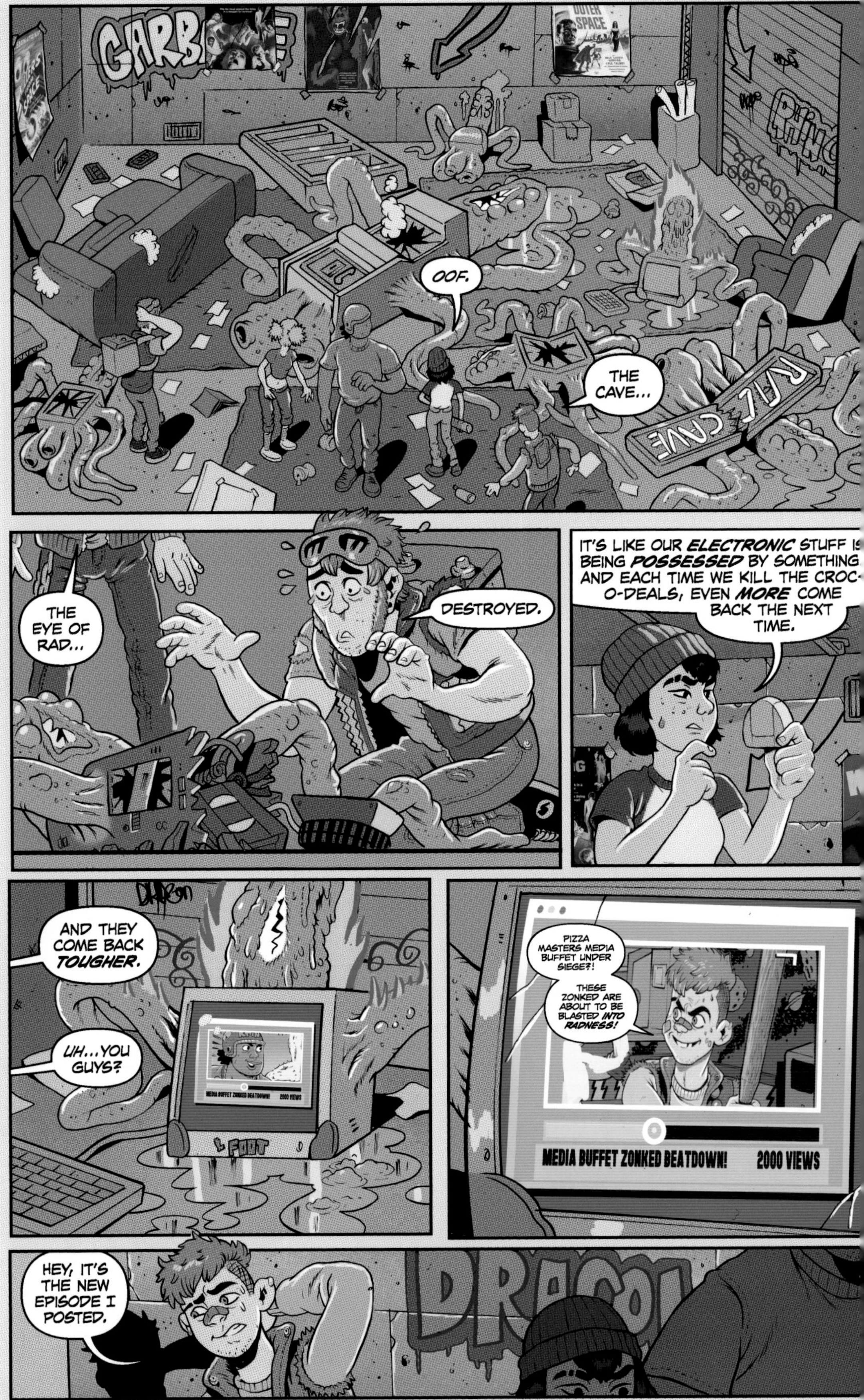
OOF.
THE CAVE...
THE EYE OF RAD...
DESTROYED.
IT'S LIKE OUR *ELECTRONIC* STUFF IS BEING *POSSESSED* BY SOMETHING AND EACH TIME WE KILL THE CROC-O-DEALS, EVEN *MORE* COME BACK THE NEXT TIME.
AND THEY COME BACK *TOUGHER.*
UH...YOU GUYS?
MEDIA BUFFET ZONKED BEATDOWN! 2000 VIEWS
PIZZA MASTERS MEDIA BUFFET UNDER SIEGE?!
THESE ZONKED ARE ABOUT TO BE BLASTED *INTO RADNESS!*
MEDIA BUFFET ZONKED BEATDOWN! 2000 VIEWS
HEY, IT'S THE NEW EPISODE I POSTED.

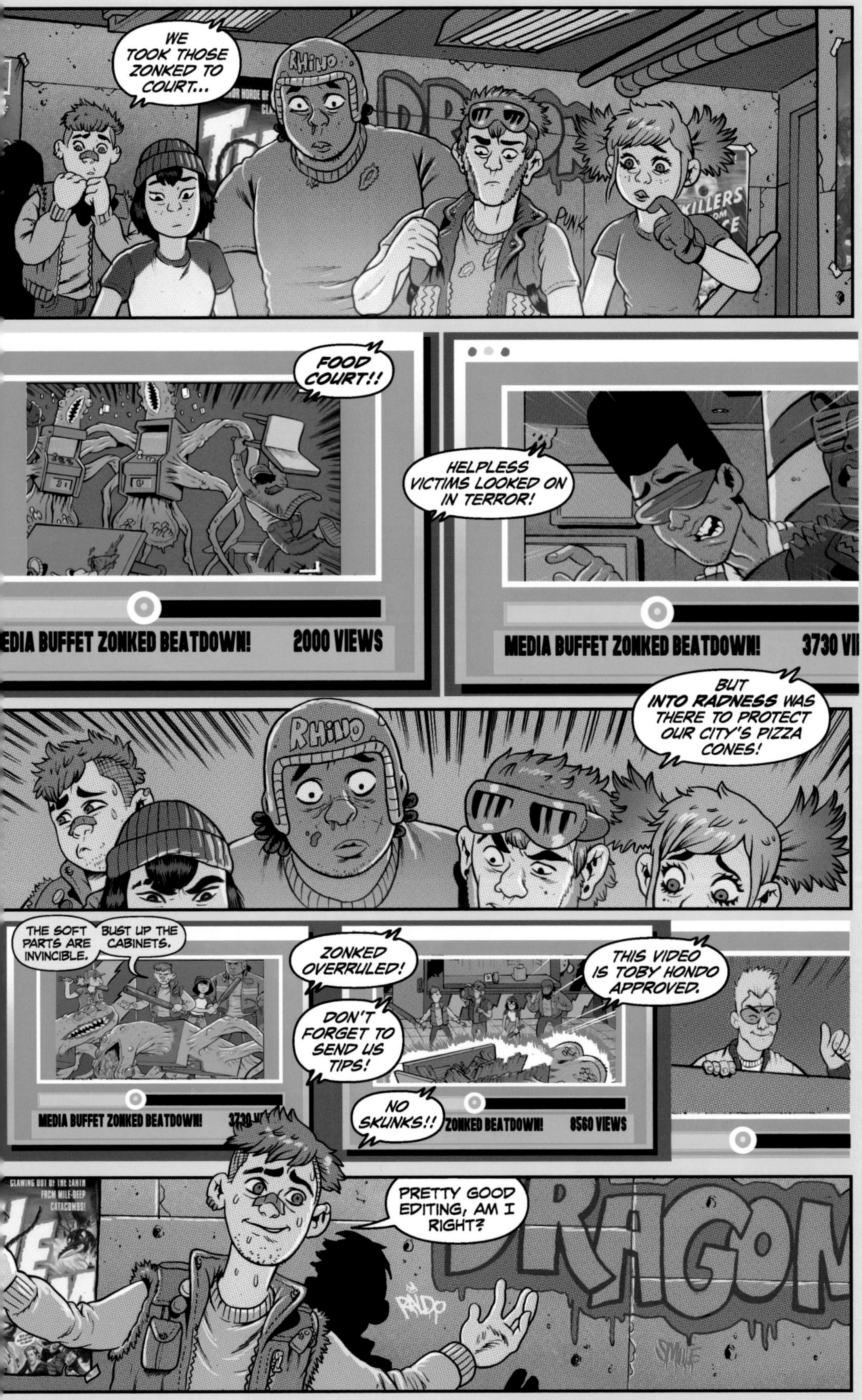
WE TOOK THOSE ZONKED TO COURT...
RHINO
PUNK
FOOD COURT!!
MEDIA BUFFET ZONKED BEATDOWN!
2000 VIEWS
HELPLESS VICTIMS LOOKED ON IN TERROR!
MEDIA BUFFET ZONKED BEATDOWN!
BUT INTO RADNESS WAS THERE TO PROTECT OUR CITY'S PIZZA CONES!
RHINO
THE SOFT PARTS ARE INVINCIBLE.
BUST UP THE CABINETS.
MEDIA BUFFET ZONKED BEATDOWN!
ZONKED OVERRULED!
DON'T FORGET TO SEND US TIPS!
THIS VIDEO IS TOBY HONDO APPROVED.
NO SKUNKS!!
ZONKED BEATDOWN!
8560 VIEWS
CLAWING OUT OF THE EARTH FROM MILE-DEEP CATACOMBS!
PRETTY GOOD EDITING, AM I RIGHT?

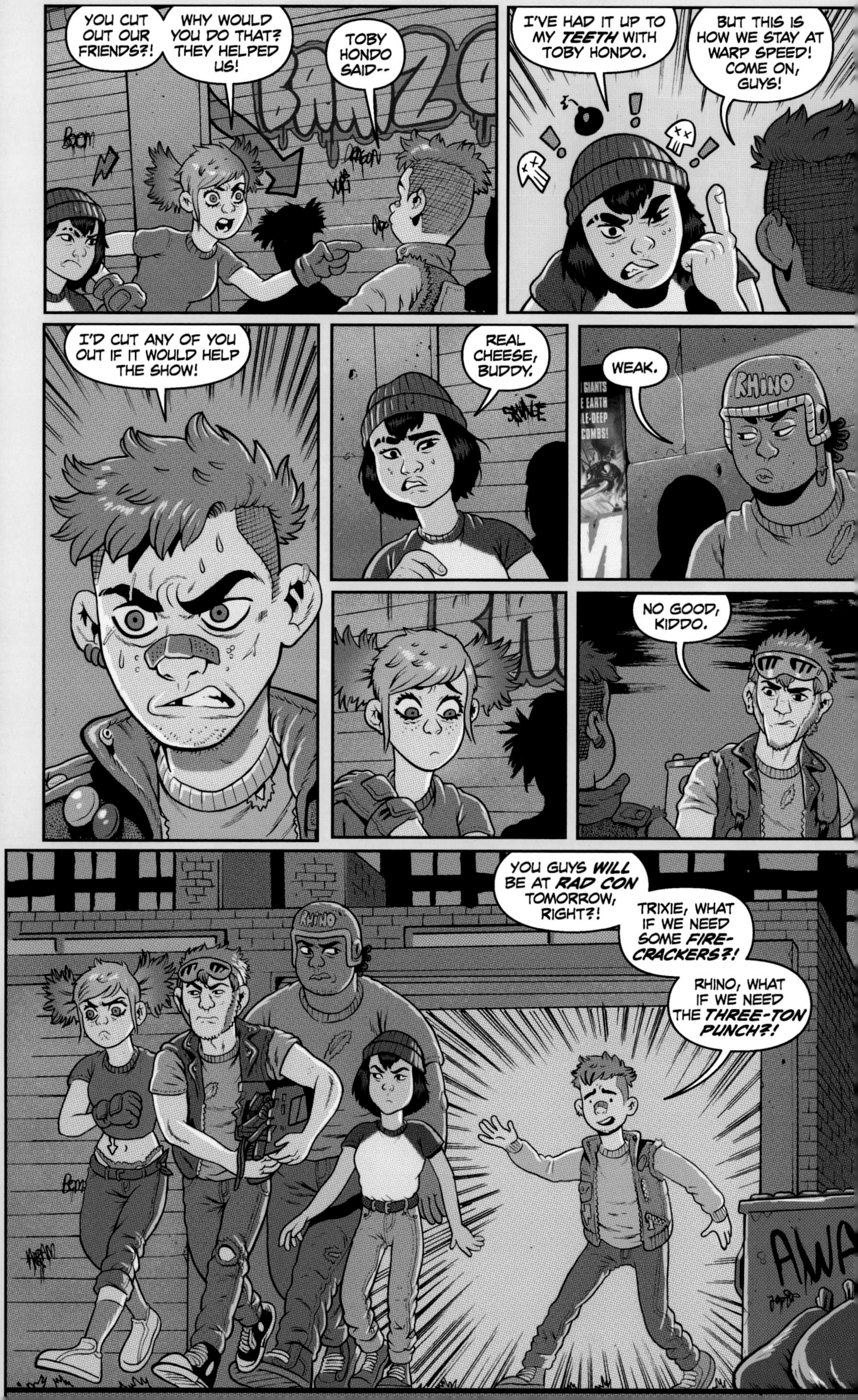
YOU CUT OUT OUR FRIENDS?!
WHY WOULD YOU DO THAT? THEY HELPED US!
TOBY HONDO SAID--
I'VE HAD IT UP TO MY TEETH WITH TOBY HONDO.
BUT THIS IS HOW WE STAY AT WARP SPEED! COME ON, GUYS!
I'D CUT ANY OF YOU OUT IF IT WOULD HELP THE SHOW!
REAL CHEESE, BUDDY.
WEAK.
NO GOOD, KIDDO.
YOU GUYS WILL BE AT RAD CON TOMORROW, RIGHT?!
TRIXIE, WHAT IF WE NEED SOME FIRE-CRACKERS?!
RHINO, WHAT IF WE NEED THE THREE-TON PUNCH?!

THERE ARE TWO KINDS OF PAIN THAT CAN KICK YOUR ASS IN THIS WORLD, MY PEOPLE.

ONE, WE ALL FEEL. THAT'S THE PAIN OF REGRET.

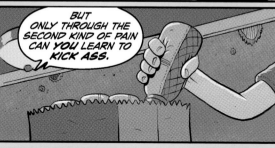

BUT ONLY THROUGH THE SECOND KIND OF PAIN CAN YOU LEARN TO KICK ASS.

I'M TALKING ABOUT THE PAIN OF DISCIPLINE.

UH... FRANK, CAN YOU DROP ME OFF DOWNTOWN NOW?

YOU BET, JASON. JUST LEMME GRAB MY KEYS.

SO WHAT'S ALL THAT STUFF IN THE PAPER BAG, BUDDY?

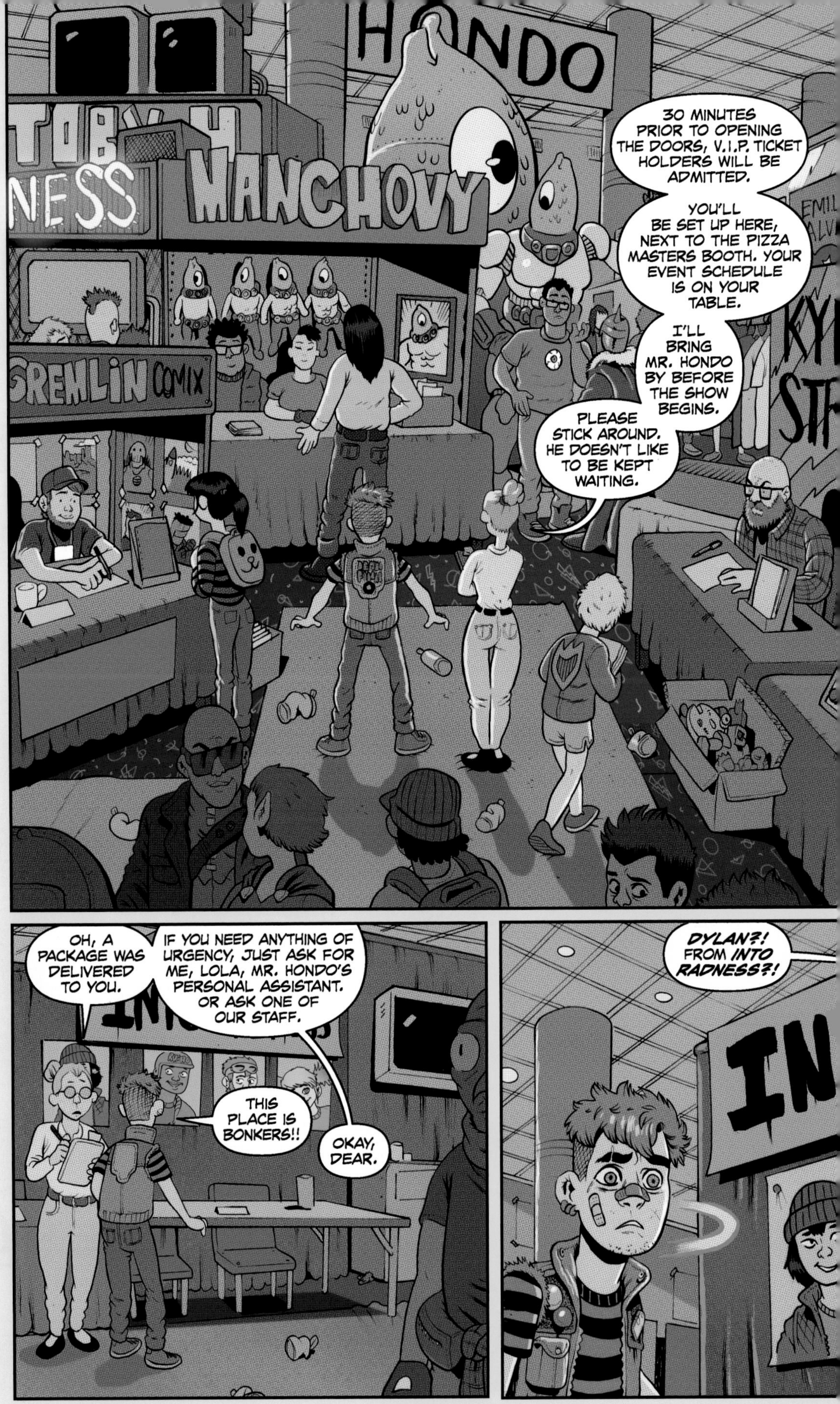
HONDO
MANCHOVY
GREMLIN COMIX
30 MINUTES PRIOR TO OPENING THE DOORS, V.I.P. TICKET HOLDERS WILL BE ADMITTED.
YOU'LL BE SET UP HERE, NEXT TO THE PIZZA MASTERS BOOTH. YOUR EVENT SCHEDULE IS ON YOUR TABLE.
I'LL BRING MR. HONDO BY BEFORE THE SHOW BEGINS.
PLEASE STICK AROUND. HE DOESN'T LIKE TO BE KEPT WAITING.
OH, A PACKAGE WAS DELIVERED TO YOU.
IF YOU NEED ANYTHING OF URGENCY, JUST ASK FOR ME, LOLA, MR. HONDO'S PERSONAL ASSISTANT. OR ASK ONE OF OUR STAFF.
THIS PLACE IS BONKERS!!
OKAY, DEAR.
DYLAN?! FROM *INTO RADNESS?!*

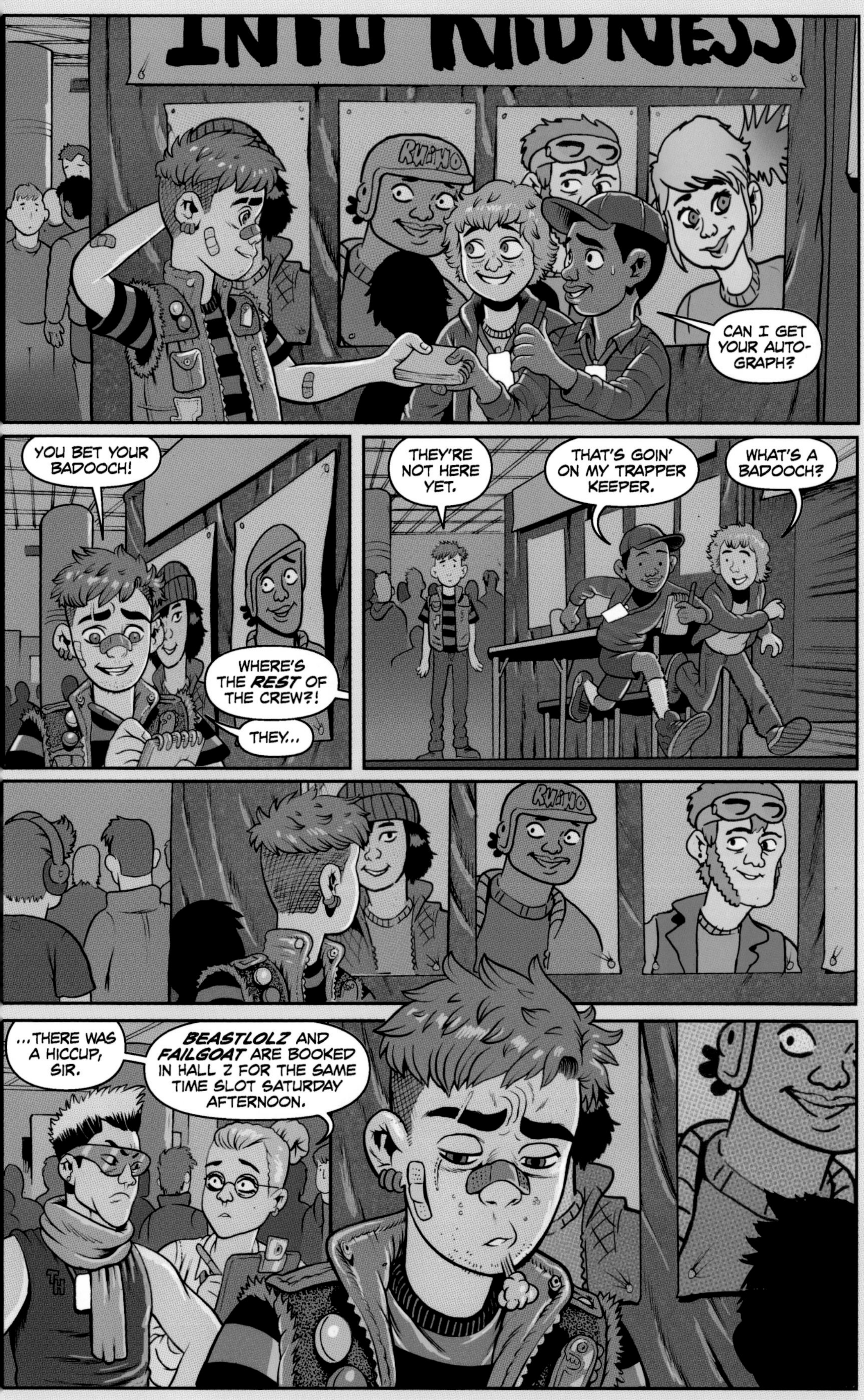
CAN I GET YOUR AUTOGRAPH?
YOU BET YOUR BADOOCH!
WHERE'S THE *REST* OF THE CREW?!
THEY...
THEY'RE NOT HERE YET.
THAT'S GOIN' ON MY TRAPPER KEEPER.
WHAT'S A BADOOCH?
...THERE WAS A HICCUP, SIR.
BEASTLOLZ AND *FAILGOAT* ARE BOOKED IN HALL Z FOR THE SAME TIME SLOT SATURDAY AFTERNOON.

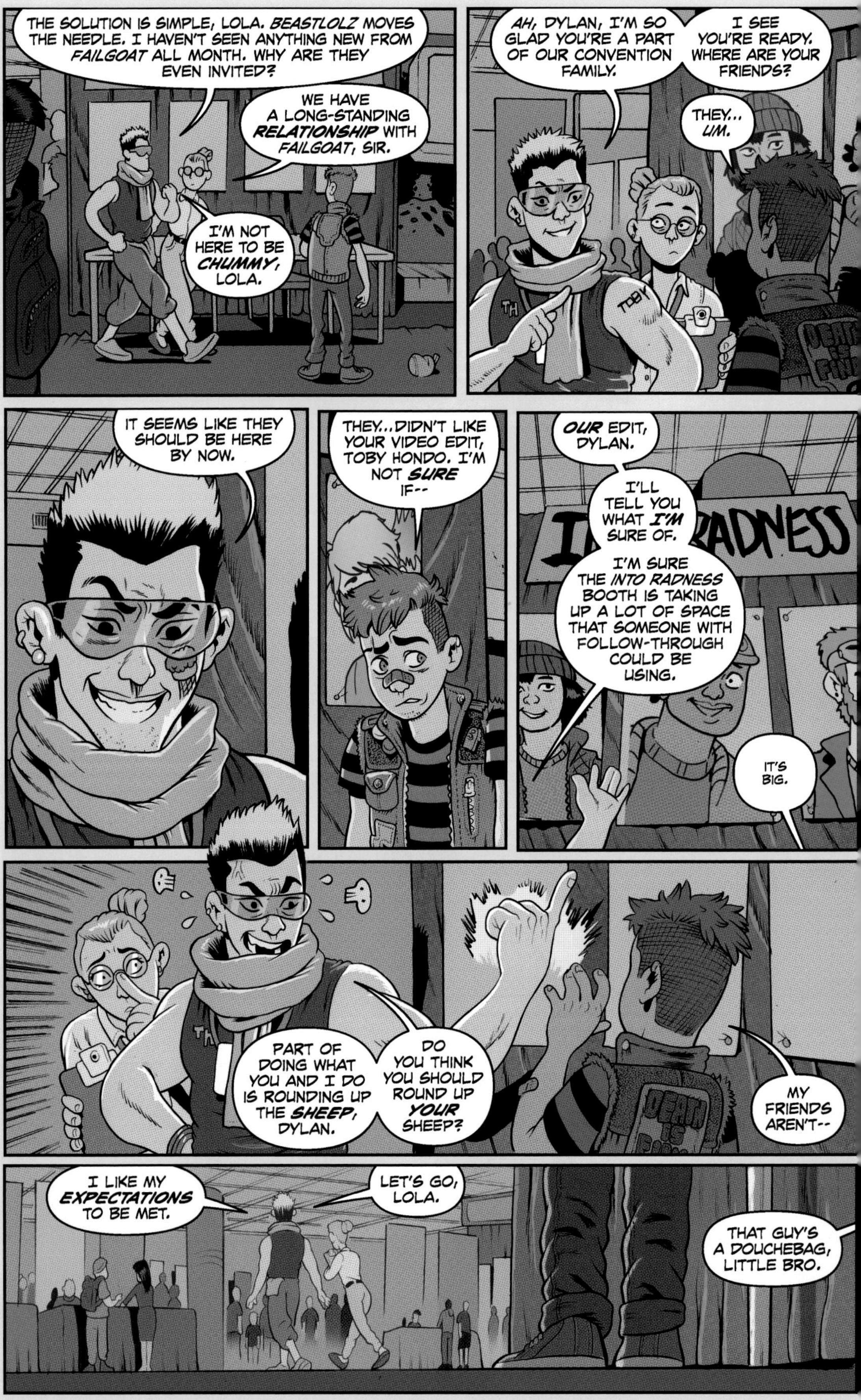
THE SOLUTION IS SIMPLE, LOLA. BEASTLOLZ MOVES THE NEEDLE. I HAVEN'T SEEN ANYTHING NEW FROM FAILGOAT ALL MONTH. WHY ARE THEY EVEN INVITED?
WE HAVE A LONG-STANDING RELATIONSHIP WITH FAILGOAT, SIR.
I'M NOT HERE TO BE CHUMMY, LOLA.
AH, DYLAN, I'M SO GLAD YOU'RE A PART OF OUR CONVENTION FAMILY.
I SEE YOU'RE READY. WHERE ARE YOUR FRIENDS?
THEY... UM.
IT SEEMS LIKE THEY SHOULD BE HERE BY NOW.
THEY...DIDN'T LIKE YOUR VIDEO EDIT, TOBY HONDO. I'M NOT SURE IF--
OUR EDIT, DYLAN.
I'LL TELL YOU WHAT I'M SURE OF.
I'M SURE THE INTO RADNESS BOOTH IS TAKING UP A LOT OF SPACE THAT SOMEONE WITH FOLLOW-THROUGH COULD BE USING.
IT'S BIG.
PART OF DOING WHAT YOU AND I DO IS ROUNDING UP THE SHEEP, DYLAN.
DO YOU THINK YOU SHOULD ROUND UP YOUR SHEEP?
MY FRIENDS AREN'T--
I LIKE MY EXPECTATIONS TO BE MET.
LET'S GO, LOLA.
THAT GUY'S A DOUCHEBAG, LITTLE BRO.

SLUDGE! YOU CAME!!

DID YOU *SEE* THIS PLACE?! THEY HAVE EVERYTHING.

THEY HAVE THREE FLAVORS OF MILK EGGS.

INTO RA

POY STATION

DNESS

ALL THIS? IT *IS* AMAZING, BUDDY.

BUT I CAN'T SHAKE THE FEELING IT'S NOT OURS.

WE'RE GUESTS, MAN. ON SOMEBODY ELSE'S CHANNEL.

WHAT DO YOU MEAN? THIS IS EVERYTHING WE WANTED.

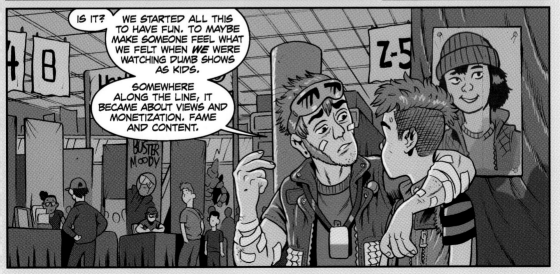

IS IT? WE STARTED ALL THIS TO HAVE FUN. TO MAYBE MAKE SOMEONE FEEL WHAT *WE* WERE WATCHING DUMB SHOWS AS KIDS.

SOMEWHERE ALONG THE LINE, IT BECAME ABOUT VIEWS AND MONETIZATION. FAME AND CONTENT.

BUSTER MOODY

Z-5

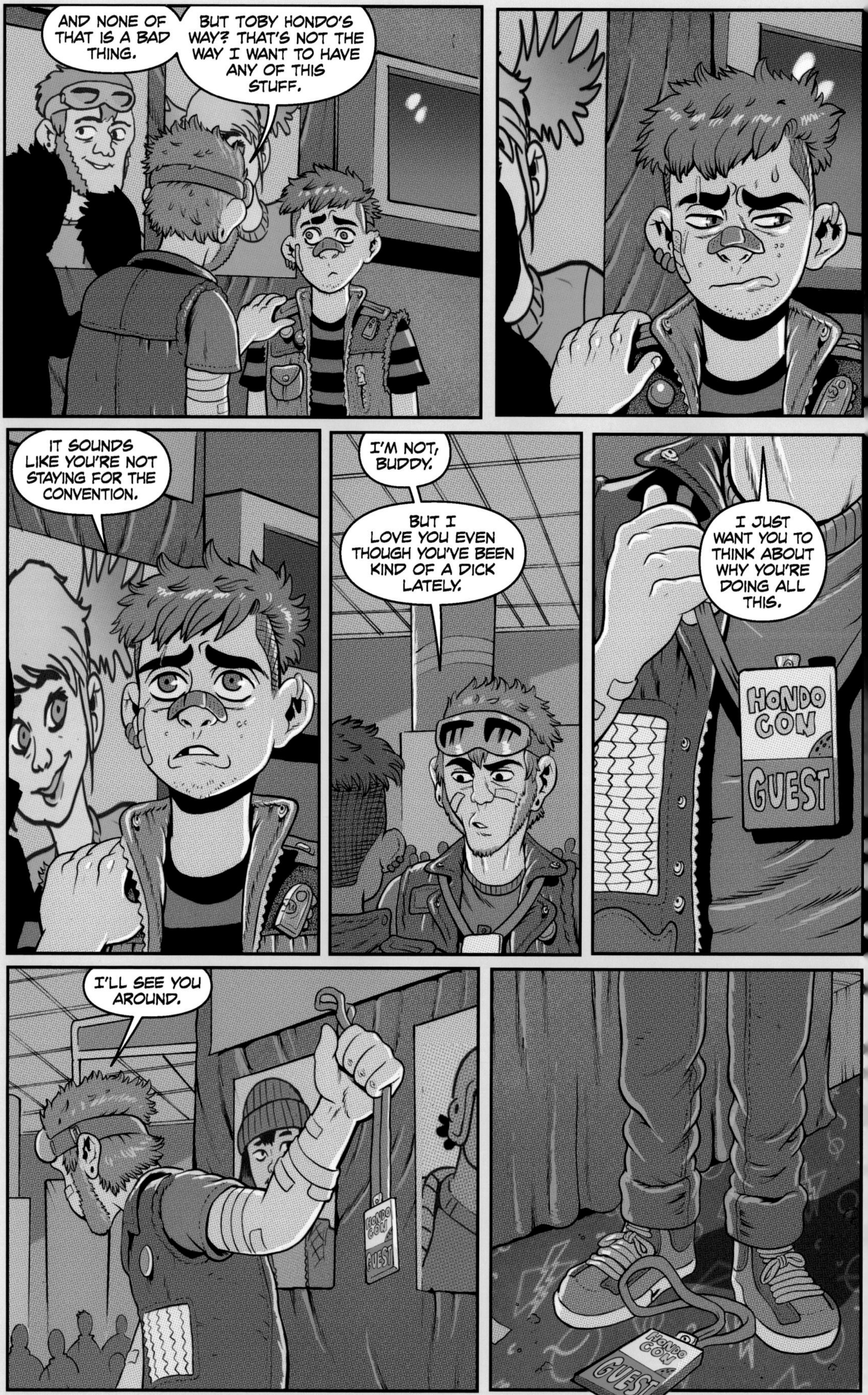
AND NONE OF THAT IS A BAD THING.
BUT TOBY HONDO'S WAY? THAT'S NOT THE WAY I WANT TO HAVE ANY OF THIS STUFF.
IT SOUNDS LIKE YOU'RE NOT STAYING FOR THE CONVENTION.
I'M NOT, BUDDY.
BUT I LOVE YOU EVEN THOUGH YOU'VE BEEN KIND OF A DICK LATELY.
I JUST WANT YOU TO THINK ABOUT WHY YOU'RE DOING ALL THIS.
HONDO CON
GUEST
I'LL SEE YOU AROUND.
HONDO CON
GUEST
HONDO CON
GUEST

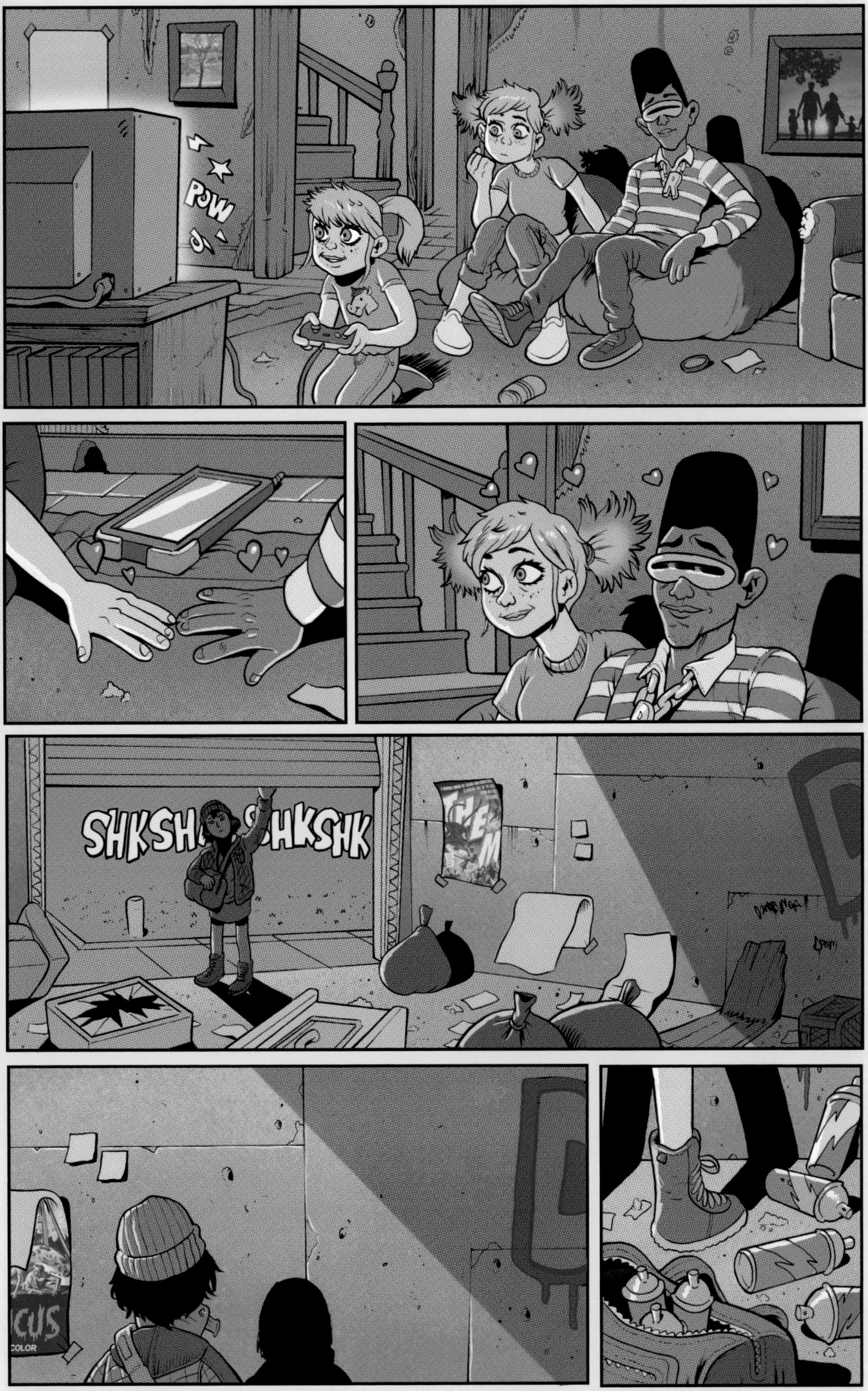
POW
SHKSHK SHKSHK

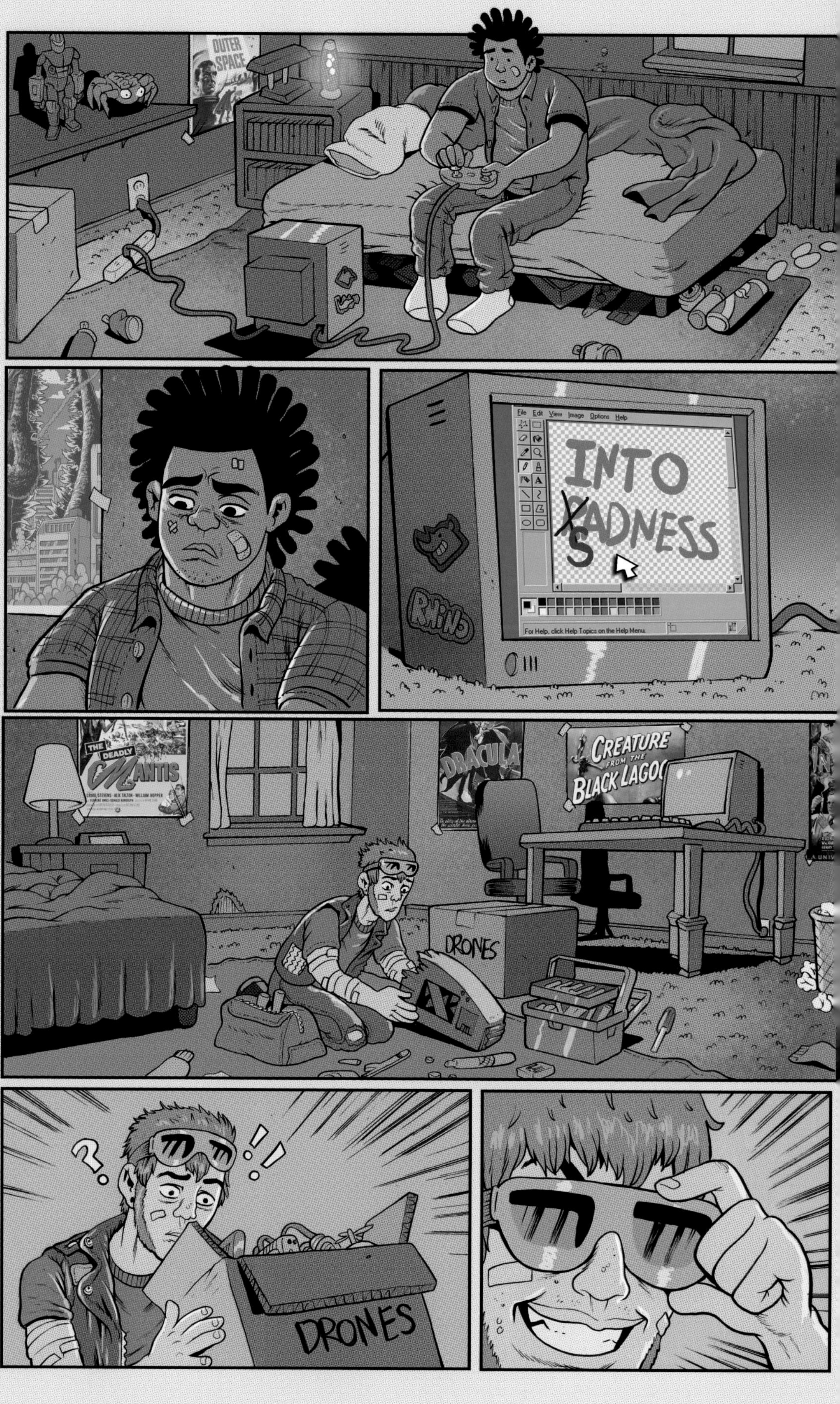
OUTER SPACE
File Edit View Image Options Help
INTO
SADNESS
For Help, click Help Topics on the Help Menu.
RHINO
THE DEADLY MANTIS
CRAIG STEVENS · ALIX TALTON · WILLIAM HOPPER
DRACULA
CREATURE FROM THE BLACK LAGOO
DRONES
?
!!
DRONES

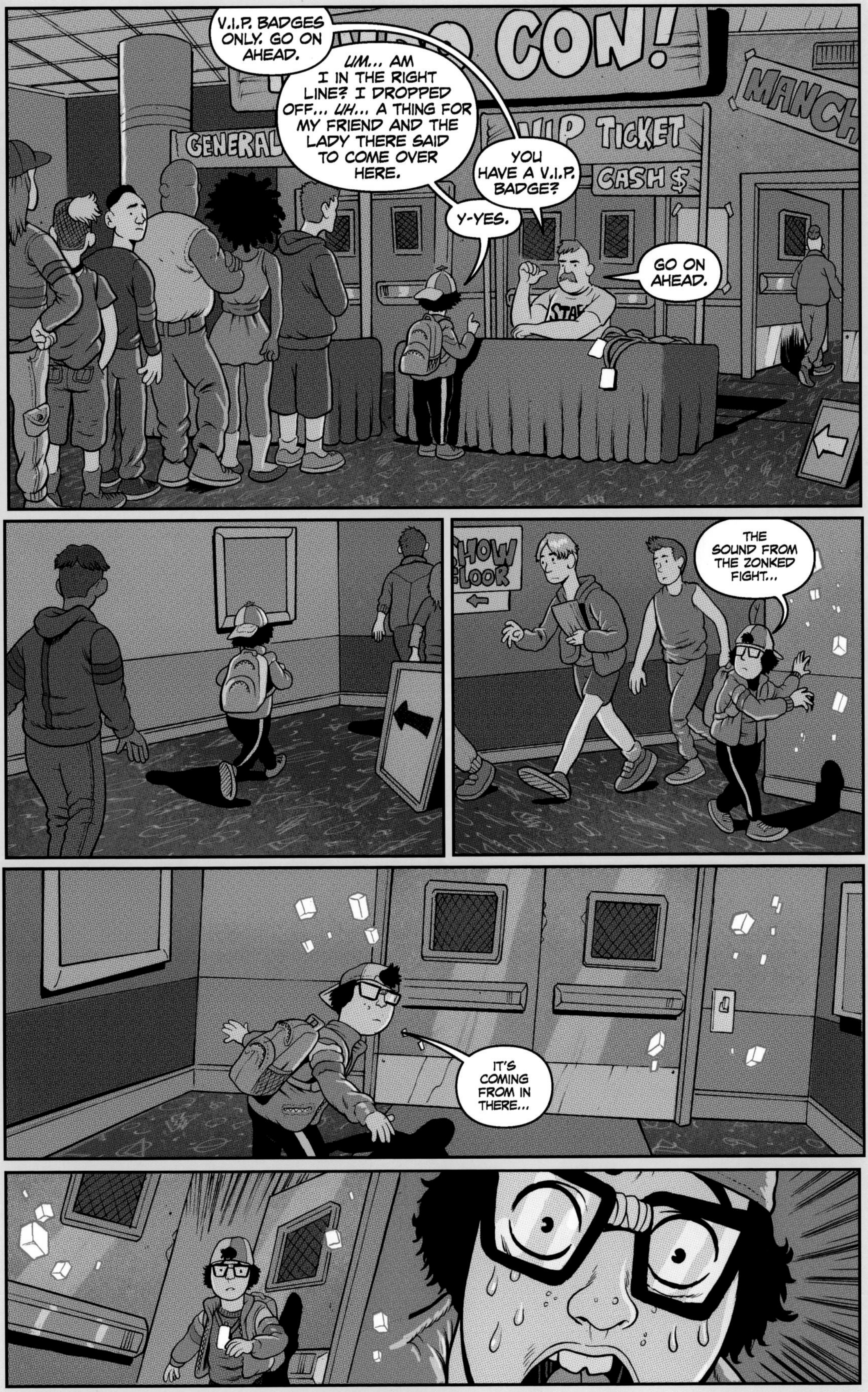
CON!
MANCH
GENERAL
VIP TICKET
CASH $
V.I.P. BADGES ONLY. GO ON AHEAD.
UM... AM I IN THE RIGHT LINE? I DROPPED OFF... UH... A THING FOR MY FRIEND AND THE LADY THERE SAID TO COME OVER HERE.
YOU HAVE A V.I.P. BADGE?
Y-YES.
GO ON AHEAD.
SHOW FLOOR
THE SOUND FROM THE ZONKED FIGHT...
IT'S COMING FROM IN THERE...

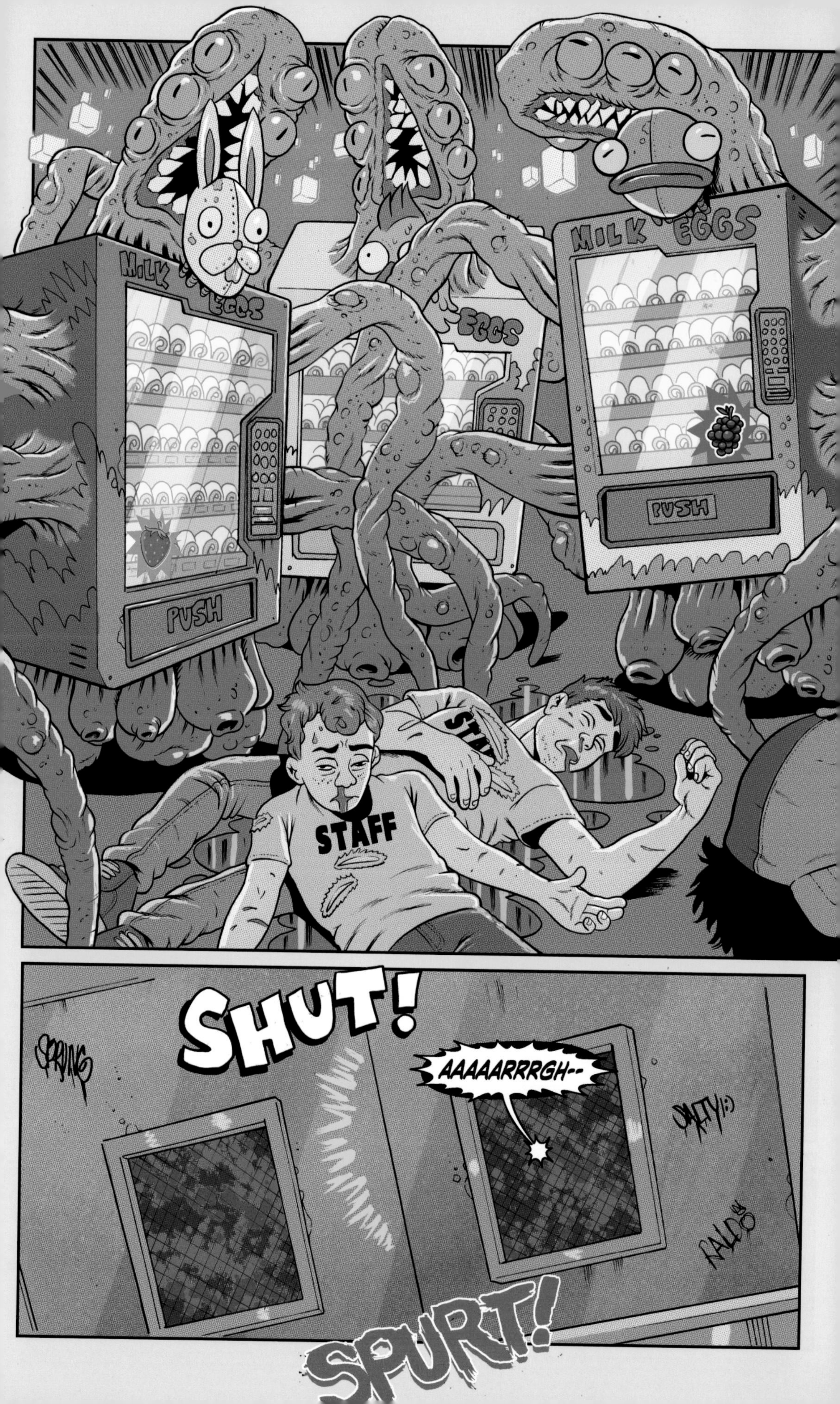
MILK EGGS
MILK EGGS
EGGS
PUSH
PUSH
STAFF
STAFF
SHUT!
AAAAARRRGH--
SPURT!

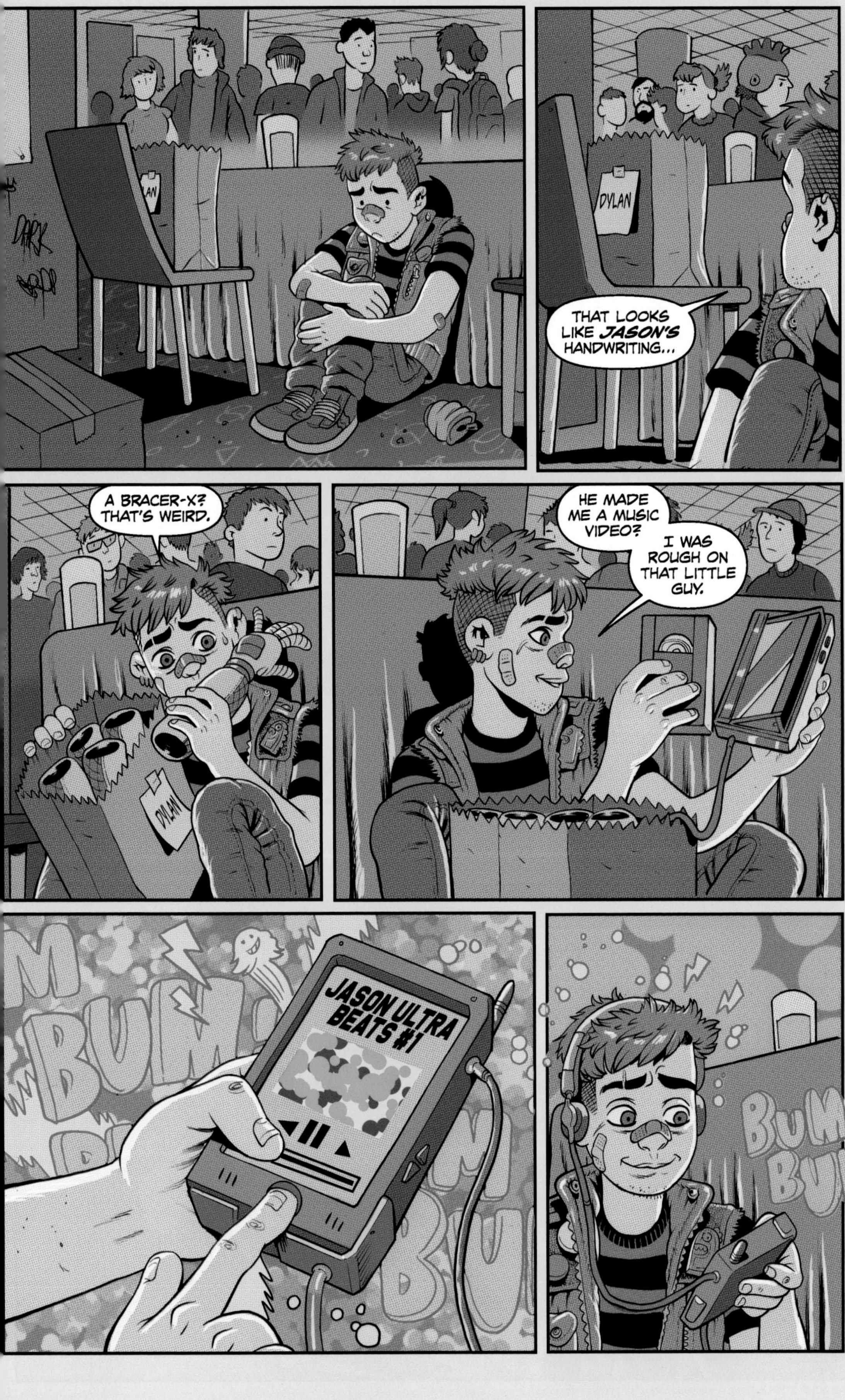
DYLAN
THAT LOOKS LIKE *JASON'S* HANDWRITING...
A BRACER-X? THAT'S WEIRD.
DYLAN
HE MADE ME A MUSIC VIDEO?
I WAS ROUGH ON THAT LITTLE GUY.
BUM
JASON ULTRA BEATS #1
BUM BUM

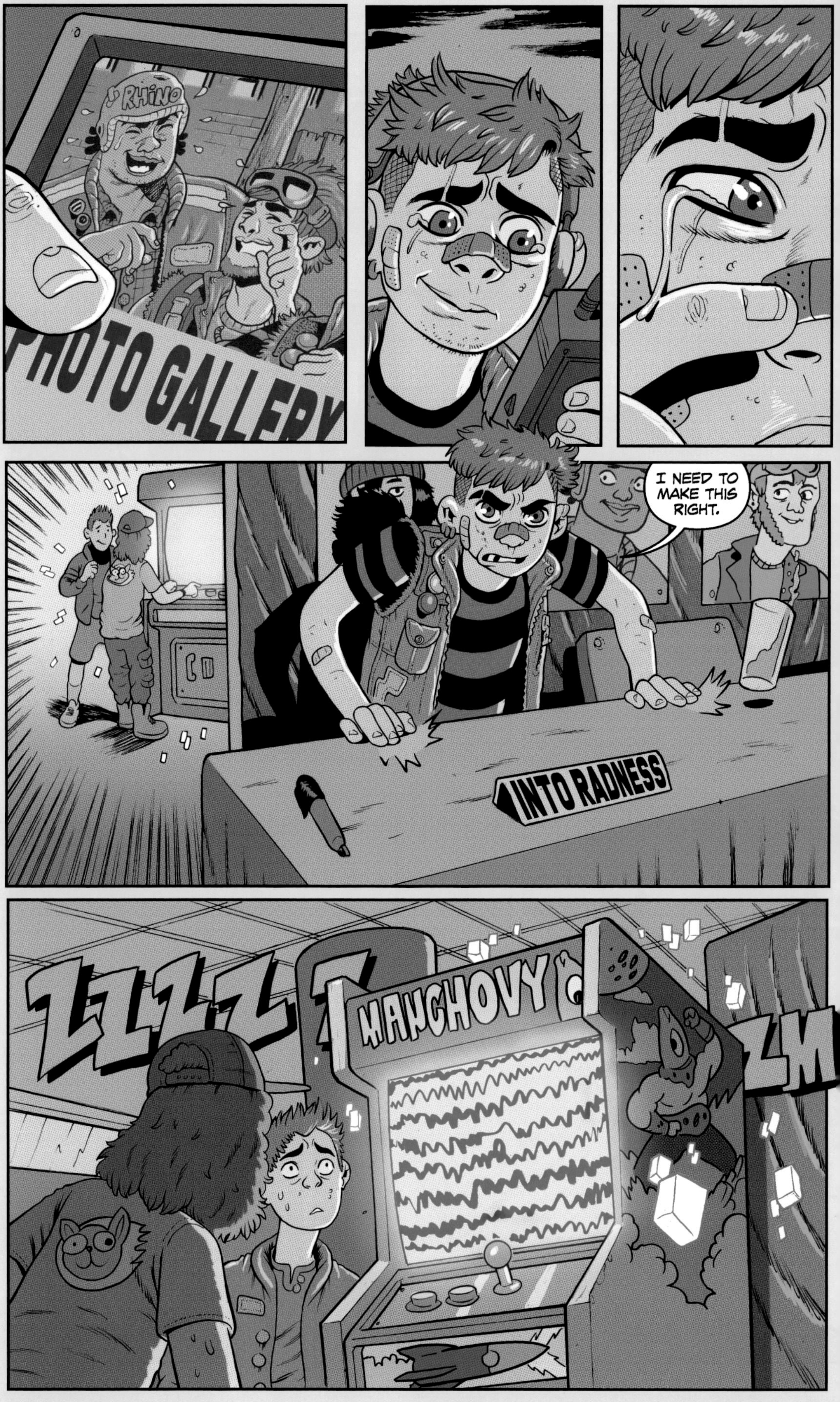
PHOTO GALLERY
RHINO
I NEED TO MAKE THIS RIGHT.
INTO RADNESS
ZZZZZ
MANCHOVY
ZM

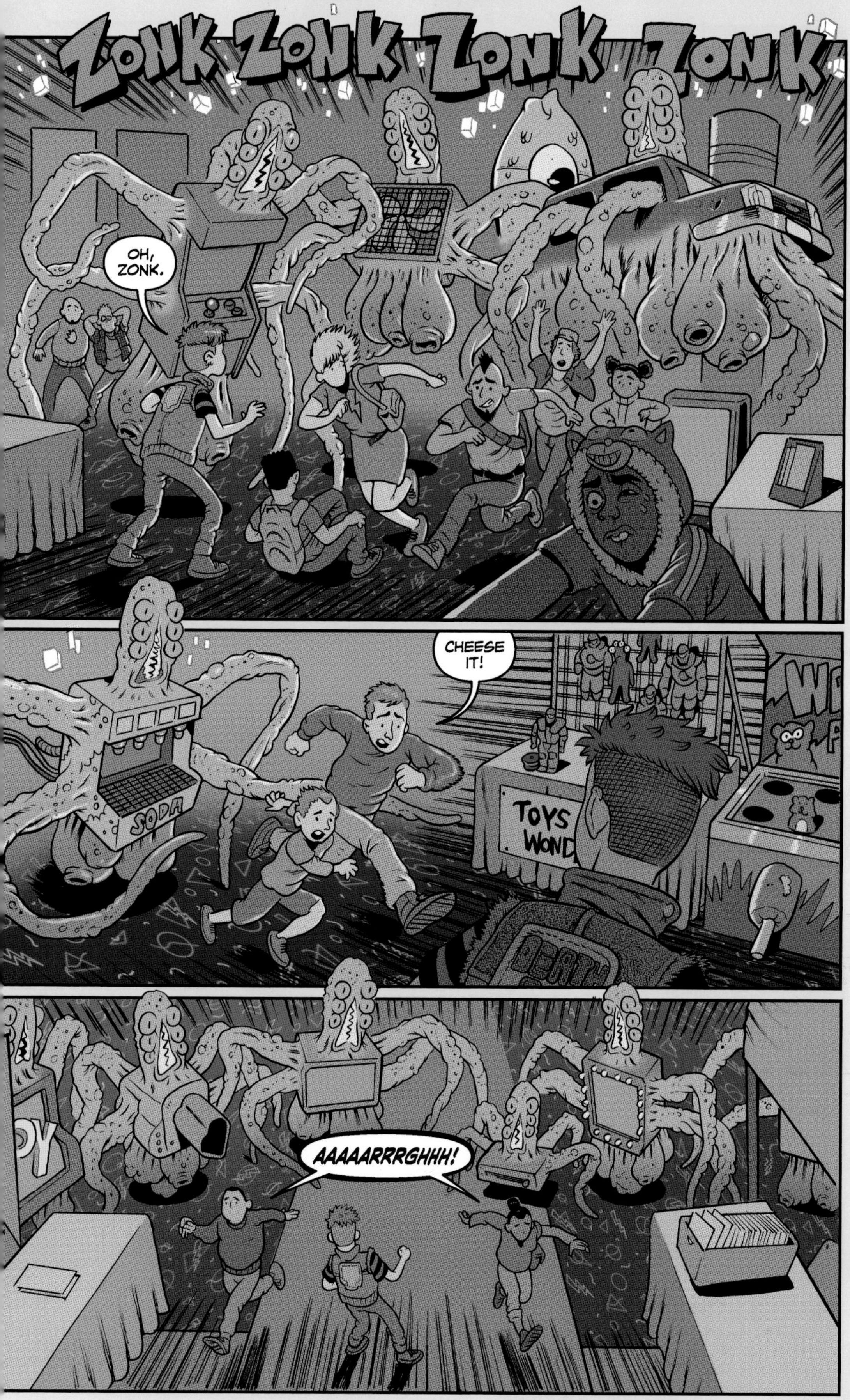
ZONK ZONK ZONK ZONK
OH, ZONK.
CHEESE IT!
TOYS WOND
SODA
AAAAARRRGHHH!

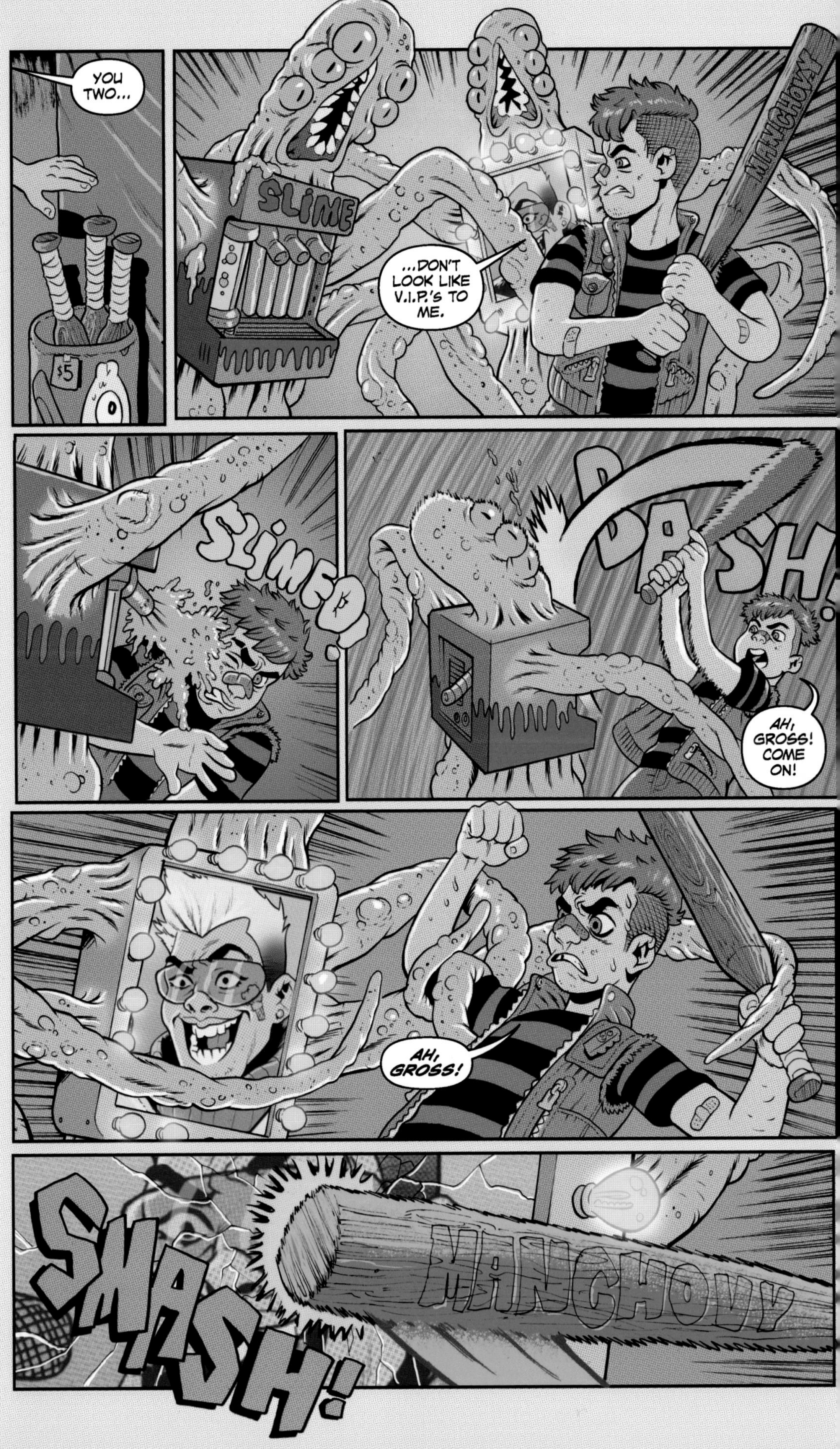
YOU TWO...
SLIME
$5
...DON'T LOOK LIKE V.I.P.'s TO ME.
MANCHOVY
SLIMED!
DASH!
AH, GROSS! COME ON!
AH, GROSS!
SMASH!
MANCHOVY

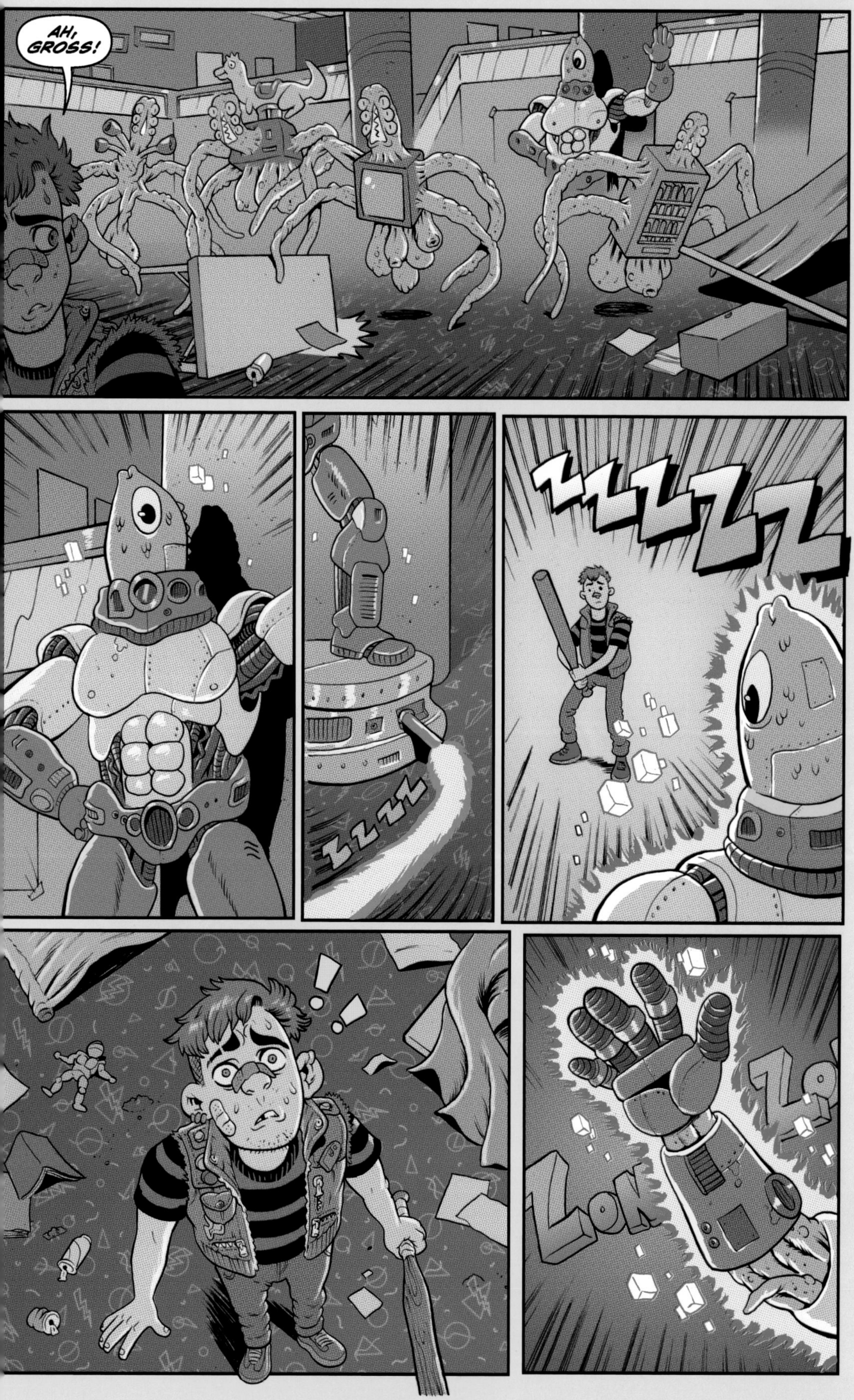
AH, GROSS!
ZZZZ
ZZZZZZ
ZONK

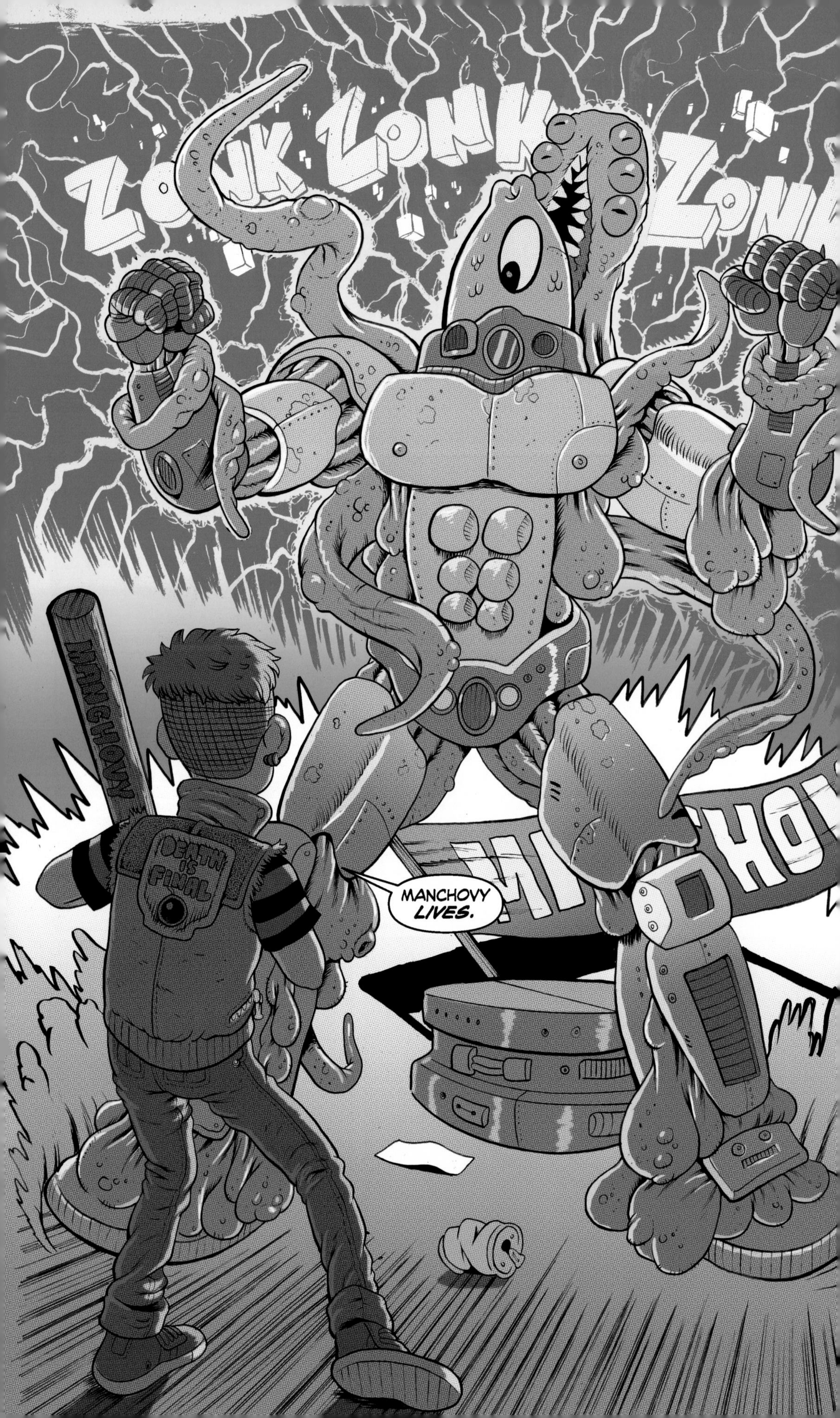
ZONK ZONK
MANCHOVY
DEATH IS FINAL
MANCHOVY LIVES.

CHAPTER FOUR

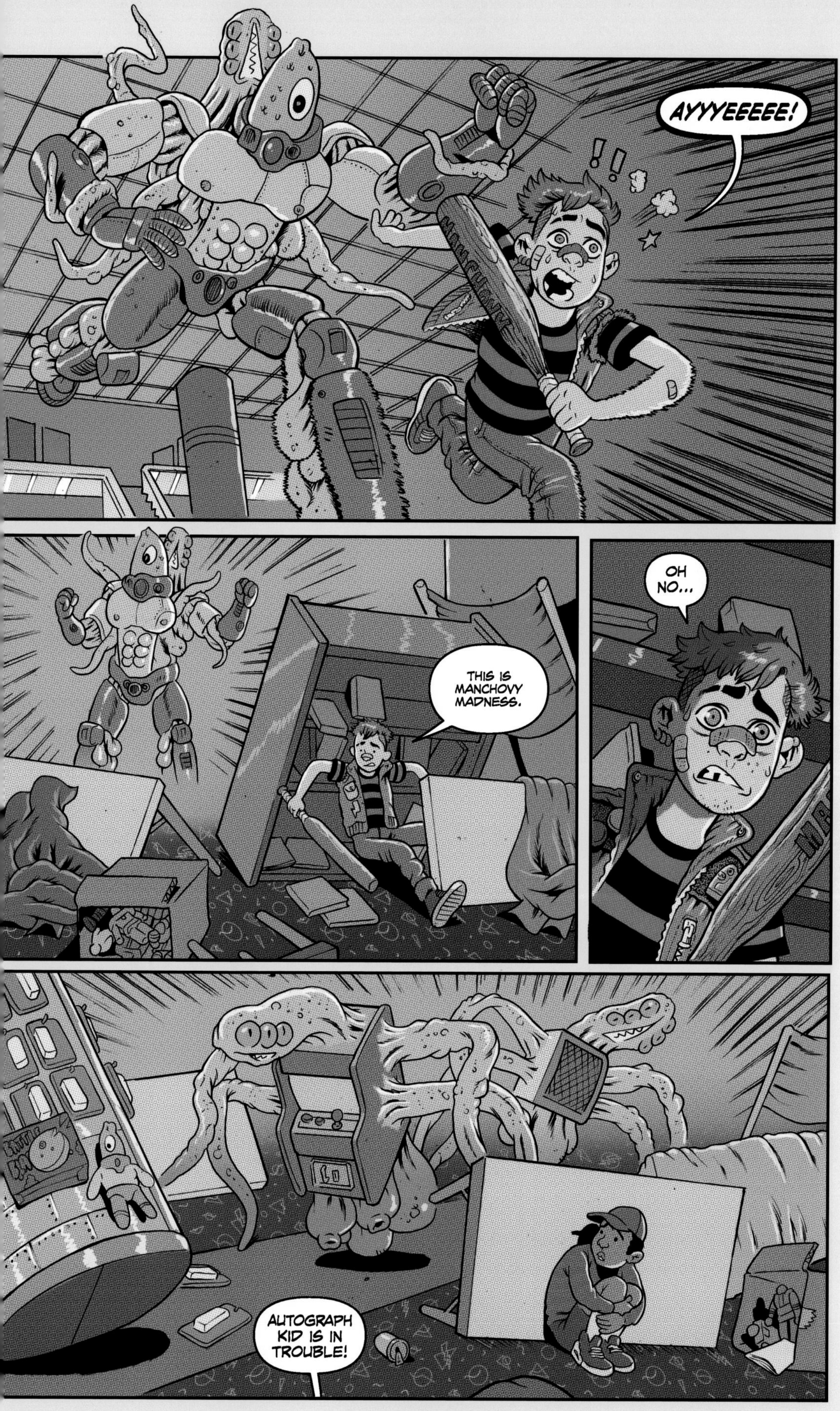
AYYYEEEEE!
!!
THIS IS MANCHOVY MADNESS.
OH NO...
AUTOGRAPH KID IS IN TROUBLE!

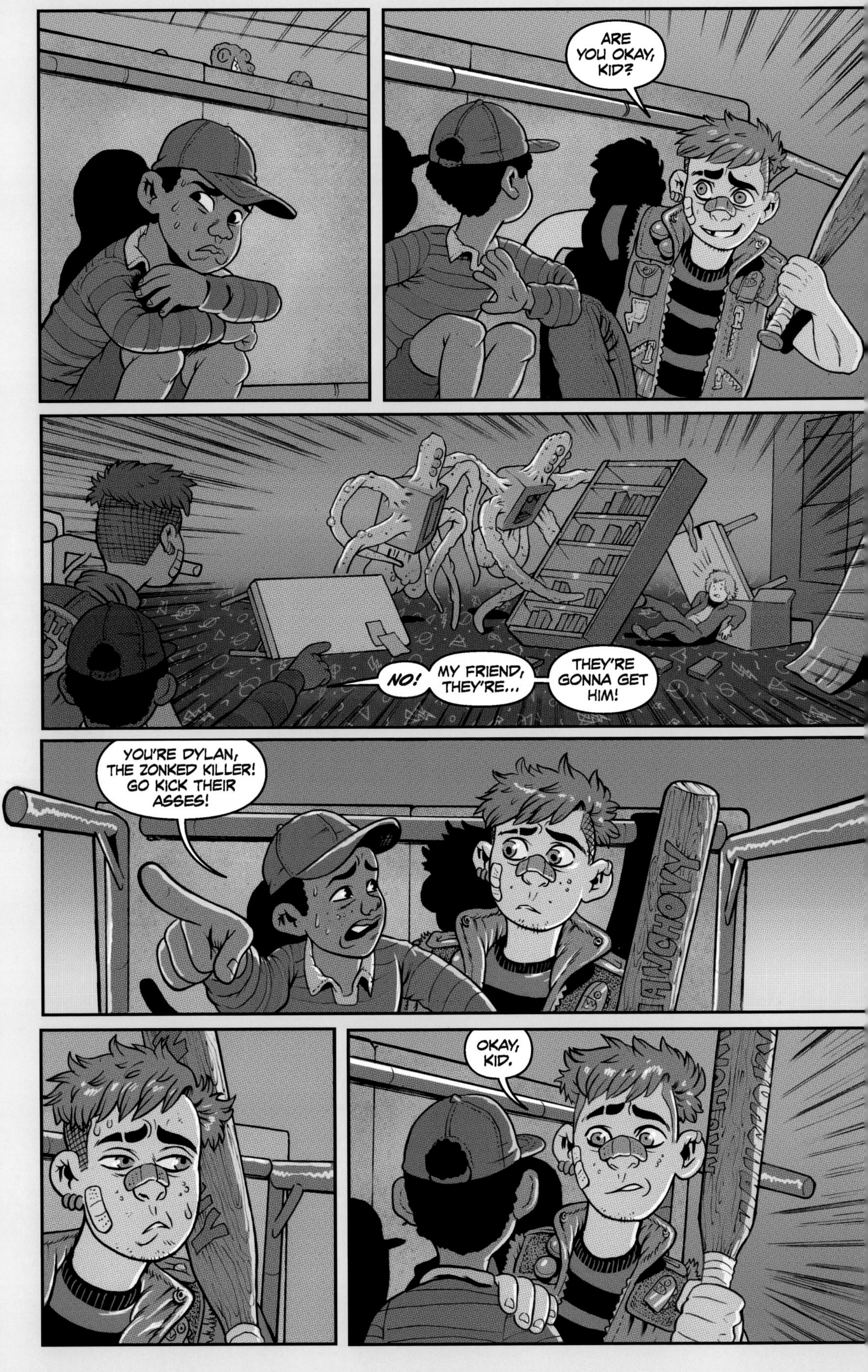
ARE YOU OKAY, KID?
NO!
MY FRIEND, THEY'RE...
THEY'RE GONNA GET HIM!
YOU'RE DYLAN, THE ZONKED KILLER! GO KICK THEIR ASSES!
OKAY, KID.

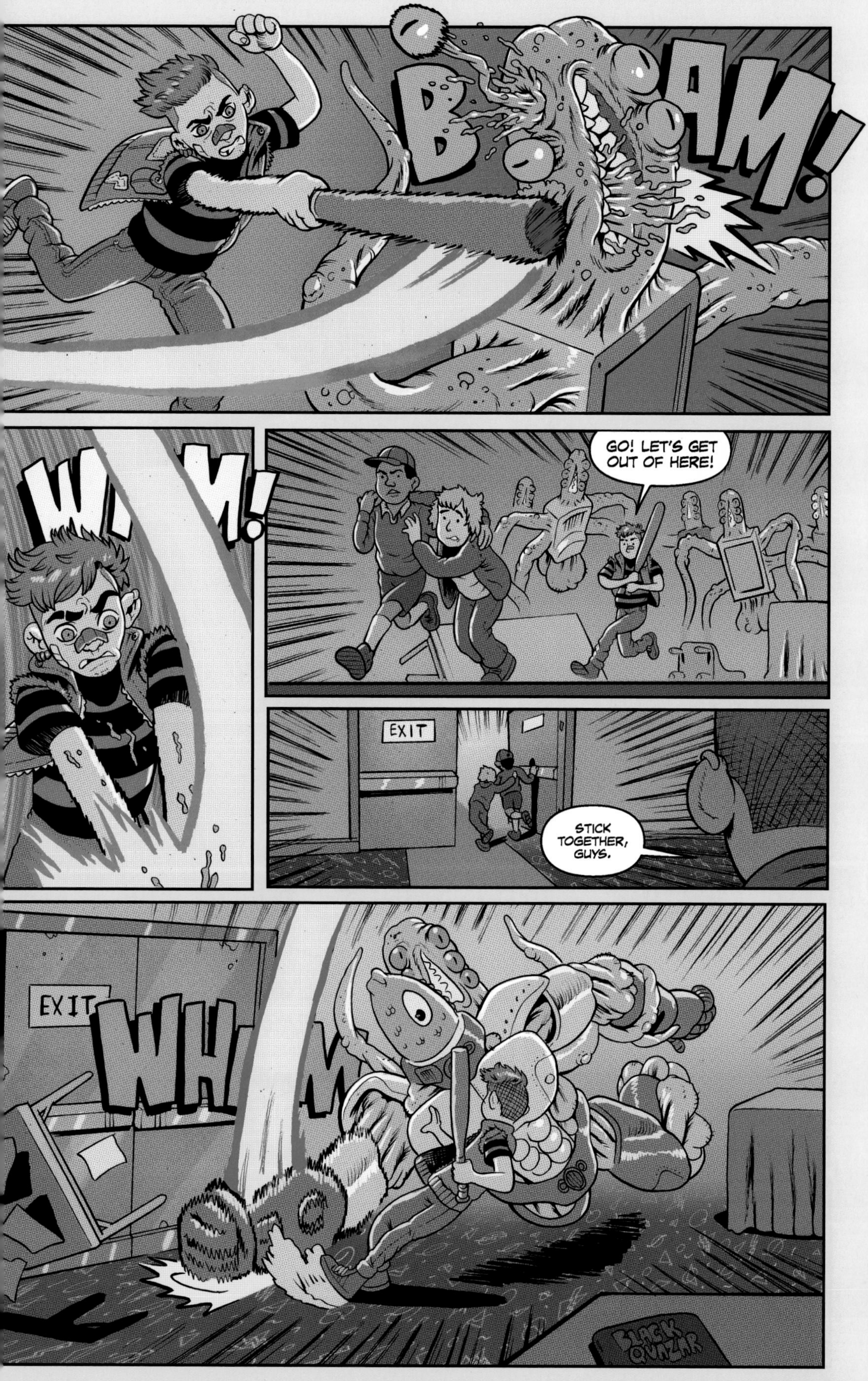
BOAM!
WHAM!
GO! LET'S GET OUT OF HERE!
EXIT
STICK TOGETHER, GUYS.
EXIT
WHAM
BLACK QUAZAR

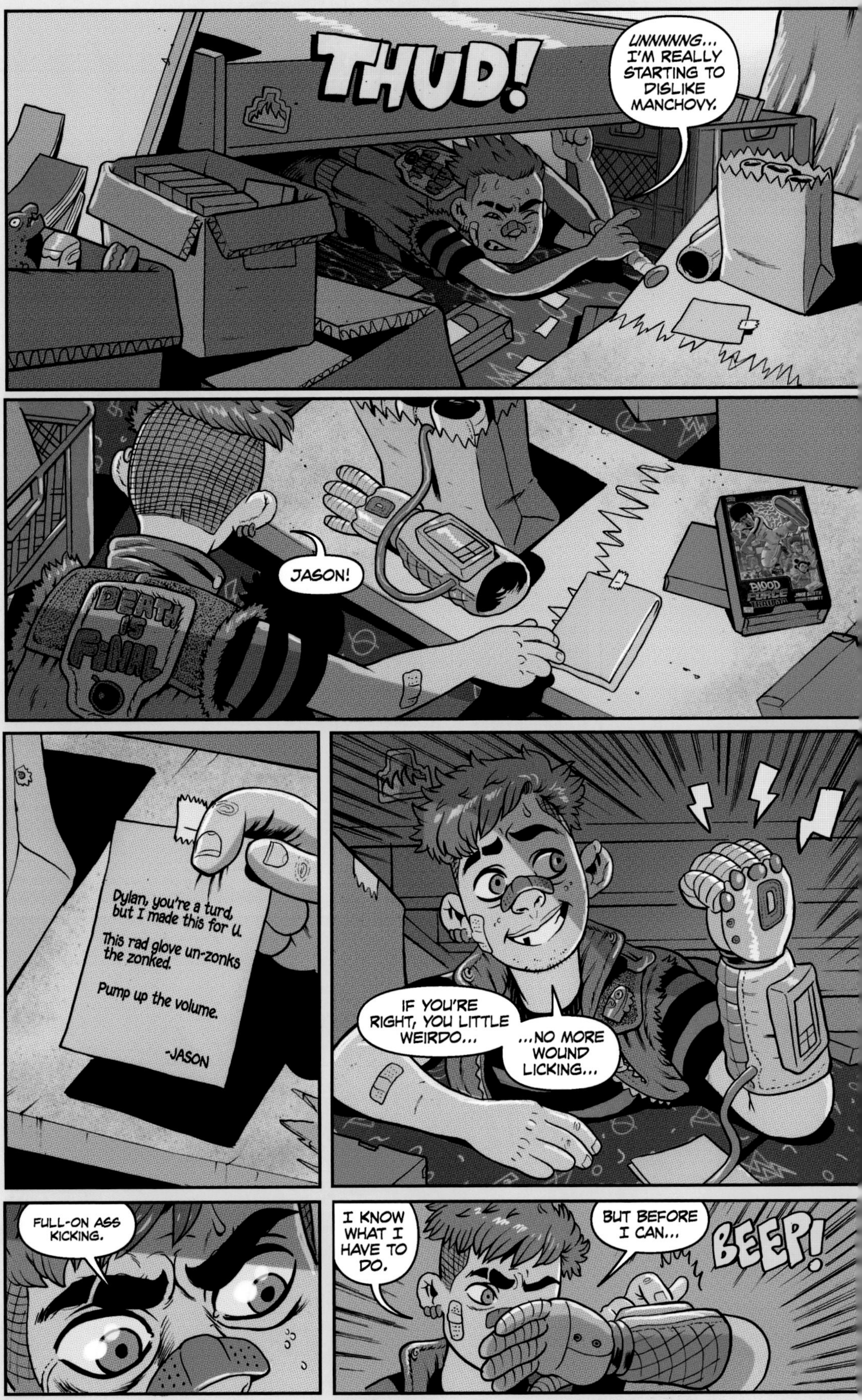
THUD!
UNNNNNG... I'M REALLY STARTING TO DISLIKE MANCHOVY.
JASON!
BLOOD FORCE TRAUMA
Dylan, you're a turd, but I made this for u.
This rad glove un-zonks the zonked.
Pump up the volume.
-JASON
IF YOU'RE RIGHT, YOU LITTLE WEIRDO...
...NO MORE WOUND LICKING...
FULL-ON ASS KICKING.
I KNOW WHAT I HAVE TO DO.
BUT BEFORE I CAN...
BEEP!

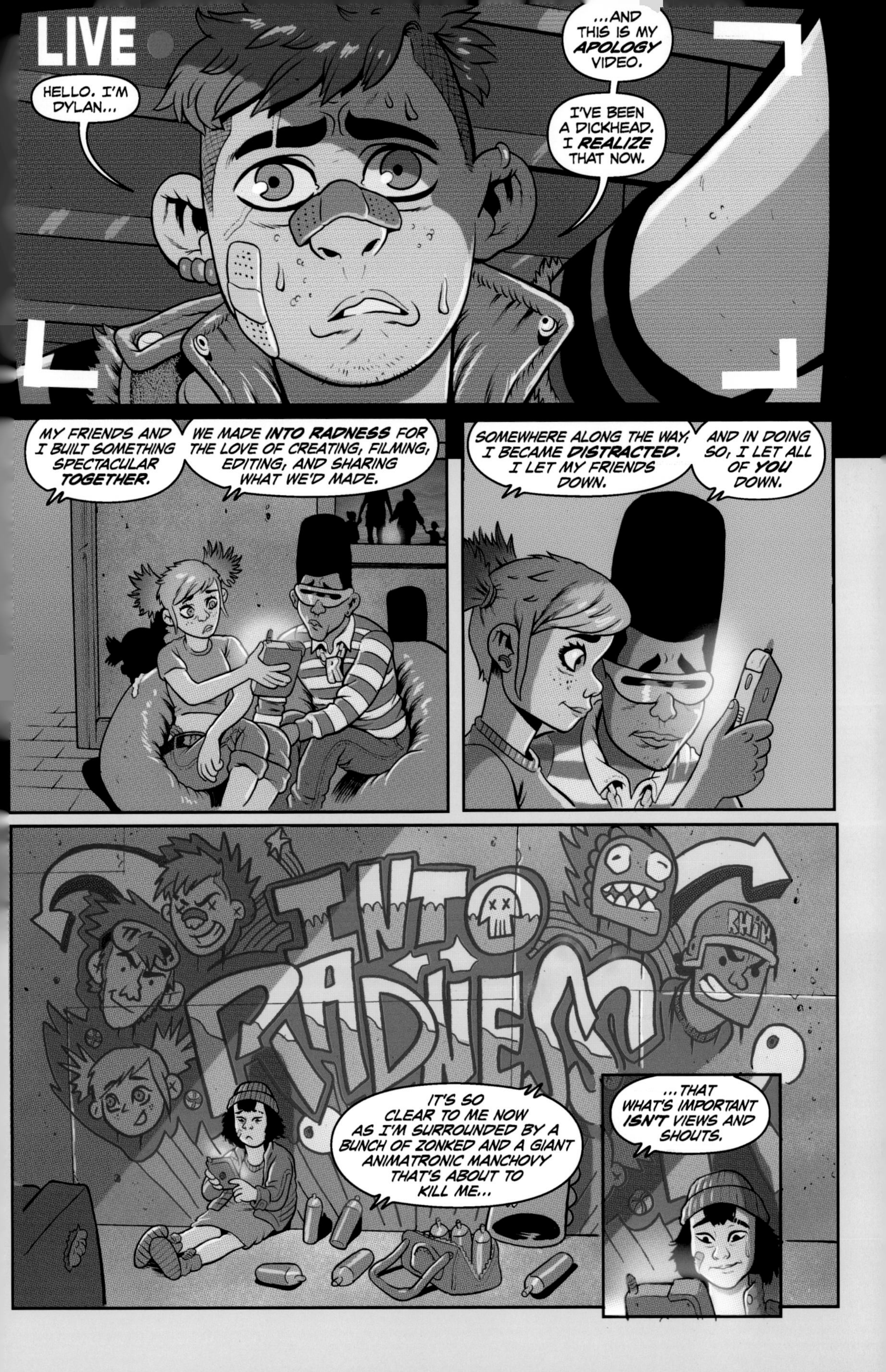
LIVE
HELLO. I'M DYLAN...
...AND THIS IS MY APOLOGY VIDEO.
I'VE BEEN A DICKHEAD. I REALIZE THAT NOW.
MY FRIENDS AND I BUILT SOMETHING SPECTACULAR TOGETHER.
WE MADE INTO RADNESS FOR THE LOVE OF CREATING, FILMING, EDITING, AND SHARING WHAT WE'D MADE.
SOMEWHERE ALONG THE WAY, I BECAME DISTRACTED. I LET MY FRIENDS DOWN.
AND IN DOING SO, I LET ALL OF YOU DOWN.
INTO RADNESS
IT'S SO CLEAR TO ME NOW AS I'M SURROUNDED BY A BUNCH OF ZONKED AND A GIANT ANIMATRONIC MANCHOVY THAT'S ABOUT TO KILL ME...
...THAT WHAT'S IMPORTANT ISN'T VIEWS AND SHOUTS.

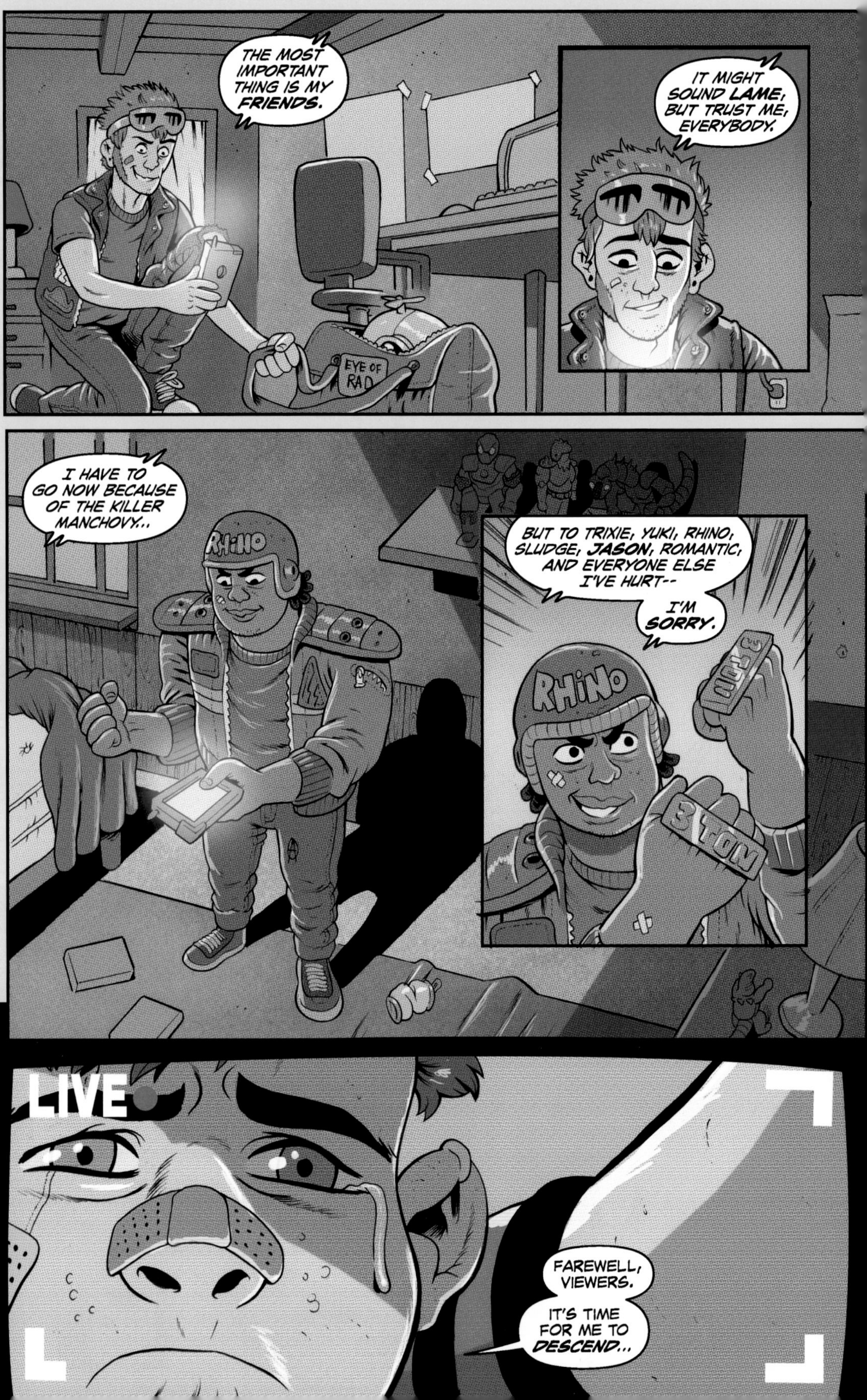
THE MOST IMPORTANT THING IS MY FRIENDS.
IT MIGHT SOUND LAME, BUT TRUST ME, EVERYBODY.
EYE OF RAD
I HAVE TO GO NOW BECAUSE OF THE KILLER MANCHOVY...
RHINO
BUT TO TRIXIE, YUKI, RHINO, SLUDGE, JASON, ROMANTIC, AND EVERYONE ELSE I'VE HURT--
I'M SORRY.
RHINO
3 TON
LIVE
FAREWELL, VIEWERS.
IT'S TIME FOR ME TO DESCEND...

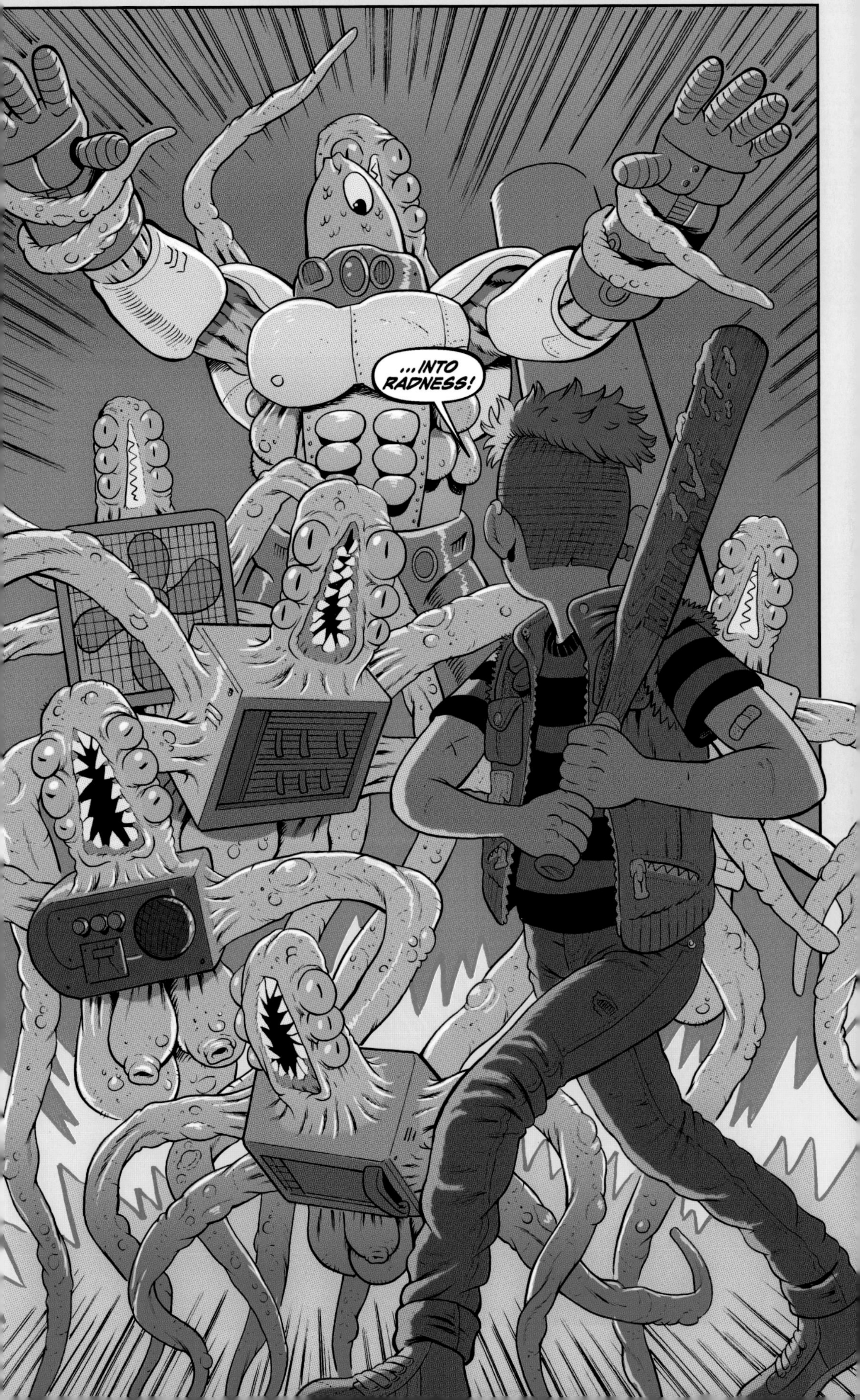
...INTO RADNESS!

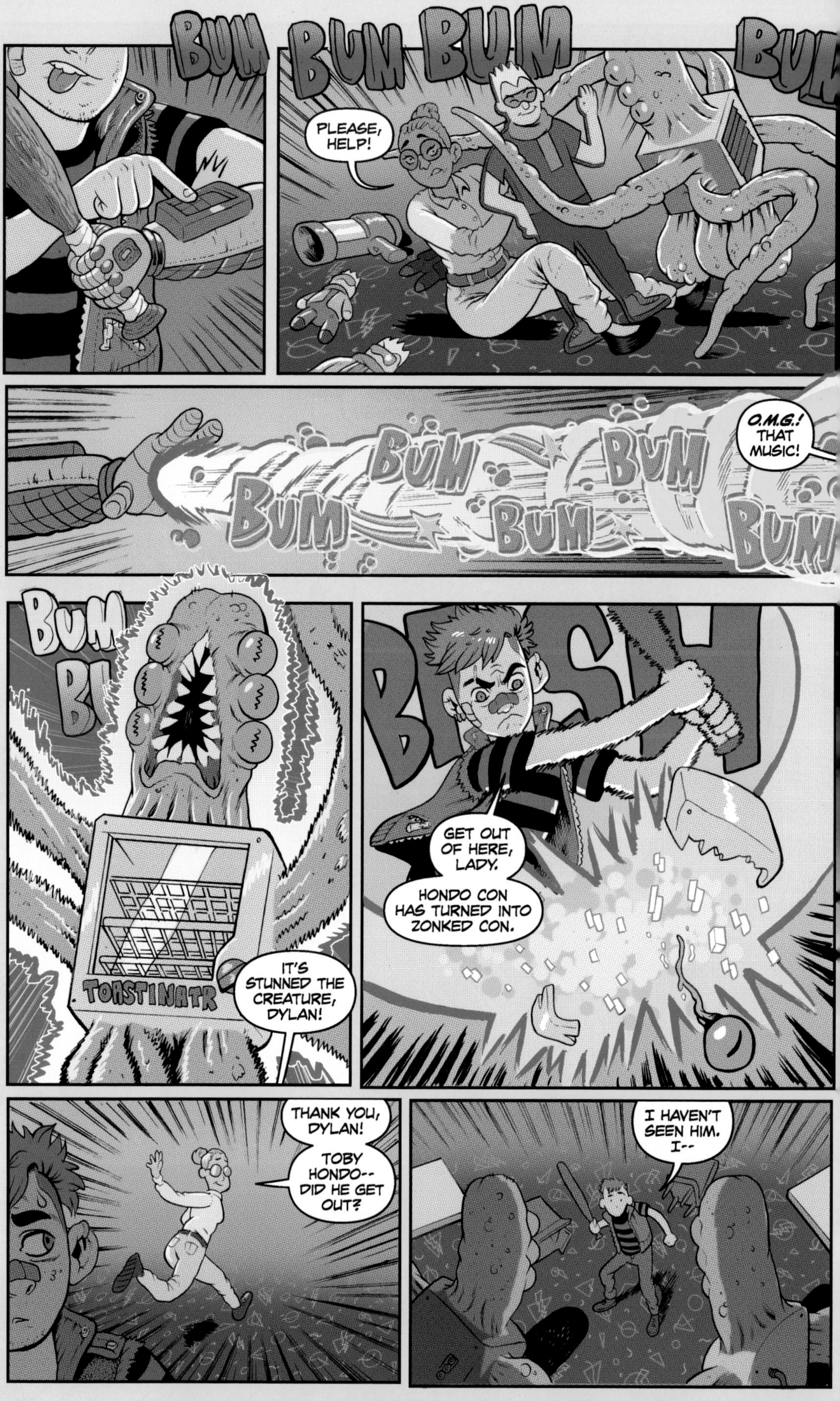
BUM BUM BUM BUM
PLEASE, HELP!
BUM BUM BUM BUM BUM
O.M.G.! THAT MUSIC!
BUM
TOASTINATR
IT'S STUNNED THE CREATURE, DYLAN!
GET OUT OF HERE, LADY.
HONDO CON HAS TURNED INTO ZONKED CON.
THANK YOU, DYLAN!
TOBY HONDO-- DID HE GET OUT?
I HAVEN'T SEEN HIM. I--

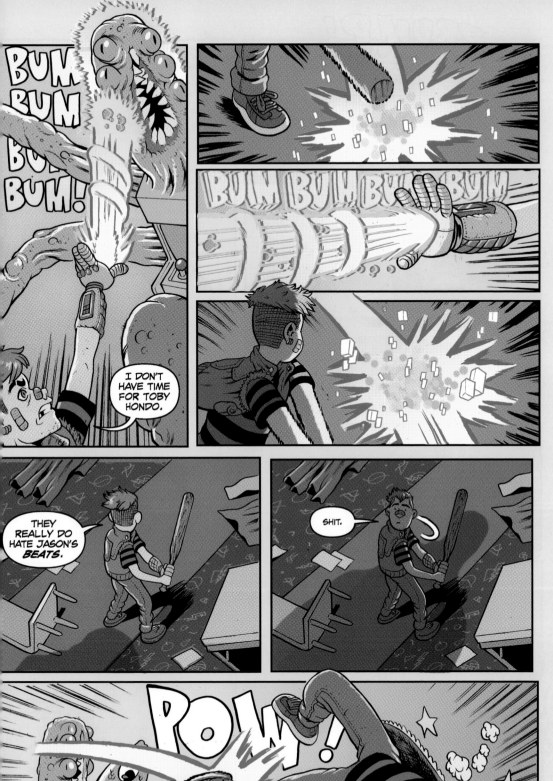

BUM
BUM
BUM
BUM!

BUM BUM BUM BUM

I DON'T HAVE TIME FOR TOBY HONDO.

THEY REALLY DO HATE JASON'S *BEATS*.

SHIT.

POW!

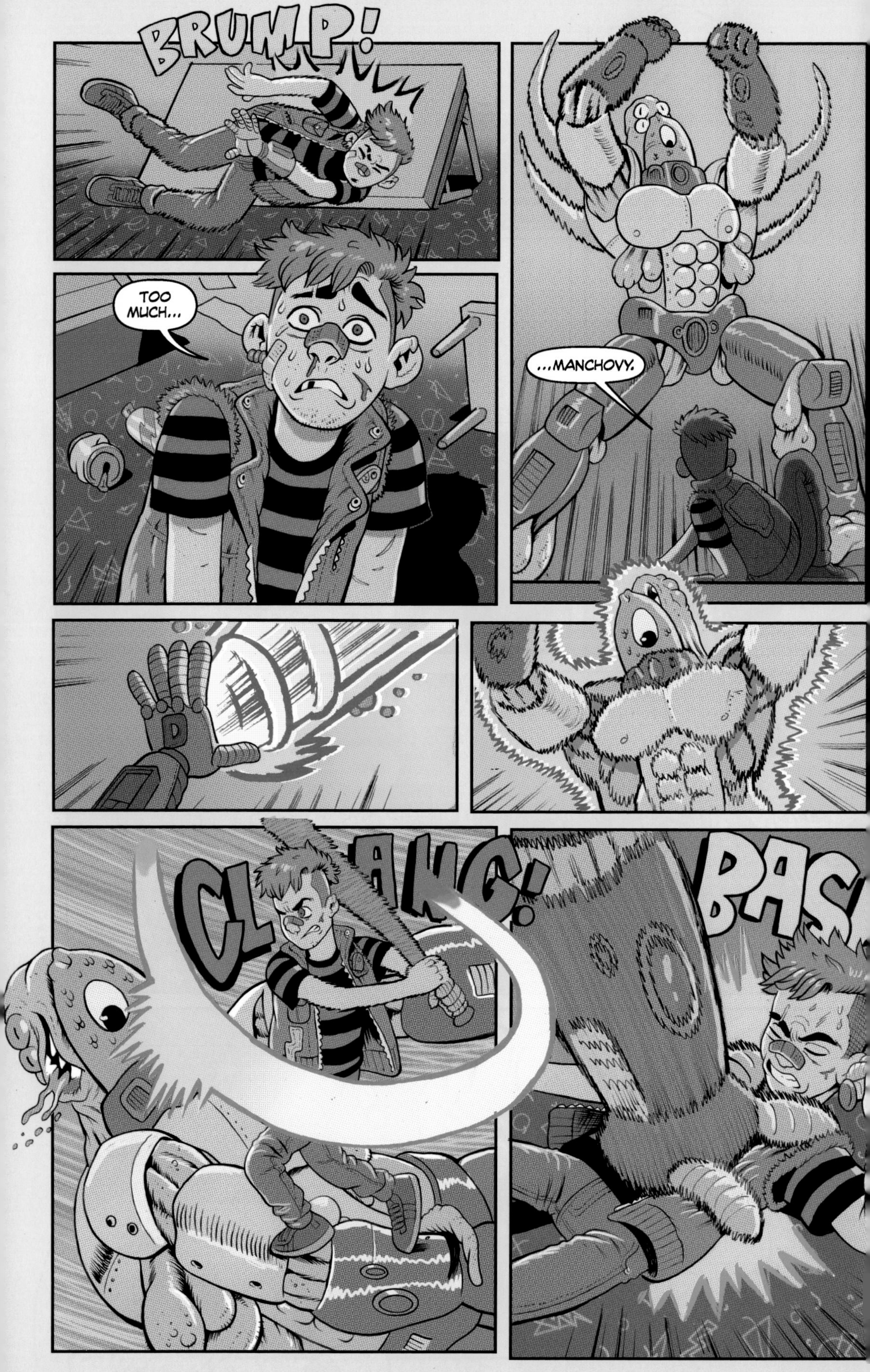
BRUMP!
TOO MUCH...
...MANCHOVY.
CLANG!
BAS

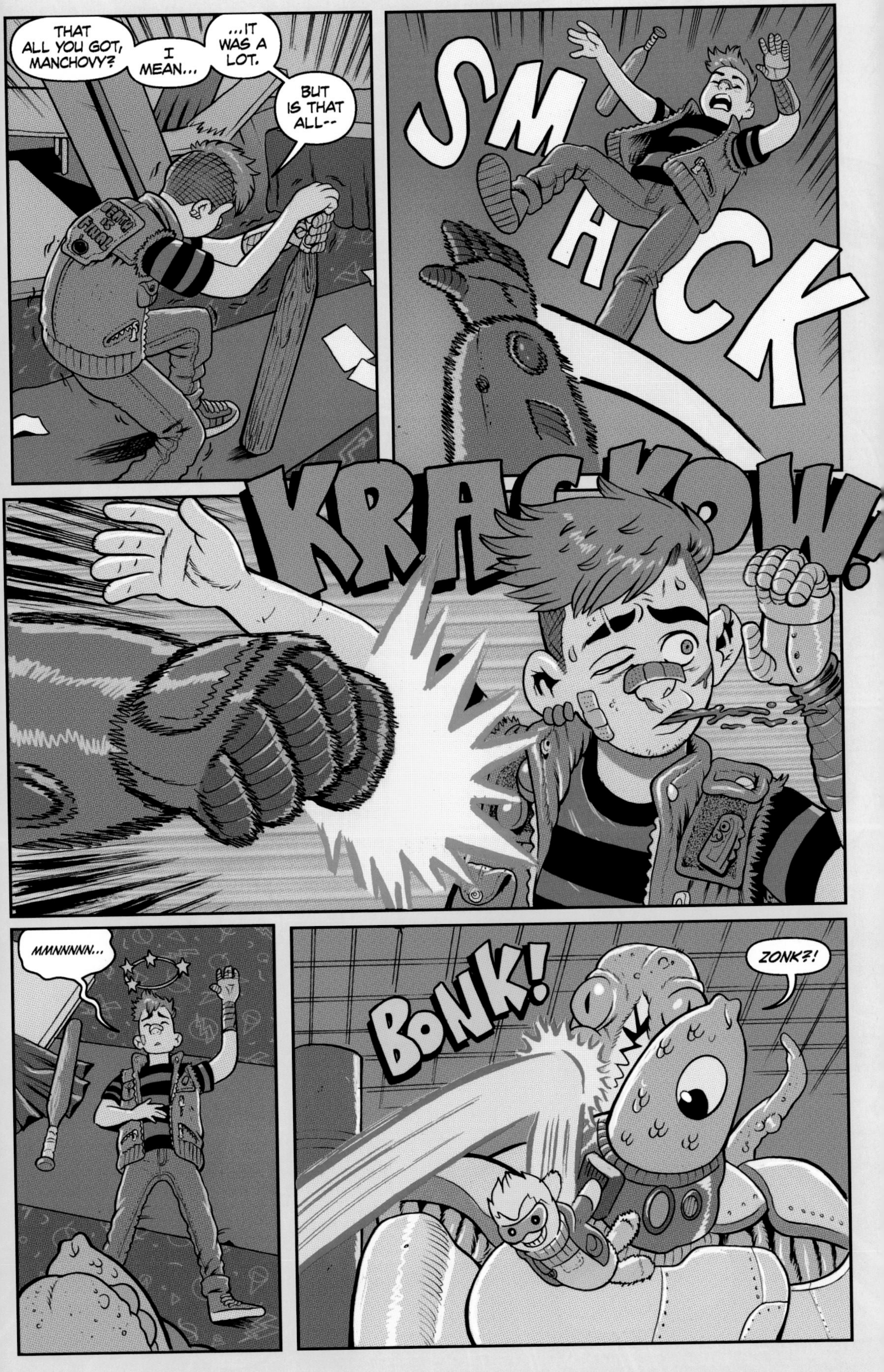

THAT ALL YOU GOT, MANCHOVY?
I MEAN...
...IT WAS A LOT.
BUT IS THAT ALL--
SMHACK
KRACKOW!!
MMNNNNN...
BONK!
ZONK?!

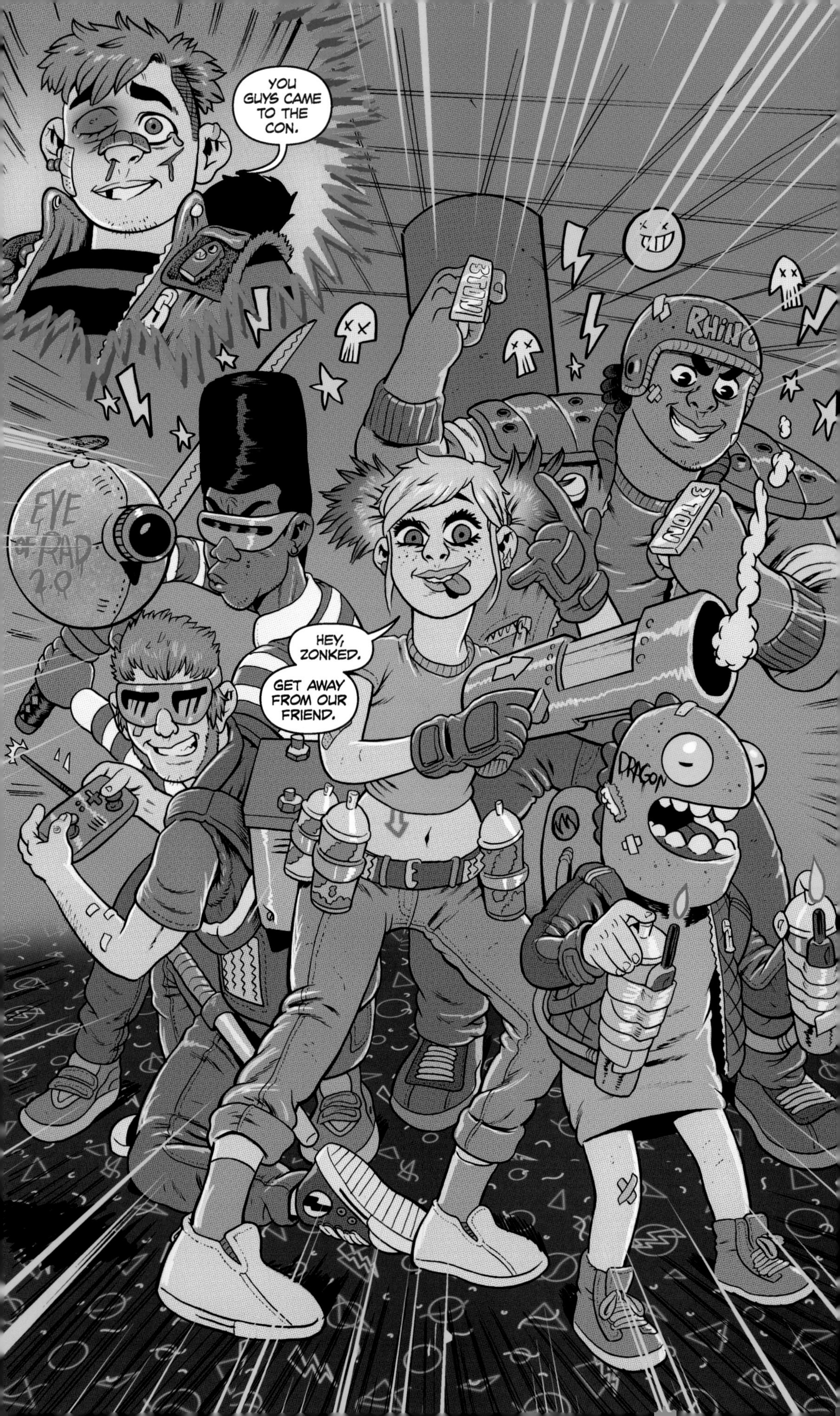

YOU GUYS CAME TO THE CON.
HEY, ZONKED.
GET AWAY FROM OUR FRIEND.
RHINO
3 TON
3 TON
EYE OF RAD 2.0
DRAGON

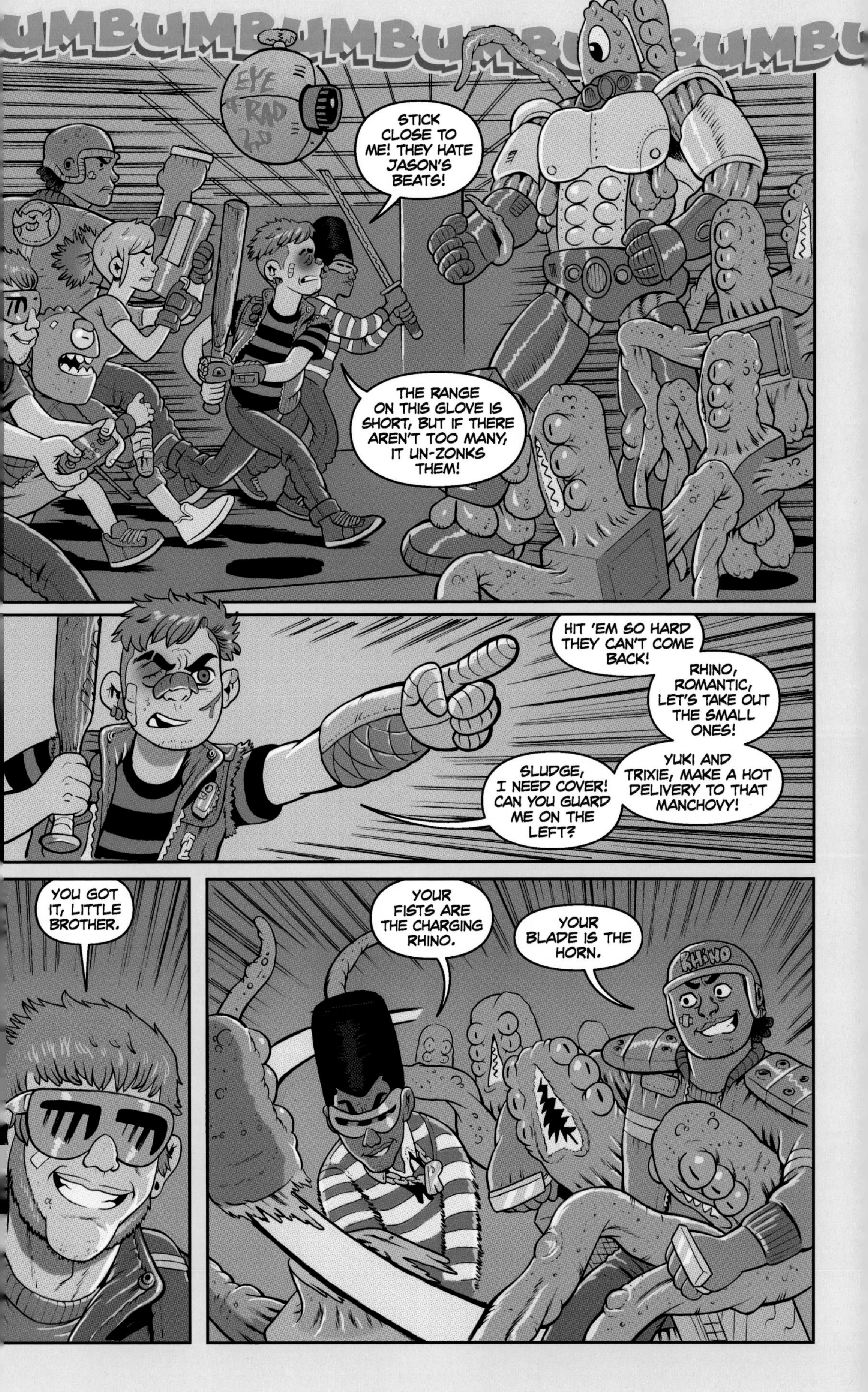
BUMBUMBUMBUMBUMBUMBUMBU
EYE RAD
STICK CLOSE TO ME! THEY HATE JASON'S BEATS!
THE RANGE ON THIS GLOVE IS SHORT, BUT IF THERE AREN'T TOO MANY, IT UN-ZONKS THEM!
HIT 'EM SO HARD THEY CAN'T COME BACK!
RHINO, ROMANTIC, LET'S TAKE OUT THE SMALL ONES!
YUKI AND TRIXIE, MAKE A HOT DELIVERY TO THAT MANCHOVY!
SLUDGE, I NEED COVER! CAN YOU GUARD ME ON THE LEFT?
YOU GOT IT, LITTLE BROTHER.
YOUR FISTS ARE THE CHARGING RHINO.
YOUR BLADE IS THE HORN.
RHINO

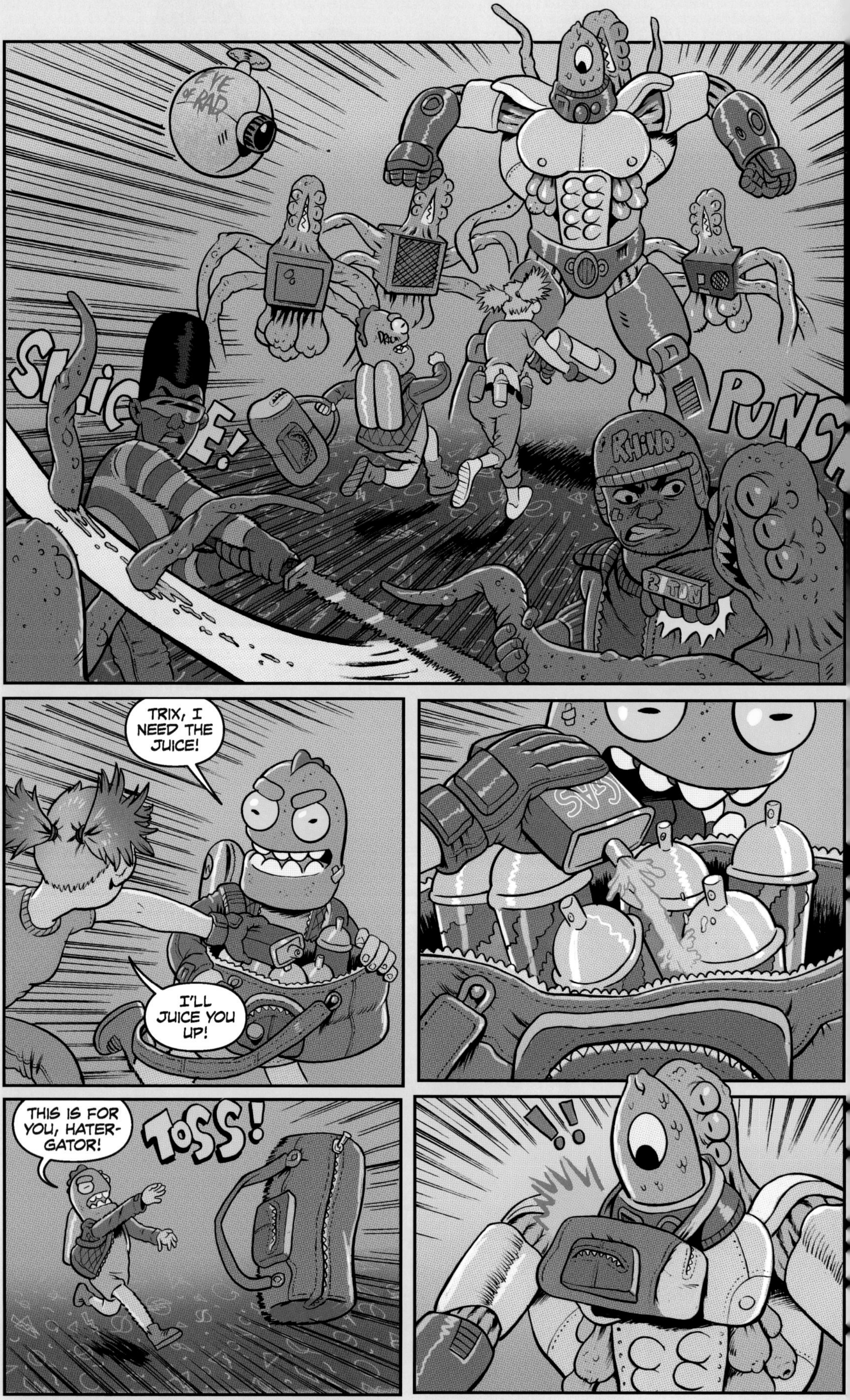
EYE OF RAD
RHINO
TRIX, I NEED THE JUICE!
I'LL JUICE YOU UP!
GAS
THIS IS FOR YOU, HATER-GATOR!
TOSS!

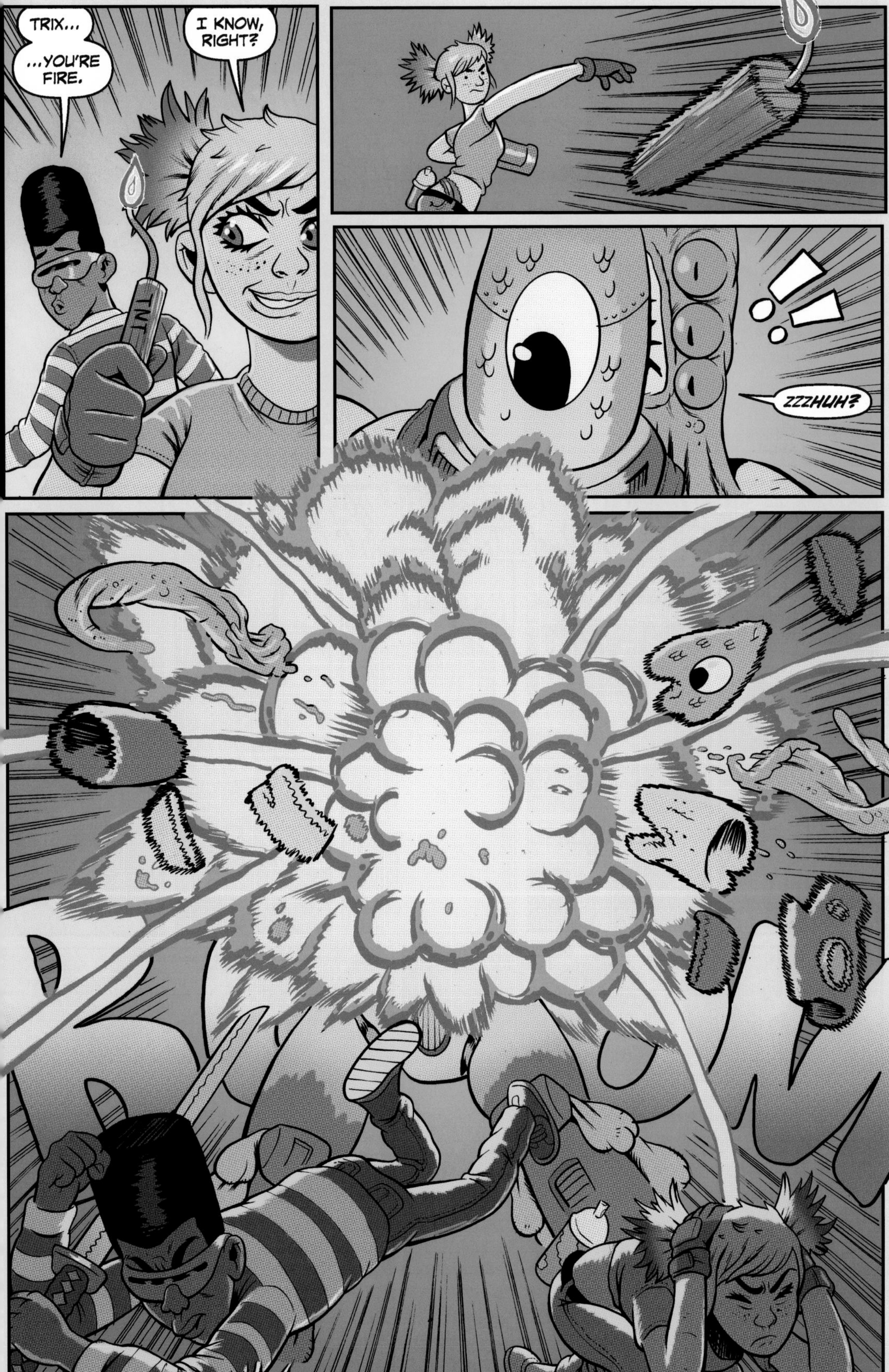
TRIX...
...YOU'RE FIRE.
I KNOW, RIGHT?
!!
ZZZHUH?

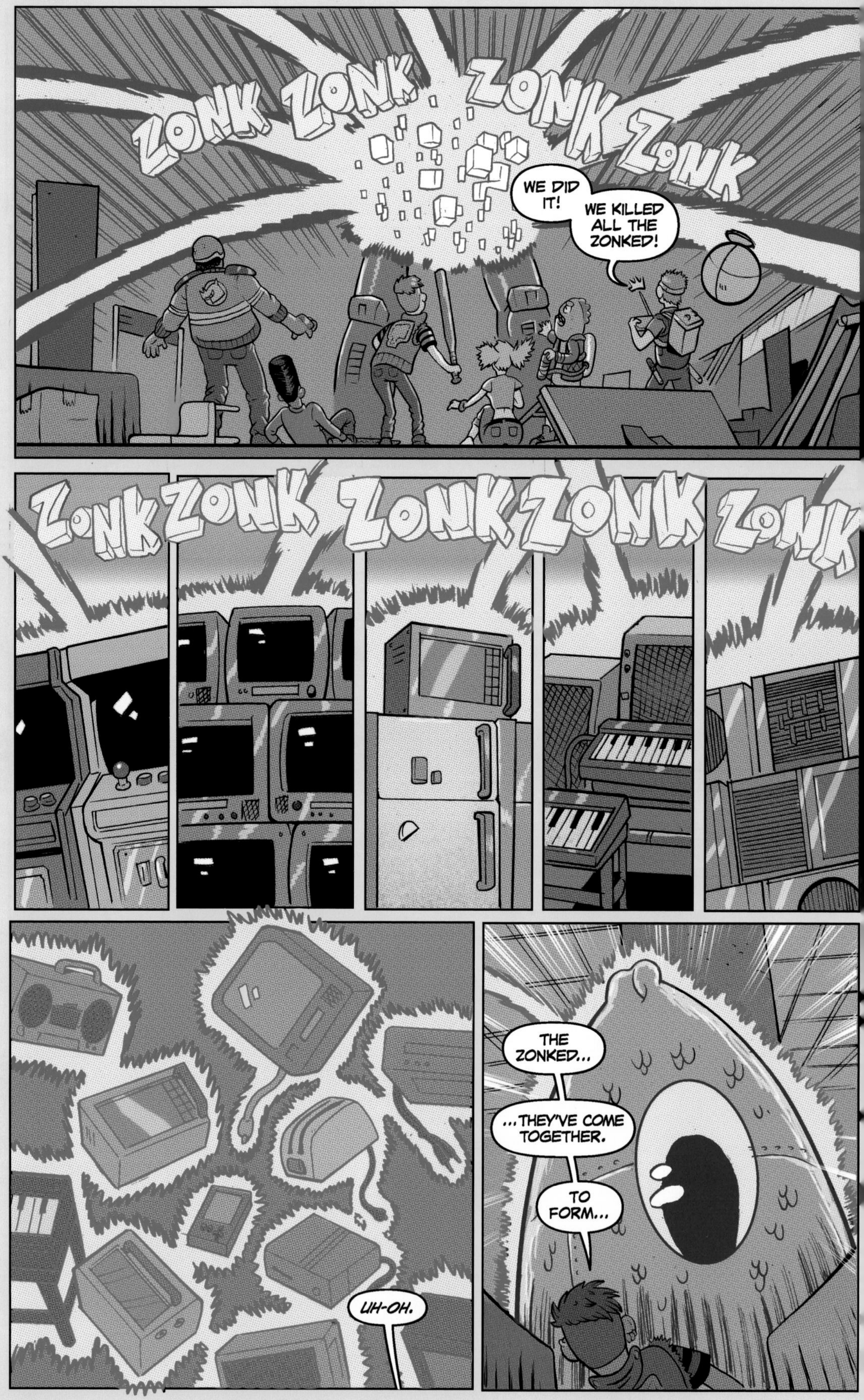
ZONK ZONK ZONK ZONK
WE DID IT!
WE KILLED ALL THE ZONKED!
ZONK ZONK ZONK ZONK ZONK
UH-OH.
THE ZONKED...
...THEY'VE COME TOGETHER.
TO FORM...

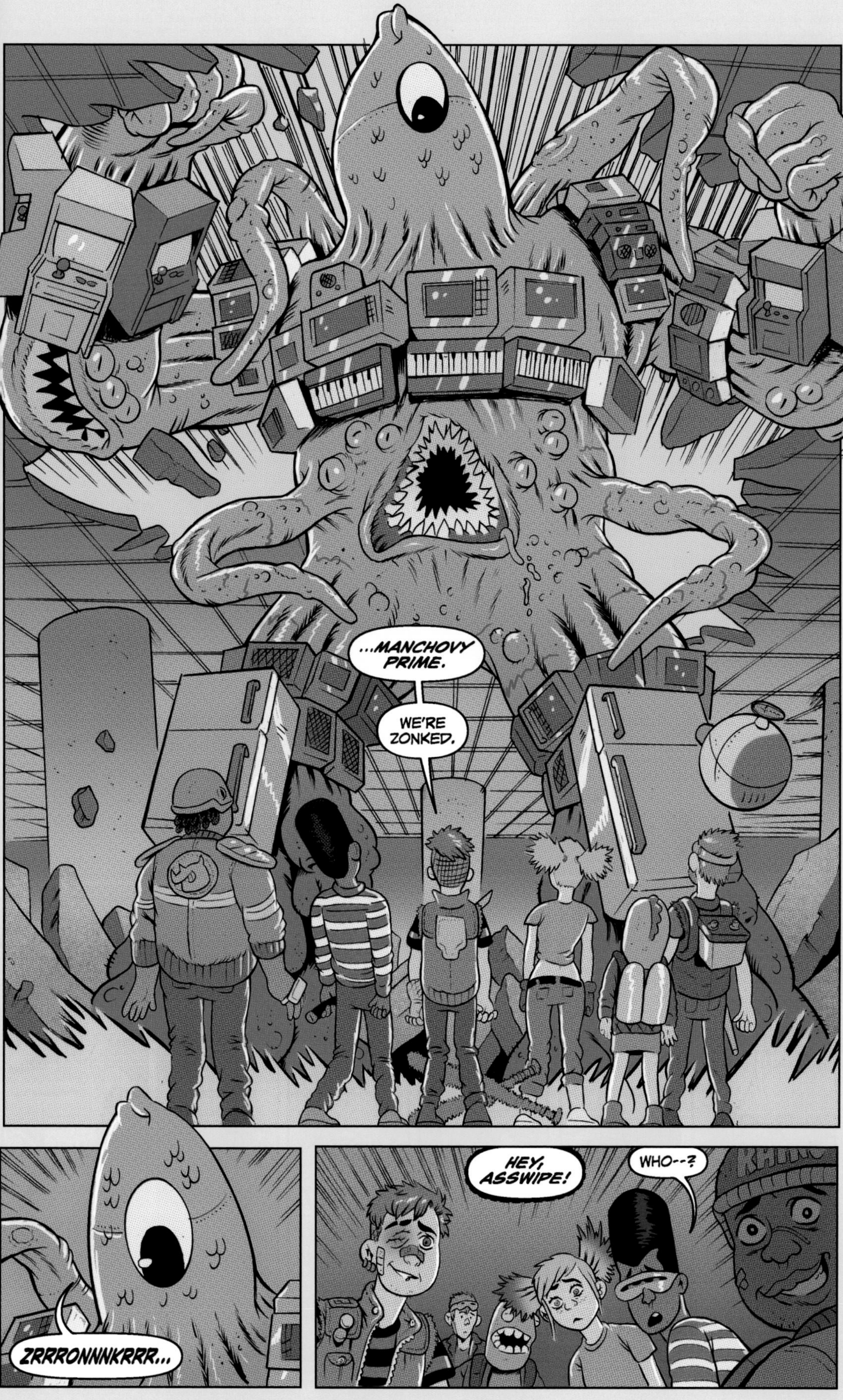
...MANCHOVY PRIME.
WE'RE ZONKED.
ZRRRONNNKRRR...
HEY, ASSWIPE!
WHO--?

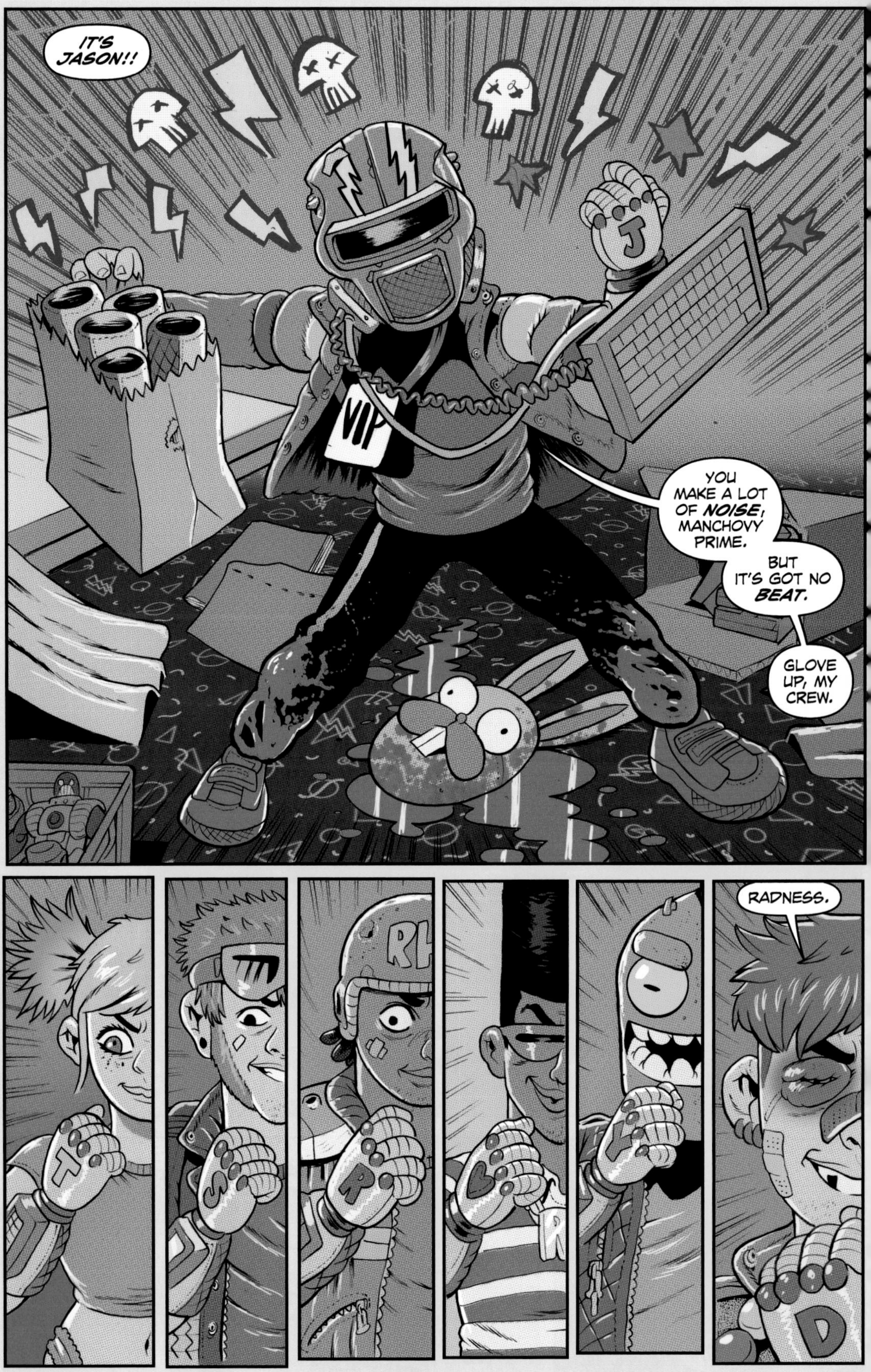
IT'S JASON!!
YOU MAKE A LOT OF NOISE, MANCHOVY PRIME.
BUT IT'S GOT NO BEAT.
GLOVE UP, MY CREW.
RADNESS.

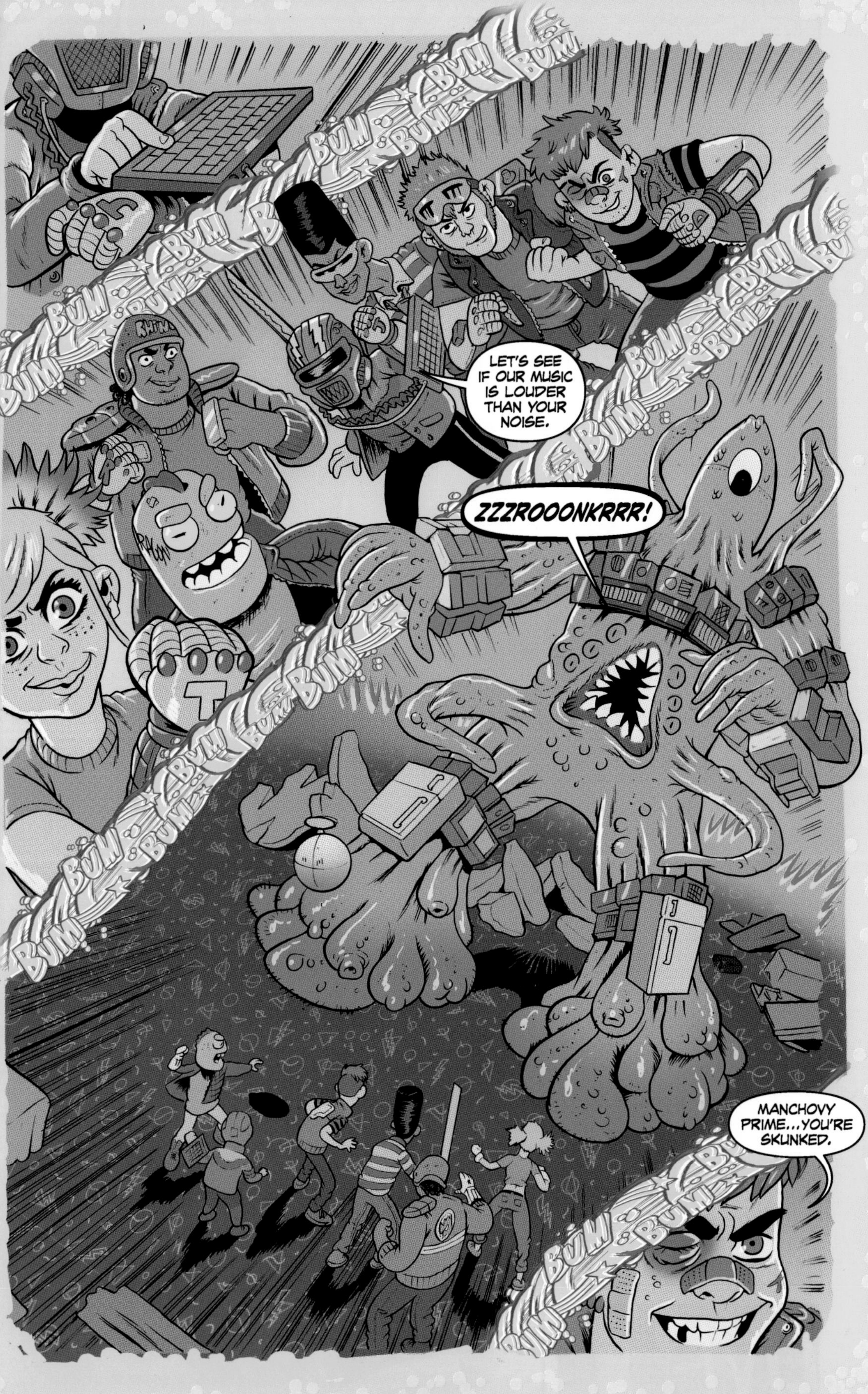
LET'S SEE IF OUR MUSIC IS LOUDER THAN YOUR NOISE.
ZZZROOONKRRR!
MANCHOVY PRIME...YOU'RE SKUNKED.
BUM BUM BUM BUM BUM BUM BUM BUM BUM BUM BUM BUM BUM BUM BUM BUM BUM BUM BUM BUM

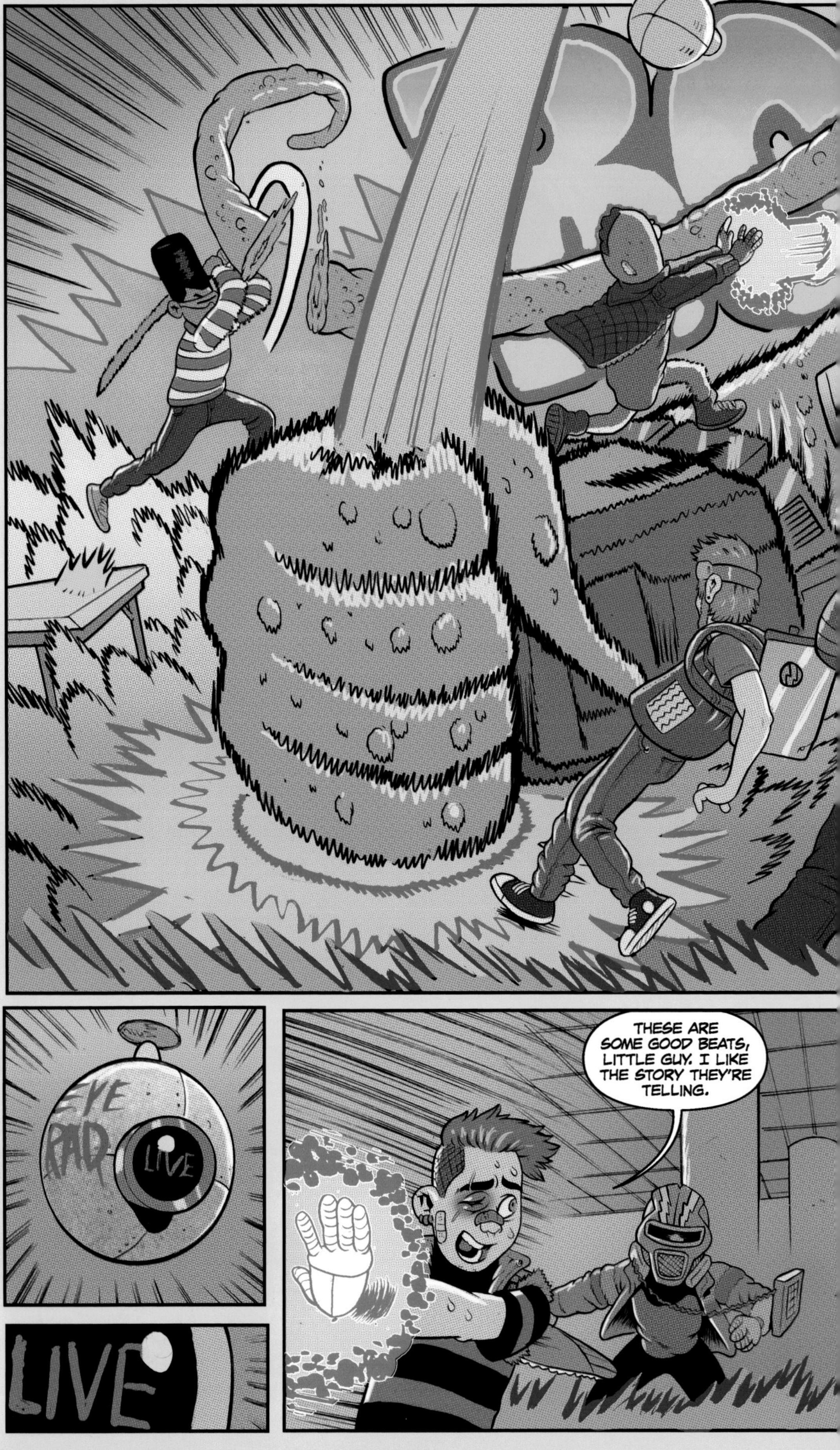
EYE
RAD
LIVE
LIVE
THESE ARE SOME GOOD BEATS, LITTLE GUY. I LIKE THE STORY THEY'RE TELLING.

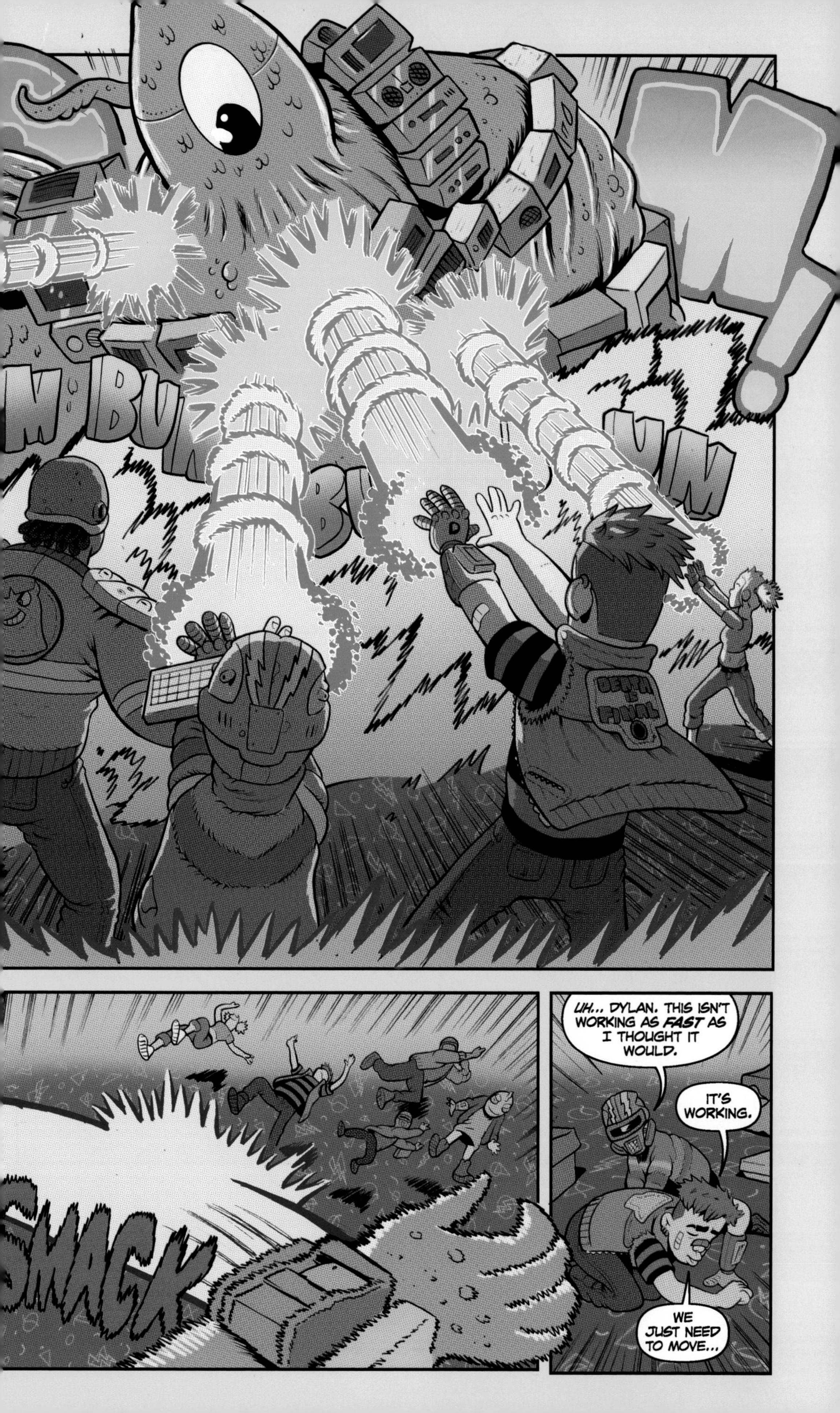
BUM BUM BUM BUM!
SMACK
UH... DYLAN. THIS ISN'T WORKING AS FAST AS I THOUGHT IT WOULD.
IT'S WORKING.
WE JUST NEED TO MOVE...

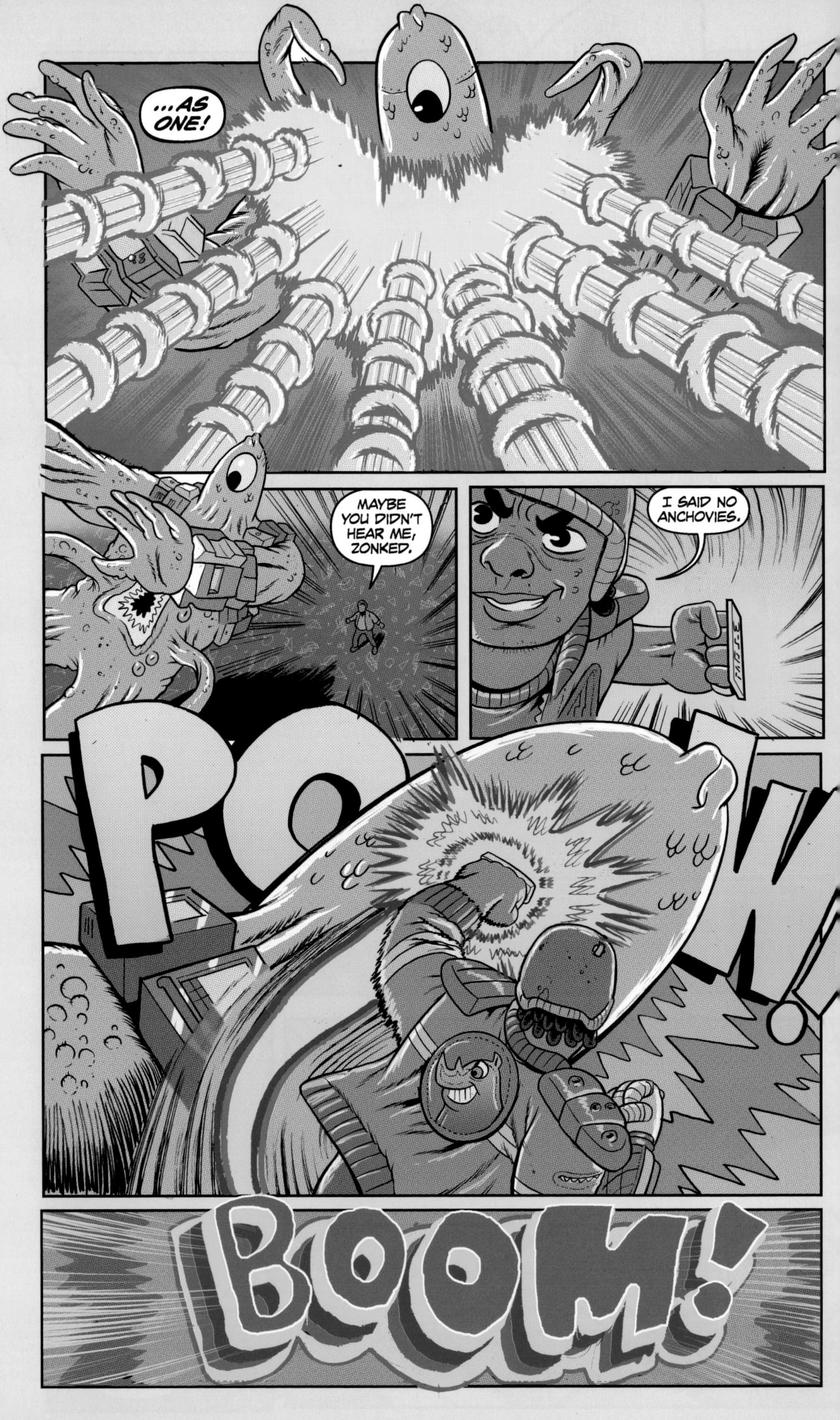
...AS ONE!
MAYBE YOU DIDN'T HEAR ME, ZONKED.
I SAID NO ANCHOVIES.
POW!
BOOM!

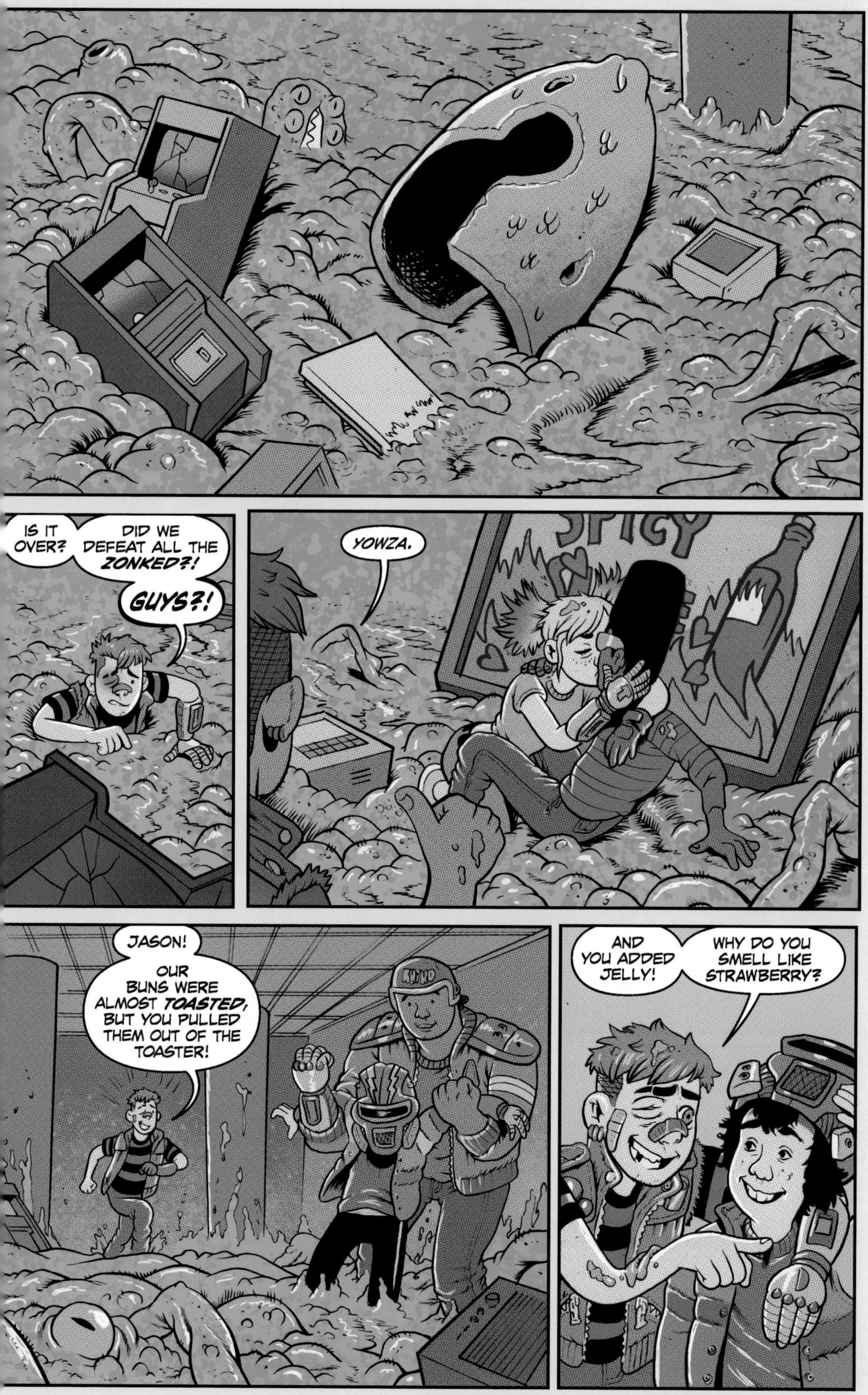
IS IT OVER?
DID WE DEFEAT ALL THE ZONKED?!
GUYS?!
YOWZA.
SPICY
JASON!
OUR BUNS WERE ALMOST TOASTED, BUT YOU PULLED THEM OUT OF THE TOASTER!
AND YOU ADDED JELLY!
WHY DO YOU SMELL LIKE STRAWBERRY?

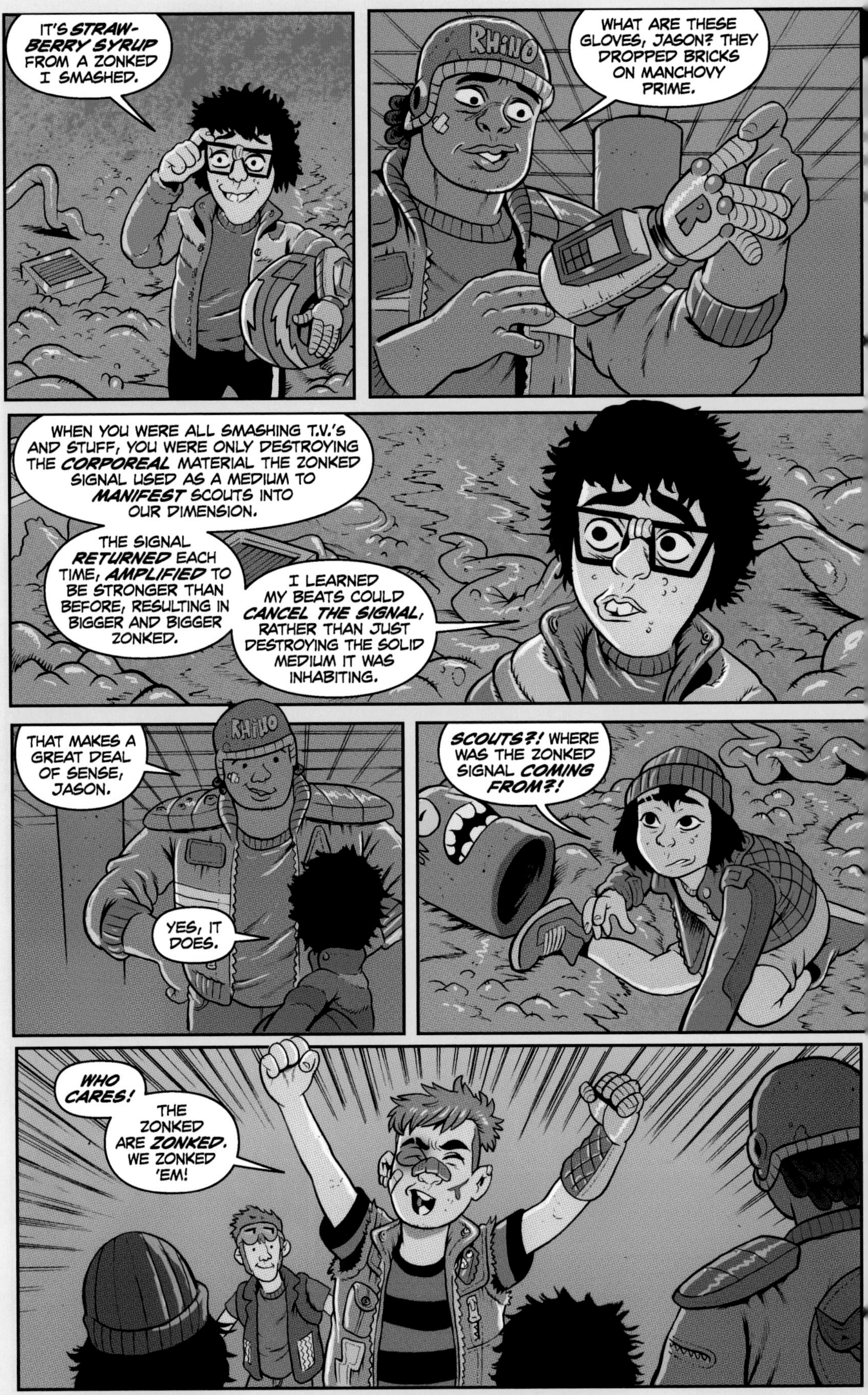
IT'S STRAWBERRY SYRUP FROM A ZONKED I SMASHED.
WHAT ARE THESE GLOVES, JASON? THEY DROPPED BRICKS ON MANCHOVY PRIME.
RHINO
WHEN YOU WERE ALL SMASHING T.V.'s AND STUFF, YOU WERE ONLY DESTROYING THE CORPOREAL MATERIAL THE ZONKED SIGNAL USED AS A MEDIUM TO MANIFEST SCOUTS INTO OUR DIMENSION.
THE SIGNAL RETURNED EACH TIME, AMPLIFIED TO BE STRONGER THAN BEFORE, RESULTING IN BIGGER AND BIGGER ZONKED.
I LEARNED MY BEATS COULD CANCEL THE SIGNAL, RATHER THAN JUST DESTROYING THE SOLID MEDIUM IT WAS INHABITING.
THAT MAKES A GREAT DEAL OF SENSE, JASON.
RHINO
YES, IT DOES.
SCOUTS?! WHERE WAS THE ZONKED SIGNAL COMING FROM?!
WHO CARES!
THE ZONKED ARE ZONKED. WE ZONKED 'EM!

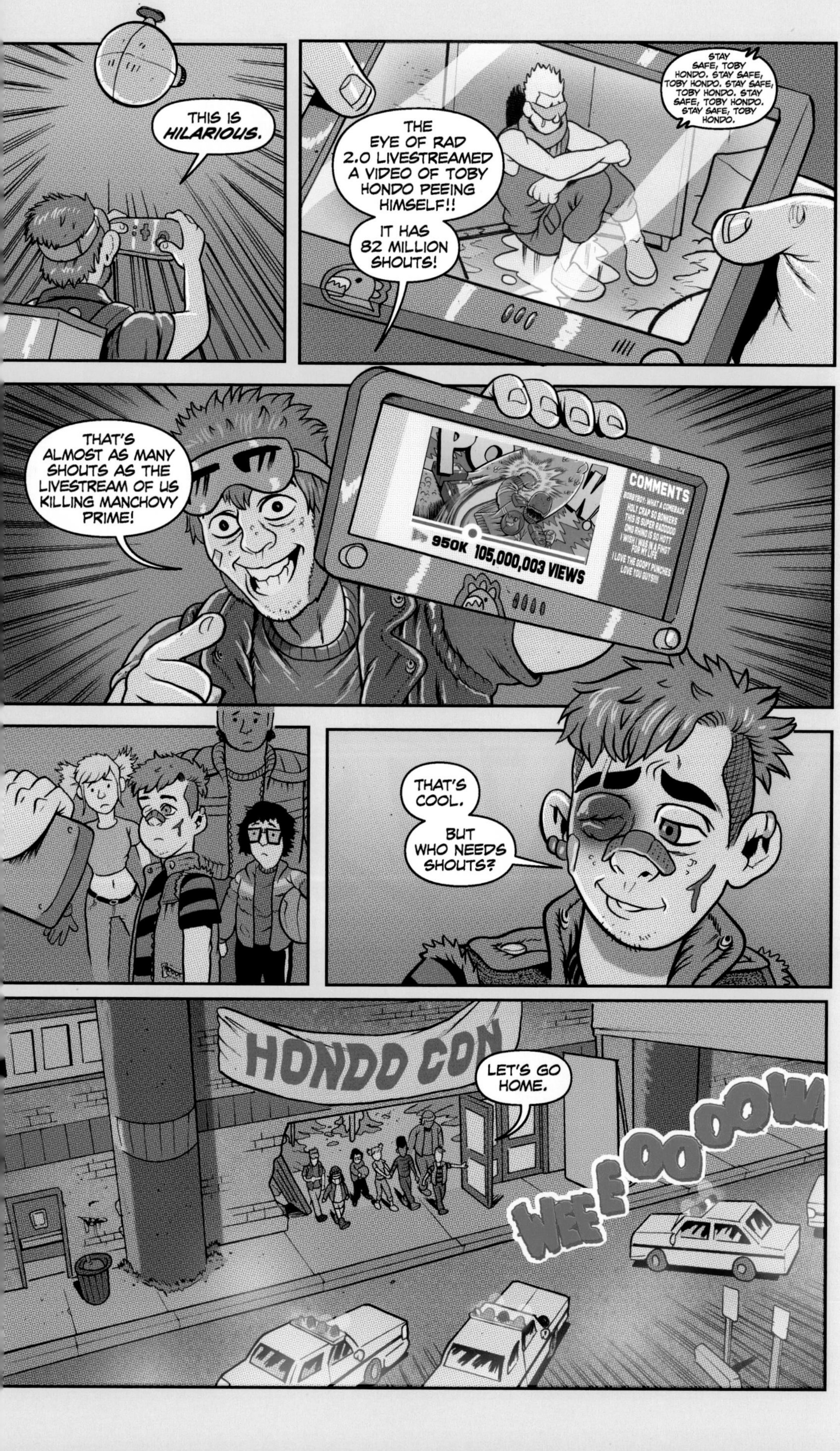
THIS IS *HILARIOUS.*
THE EYE OF RAD 2.0 LIVESTREAMED A VIDEO OF TOBY HONDO PEEING HIMSELF!!
IT HAS 82 MILLION SHOUTS!
STAY SAFE, TOBY HONDO. STAY SAFE, TOBY HONDO. STAY SAFE, TOBY HONDO. STAY SAFE, TOBY HONDO. STAY SAFE, TOBY HONDO.
THAT'S ALMOST AS MANY SHOUTS AS THE LIVESTREAM OF US KILLING MANCHOVY PRIME!
COMMENTS
BOBBYBOY: WHAT A COMEBACK
HOLY CRAP SO BONKERS
THIS IS SUPER RADDDDD
OMG RHINO IS SO HOTT
I WISH I WAS IN A FIHGT FOR MY LIFE
I LOVE THE GOOPY PUNCHES
LOVE YOU GUYS!!!!!
950K 105,000,003 VIEWS
THAT'S COOL.
BUT WHO NEEDS SHOUTS?
HONDO CON
LET'S GO HOME.
WEE E OO OOW

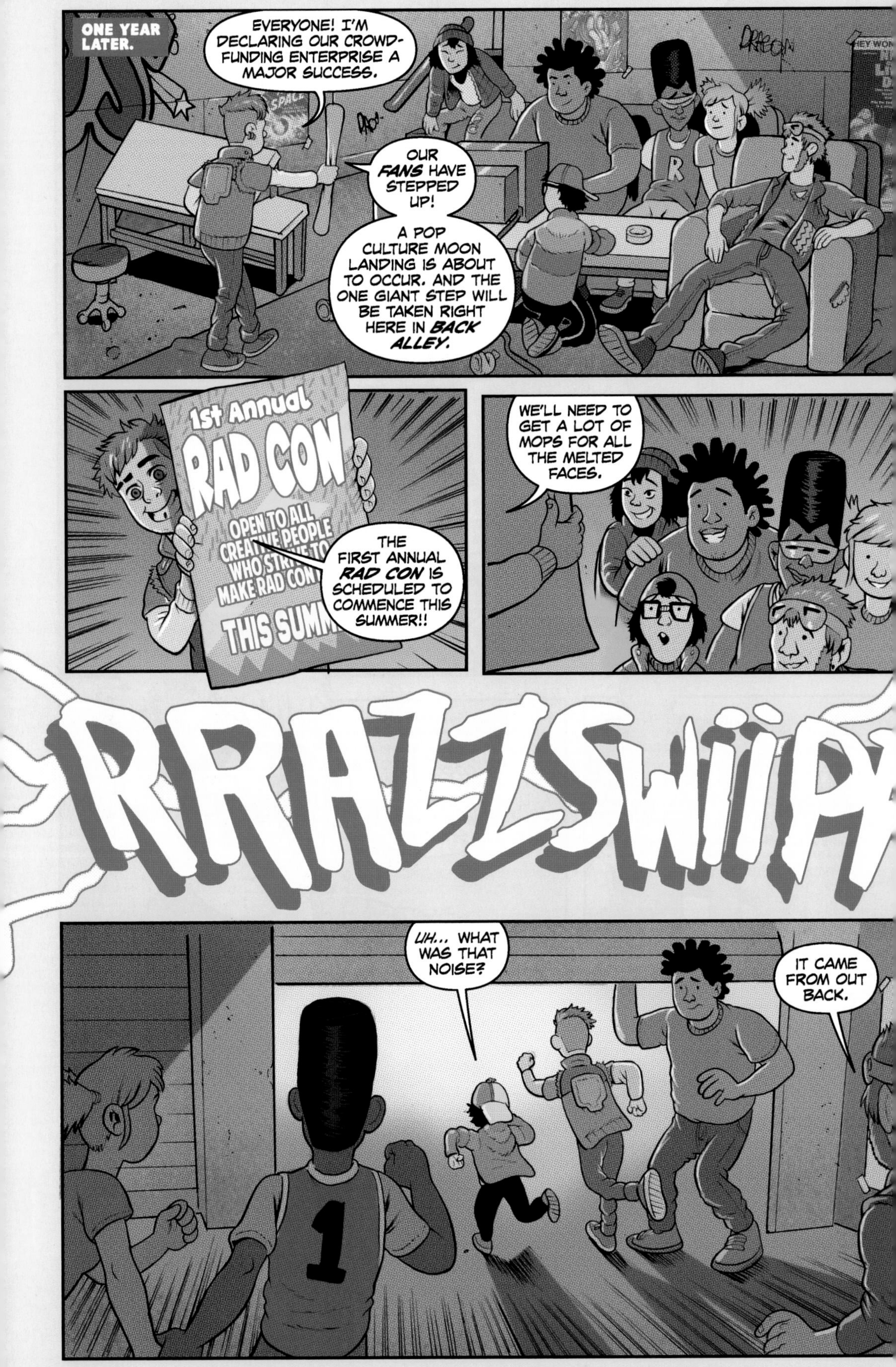
ONE YEAR LATER.
EVERYONE! I'M DECLARING OUR CROWD-FUNDING ENTERPRISE A MAJOR SUCCESS.
OUR FANS HAVE STEPPED UP!
A POP CULTURE MOON LANDING IS ABOUT TO OCCUR. AND THE ONE GIANT STEP WILL BE TAKEN RIGHT HERE IN BACK ALLEY.
1st Annual RAD CON
OPEN TO ALL CREATIVE PEOPLE WHO STRIVE TO MAKE RAD CON
THIS SUMM
THE FIRST ANNUAL RAD CON IS SCHEDULED TO COMMENCE THIS SUMMER!!
WE'LL NEED TO GET A LOT OF MOPS FOR ALL THE MELTED FACES.
RRAZZSWIIP
UH... WHAT WAS THAT NOISE?
IT CAME FROM OUT BACK.

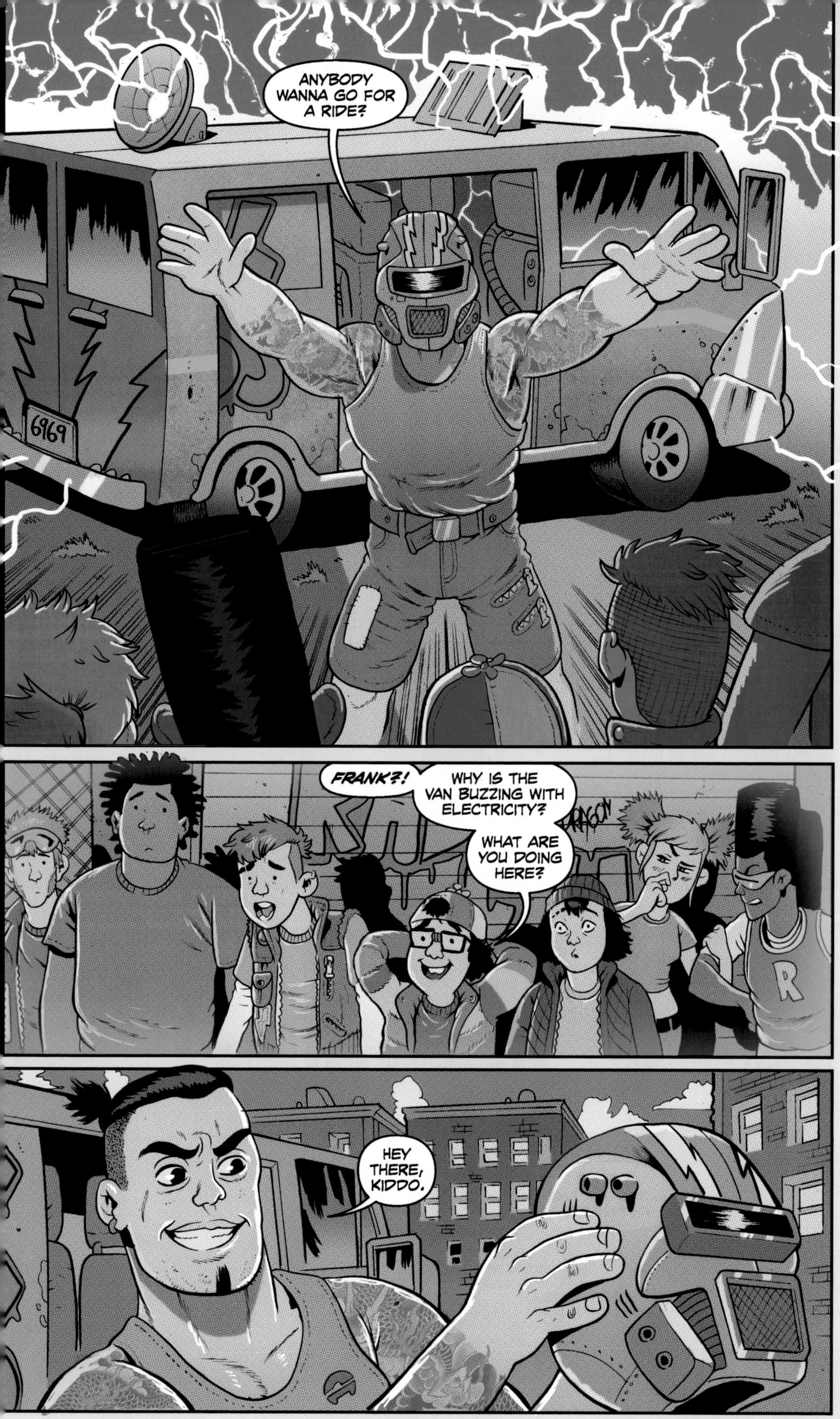
ANYBODY WANNA GO FOR A RIDE?
6969
FRANK?!
WHY IS THE VAN BUZZING WITH ELECTRICITY?
WHAT ARE YOU DOING HERE?
R
HEY THERE, KIDDO.

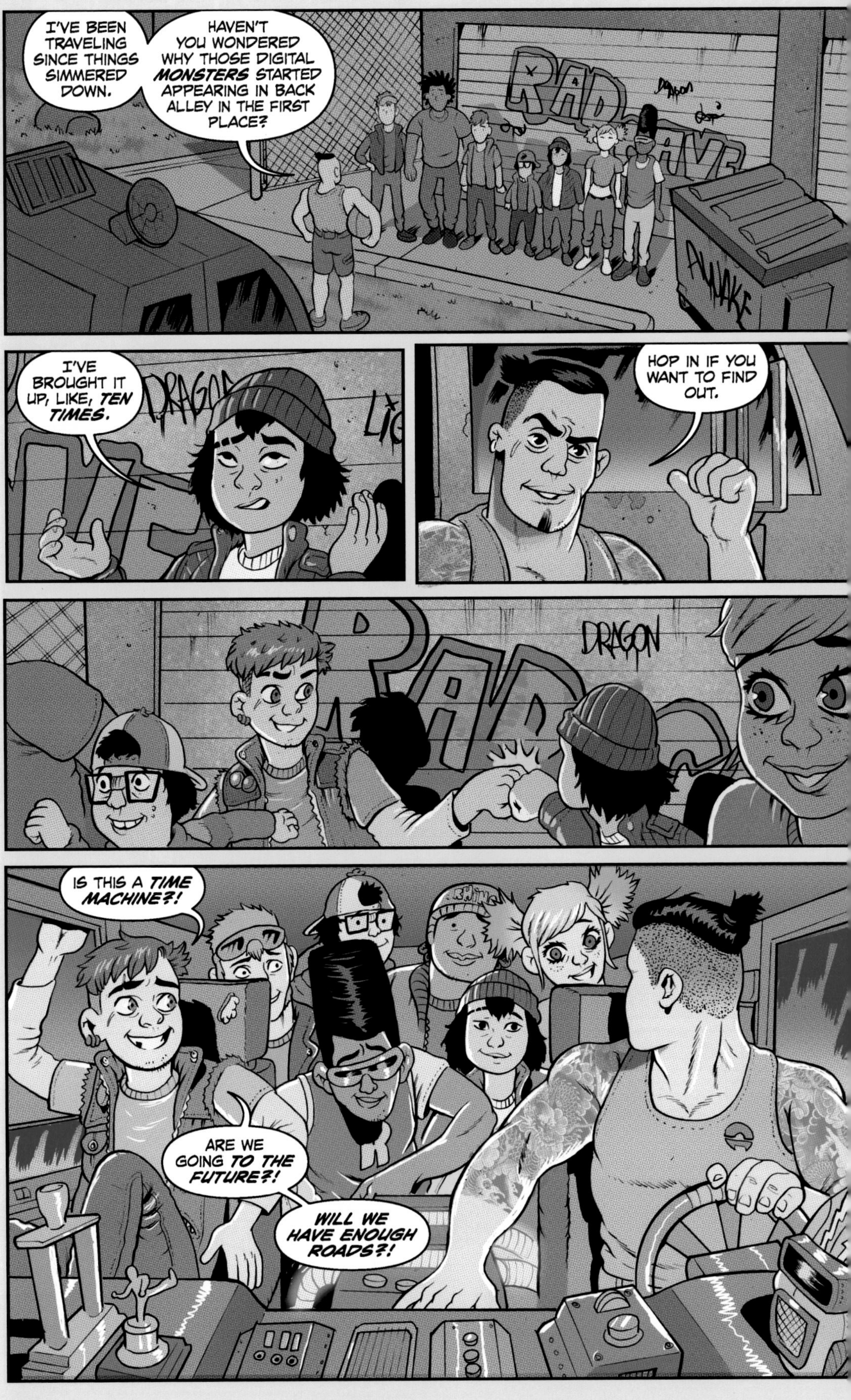
I'VE BEEN TRAVELING SINCE THINGS SIMMERED DOWN.
HAVEN'T YOU WONDERED WHY THOSE DIGITAL *MONSTERS* STARTED APPEARING IN BACK ALLEY IN THE FIRST PLACE?
RAD
AWAKE
I'VE BROUGHT IT UP, LIKE, *TEN TIMES*.
HOP IN IF YOU WANT TO FIND OUT.
DRAGON
IS THIS A *TIME MACHINE?!*
ARE WE GOING *TO THE FUTURE?!*
WILL WE HAVE ENOUGH ROADS?!

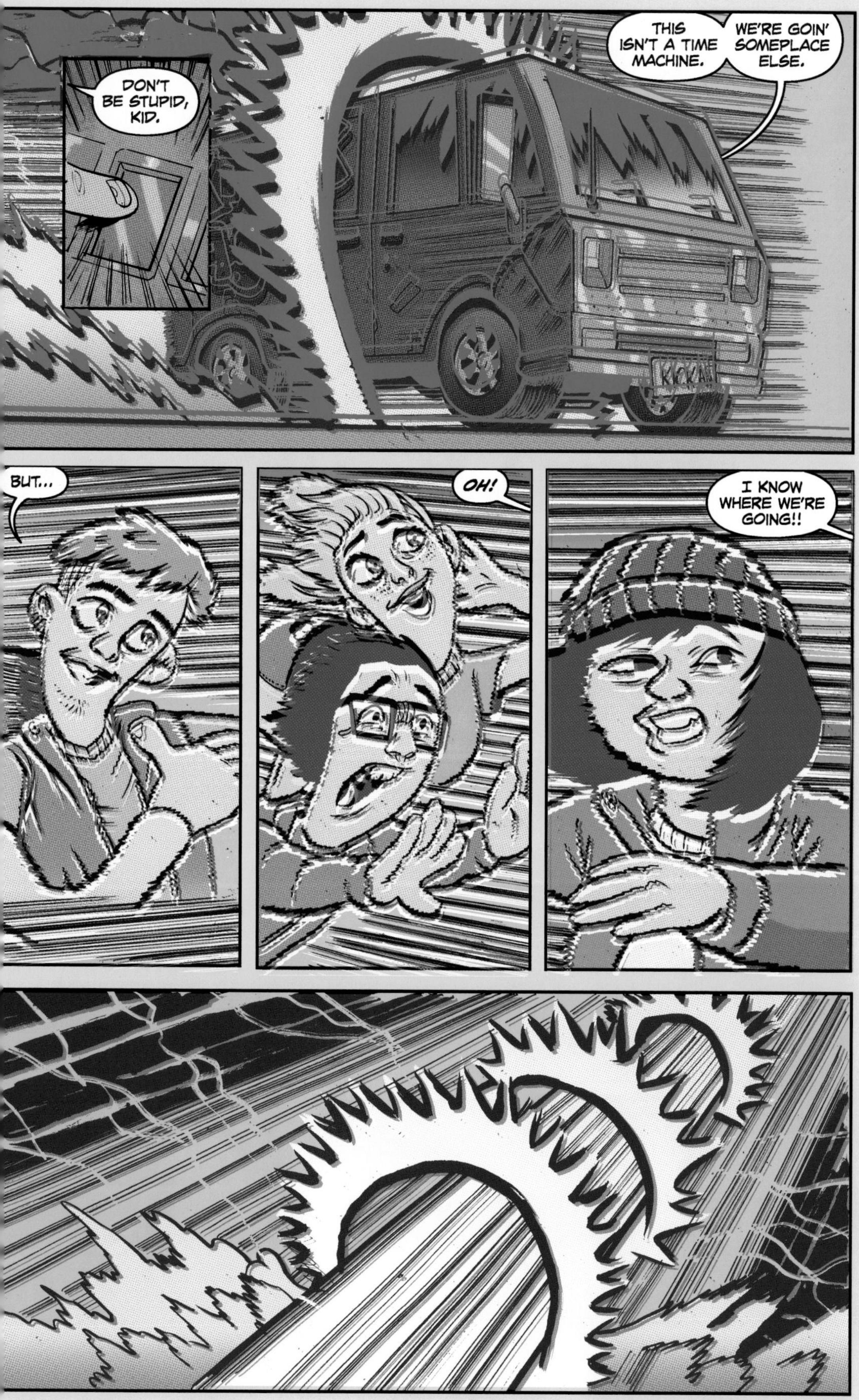
DON'T BE STUPID, KID.
THIS ISN'T A TIME MACHINE.
WE'RE GOIN' SOMEPLACE ELSE.
KICKAN
BUT...
OH!
I KNOW WHERE WE'RE GOING!!

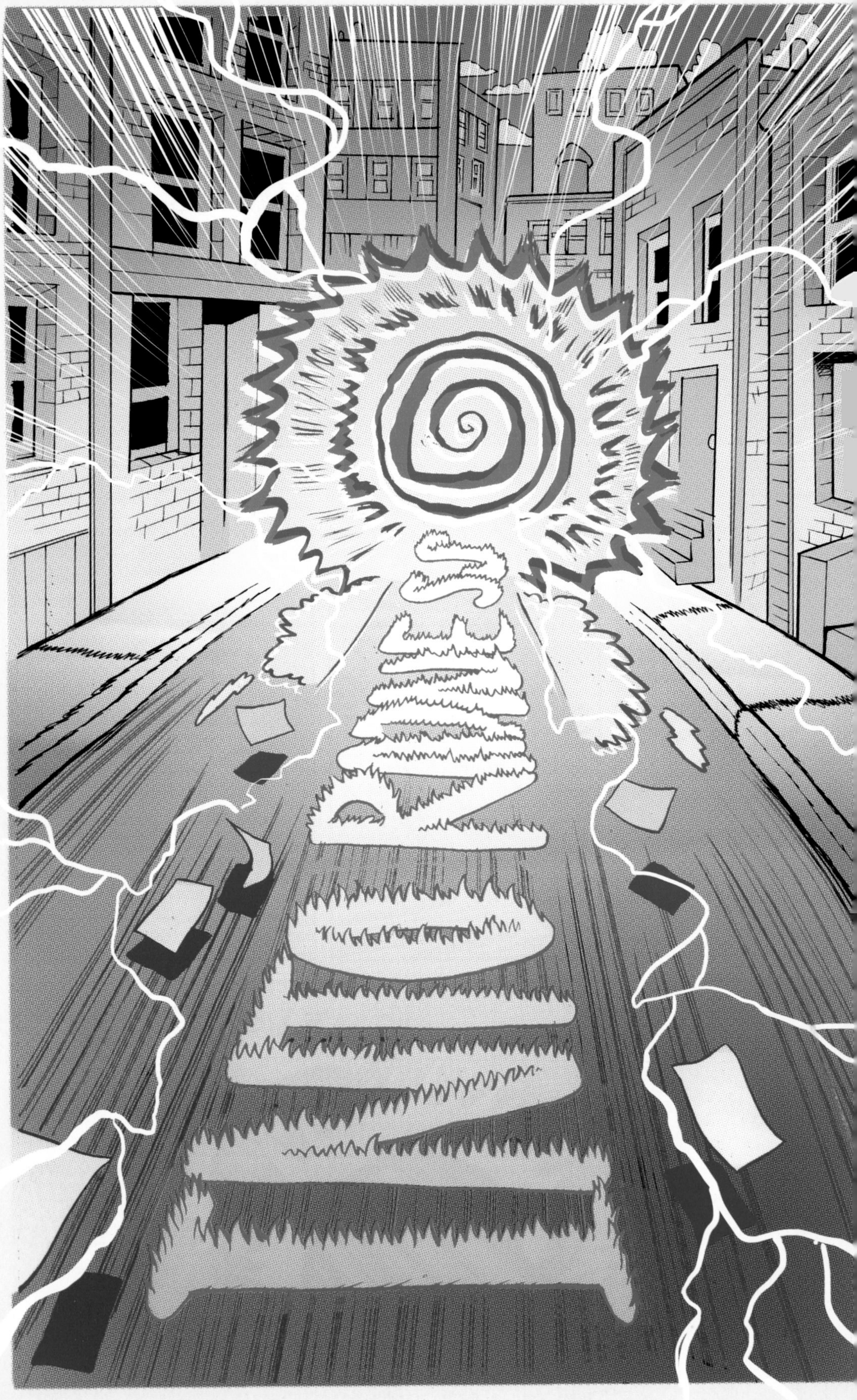